D1277307
:ion

The Object Primer

Managing Object Technology Series

Charles F. Bowman
Series Editor
Editor
The X Journal
SIGS Publications, Inc.
New York, New York

and

President
SoftWright Solutions,
Suffern, New York

1. What Every Software Manager Must Know
to Succeed with Object Technology, *John D. Williams*

2. Managing Your Move to Object Technology:
Guidelines and Strategies for a Smooth Transition,
Barry McGibbon

3. The Object Primer: The Application Developer's Guide to
Object-Orientation, *Scott W. Ambler*

Additional Volumes in Preparation

The Object Primer

The Application Developer's Guide to Object-Orientation

Scott W. Ambler

**Mark Winter & Associates Inc.
Toronto, Ontario, Canada**

SIGS
BOOKS

New York • London • Paris • Munich • Cologne

005.11
Am 160
1995 a

Library of Congress Cataloging-in-Publication Data

Ambler, Scott W., 1966–
   The object primer : the application developer's guide to object-
   orientation / Scott W. Ambler.
      p. cm. — (Managing object technology series ; 3)
   Includes index.
   ISBN 1-884842-17-8 (pbk. : alk. paper)
   1. Object-oriented programming (Computer science)   I. Title.
   II. Series.
   QA76.64.A494 1995
   005.1'1—dc20   95-41884
                                                         CIP

The names, characters, places and incidents in this book are either products
of the author's imagination or are used fictitiously. Any resemblance to
actual events, locales, or persons, living or dead, is entirely coincidental.

PUBLISHED BY
SIGS Books
71 W. 23rd Street, Third Floor
New York, New York 10010

Copyright © 1995 by SIGS Books. All Rights Reserved.   Neither this book
nor any part may be reproduced or transmitted in any form or by any
means, electronic or mechanical, including photocopying, microfilming,
and recording, or by any information storage and retrieval system, without
permission in writing from the publisher.
Any product mentioned in this book may be a trademark of its company.

Design and composition by Kevin Callahan.
Cover design by Jean Cohn.
Illustration on p. 153 ©1995 by David J. Pullman.
Printed on acid-free paper.

SIGS Books ISBN 1-884842-17-8
Prentice-Hall ISBN 0-13-242496-7

Printed in the United States of America
99 98 97 96 95   10 9 8 7 6 5 4 3 2 1
First Printing November 1995

To the memory of Gene Rodenberry

(1921–1991)

Thank you for your vision.

About the Author

SCOTT AMBLER IS AN INSTANCE of an **OOConsultant** based in Toronto, Ontario. Customer and **PotentialCustomer** objects can also communicate with him via electronic mail by sending messages to

AMBLER@HOOKUP.NET

Scott Ambler is a very versatile object that will change type in order to meet the needs of his clients. For example, he often becomes an **OOMentor, OOTrainer**, or an **OODeveloper** object. Scott has been an instance of an OOConsultant since 1991. He used to be a **MastersStudent** object, he received an InformationScienceDegree from the UniversityOfToronto. As a **MastersStudent**, Scott did a lot of work in OO CASE and instantiated a Thesis object in computer-supported co-operative work (an academic alias used to describe groupware). The only message Scott's Thesis responds to is **sitOnShelfAndGatherDust**, which Scott finds disappointing but predictable. Before being a **MastersStudent**, Scott was an instance of a **TechnicalSystemAnalyst** at **RoyalBankOfCanada**, where he originally became interested in object-orientation.

Objects that have been declared as friends of Scott often send him the message **youTakeThisObjectStuffTooFar**, to which he responds with the text string "But I think it's funny!" In his spare time Scott likes to write, producing columns for *Computing Canada* and *Computer Freelancer*. Scott reviews OO development tools for *Computing Canada*, which effectively means he gets paid to play with new toys. Scott also submits freelance articles to magazines and has been published in *ClientServer Computing* and *Object Magazine*. Scott is an avid watcher of **StarTrekEpisodes** and one day hopes to do his Ph.d. at **StarFleetAcademy** (Scott's not holding his breath on this one).

Foreword

*T*HE *OBJECT PRIMER* performs an all too rare function: It places the object-oriented paradigm squarely within the context of real-world systems development. Mr. Ambler tells why something should be done as well as how it should be done. This approach should be especially useful to practitioners in the field.

The tables and analyses of advantages and disadvantages are extremely useful: It is refreshing to read a book on object technology that admits that it does not have all the answers. An appropriate tone of realism permeates the book.

By this time, even the extreme enthusiasts know, on some, level, that there are no more silver bullets. I differ with the author on two points: The book calls itself a "primer." However, it is *not* a primer in the sense of being an extremely basic text that readers will soon put down, never to pick up again. Many of the passages will both repay repeated readings and will be consulted when faced with real-world problems. Similarly, Mr. Ambler is too modest when he discounts *The*

Object Primer's use by researchers or academics. Perhaps they will not be inclined to read anything called a primer—but they should. I have read hundreds of manuscripts by researchers and academics. The biggest flaw of these manuscripts is the lack of evidence that their authors appreciate how software and software tools are actually used.

There are some valuable books that provide advice on how to collect and understand user requirements; there are also increasing numbers of books that explain how to perform object-oriented development. Scott Ambler's book brings these two strands together in a way that allows readers (users) to carry through development from start to finish within an object environment.

Thomas O'Flaherty
INPUT
Teaneck, NJ

Preface

*T*HE *OBJECT PRIMER: APPLICATION DEVELOPER'S GUIDE TO OBJECT-ORIENTATION* is a straightforward, easy-to-understand introduction to object-oriented analysis and design techniques. Object-orientation (OO) is the most important change to system development since the advent of structured methods. Although OO is often used to develop complex systems, OO itself does not need to be complicated. This book is different from any other book ever written about object-orientation—it is written from the point of view of a real-world developer, somebody who has lived through the difficulty of learning this exciting new approach to systems development.

Who Should Read *The Object Primer*?

If you're a mainframe COBOL or PL/1 programmer who is working on his or her first OO project, *The Object Primer* is for you. If you're a business analyst or user representative involved in the documentation of user requirements for an OO application, *The Object Primer* is for you. If you're a project manager who needs to get up to speed on OO, *The Object Primer* is for you. If you're a systems designer whose organization is just getting into OO, *The Object Primer* is for you. If you are a student taking your first course in C++ or Smalltalk, *The Object Primer* is for you. If you're a researcher or an academic, sorry, I can't please everybody.

The Object Primer is written for you, the developers of information systems.

Throughout this book I use the term *developer* very broadly: A developer is anyone involved in the development of an application. This includes programmers, analysts, designers, user representatives, database administrators, and so on. Although many people wouldn't include user representatives in this list, I feel that because they are actively involved in development it makes sense to consider them developers. Call me a radical.

What Does *The Object Primer* Cover?

The Object Primer covers leading-edge OO concepts and techniques that have been proven in the development of real-world applications. We're going to cover in detail why we need this new approach called object-orientation, as well as the need for analysis techniques, such as CRC modeling and use-case scenarios, OO concepts, and Class modeling, an OO analysis and design technique. The book ends by putting everything into the context of an OO system development life cycle, which is basically a game plan for developing OO applications. In short, *The Object Primer* covers everything that you need to know to get you started in OO development.

The Need for a New Paradigm

Chapter 1 introduces the concept of the object-oriented paradigm. In this introductory chapter we will appreciate the potential benefits of OO.

Chapter 2 discusses several pressing problems currently faced by the systems industry, such as the application backlog, the maintenance burden, and the difficulties of gathering accurate requirements from our users. In addition, chapter 2 covers both the benefits and drawbacks of OO, providing a strategy for when and when not to use it.

CRC Modeling

Chapter 3 covers CRC modeling in detail, indicating its usefulness as an incredibly effective way to gather user requirements. CRC modeling provides a low-tech, straightforward technique for working with your users. Originally an object-oriented teaching technique, CRC cards have emerged as a mainstream OO requirements-gathering method.

Use Cases

Chapter 4 follows up with a discussion of use-case scenario testing, also called OO analysis testing, a technique that helps to ensure that your system analysis is complete and mistake free. As we'll see, the cost of fixing errors rises exponentially throughout the system development life cycle: By finding our mistakes early on, we dramatically reduce the development cost of our systems. Use-case scenario testing in combination with CRC modeling greatly increases the chance of project success, and I highly recommend that you read this chapter.

Object-Oriented Analysis and Design

Chapter 5 introduces the fundamental concepts of OO. I have found out the hard way that teaching OO concepts before CRC modeling is actually detrimental to the learning effort. The basic idea is that you don't need to have any OO knowledge to gather user requirements using either CRC modeling or use-case scenario testing, so why confuse the process? In fact, one of the most common mistakes made by people who are inexperienced in OO is that they complicate the CRC modeling process by dealing with issues such as inheritance when their users aren't ready for these concepts. Remember the KISS rule—Keep It Simple, Stupid.

Not only are OO concepts important, you also need to be able to apply them. That's why chapter 5 includes a description of my OO modeling notation. When I first considered writing a book I was very hesitant about introducing yet another OO modeling notation, seeing as there are several that are already widely accepted. In my opinion, however, there isn't a good, popular notation that is suitable for introductory purposes (until now). They're all either too complicated or have problems that I just can't live with. Don't worry, there isn't anything weird or strange about my notation, and once you learn it you'll have no problem at all moving into somebody else's. Besides, all OO notations are based on the same fundamental concepts, so who really cares if you draw a class as a rounded rectangle, a cloud, or just a plain old rectangle?

Chapter 6 covers basic class modeling, which some books inaccurately call object modeling. This is an interesting mistake because we model classes, not objects! Therefore, the term *Class Model* is obviously more appropriate than *Object Model*. We'll see how the results of our analysis (the combination of CRC modeling, prototyping, and use-case scenario testing) dovetail nicely into class modeling.

An Object-Oriented System Development Life Cycle

Chapter 7 summarizes the steps of OO development, discussing why the traditional Waterfall SDLC (system development life cycle) may not be appropriate for OO development. We are then introduced to an iterative, object-oriented SDLC called the Pinball SDLC. Following the Pinball SDLC will dramatically help to increase the chance of project success. We end chapter 7 with a discussion of what you need to do to further continue your OO learning process.

Wrapping It All Up

Chapter 8 suggests some further reading, and chapter 9 presents a glossary of all of the terms used throughout this book. Chapter 10 includes a summary of the class-modeling notation, as well as a summary of the Pinball SDLC (system development life cycle).

How to Read this Book

Programmers, Designers, and Project Managers

Read the entire book, cover to cover. It's very tempting to skip to chapter 5 and start reading from there, but that would be a major mistake. Chapter 5 builds on many of the ideas presented in the first three chapters, so please don't read ahead.

Business Analysts and User Representatives

Chapters 3 and 4 are written specifically for you, describing in detail techniques for gathering user requirements for an OO application. Although business analysts may want to read the entire book to gain a better understanding of what OO is all about, user representatives probably don't need to .

Students

Like the first group of people, you should also read this book cover to cover. Furthermore, you should read this book 2 or 3 weeks BEFORE your mid-term test on object-orientation, and not the night of the test! This stuff takes a while to sink in (actually, much longer than a few weeks, but hey, there's only so much time in a school term you know!) P.S. There's some really good cheat sheets scattered throughout the book, so keep your eye out for them.

What Will You Get From Reading *The Object Primer*?

By reading *The Object Primer,* you will gain a solid understanding of object-oriented concepts and objected-oriented analysis techniques. You will also be introduced to object-oriented design in the context of class modeling. These are the fundamental skills needed to develop object-oriented applications.

About This Book Series

This book is the first in a three volume series describing OO development techniques and issues. The topics covered by each volume are:

> *Volume 1*   describes OO analysis and introductory OO design.
>
> *Volume 2*   explores advanced OO design, OO construction, and OO testing.
>
> *Volume 3*   examines management issues for OO development.

ADVANTAGES OF THIS BOOK SERIES

It is short, straightforward, and to the point—it's not wasting your time.

It presents a full development life cycle—there's more to OO than just programming.

It takes complicated concepts and makes them simple—it'll shorten your learning curve.

It is written in the language of developers, not academics—you can understand it.

It uses real-world examples and case studies—it describes realistic applications.

It relates new techniques with your current practices—you can see where OO fits in.

It provides a smooth transition to a new technology—your first project can succeed.

Acknowledgments

Special thanks to the people who provided insightful comments that lead to significant improvements in this book: Jennifer Barzso, Jo-Anne Odell, and the people at SIGS.

Contents

About the Author   *v*
Foreword   *vii*
Preface   *ix*

Chapter 1
Introduction   **1**
1.1   Object-Orientation: A New Development Paradigm   2

      1.1.1 The Structured Paradigm Versus the
            Object-Oriented Paradigm   2

Chapter 2
Object-Orientation:
A New Development-Strategy Paradigm   **5**
2.1   Potential Benefits of Object-Orientation   6

Contents

$\boxed{xvi}$

2.1.1	OO Increases the Chance of Project Success	8
2.1.2	OO Reduces the Maintenance Burden	12
2.1.3	OO Reduces the Application Backlog	14
2.1.4	OO Deals with Complexity	16
2.2	Potential Drawbacks of OO	19
2.3	What We've Learned	22
2.3.1	The Object-Oriented Paradigm	22

Chapter 3
Gathering User Requirements: CRC Modeling — **25**

3.1	Putting the CRC Team Together	28
3.1.1	How to Become a Facilitator	32
3.2	Running a CRC Section	32
3.2.1	Organizing the CRC Modeling Room	34
3.2.2	Do Some Initial Brainstorming	34
3.2.3	Finding Classes	36
3.2.4	Finding Responsibilities	44
3.2.5	Defining Collaborators	47
3.2.6	Defining Use Cases	52
3.2.7	Arranging the CRC Cards	55
3.2.8	Prototyping	58
3.3	CRC Modeling Tips	62
3.4	Advantages and Disadvantages of CRC Modeling	64
3.5	CRC Modeling Case Study	69
3.5.1	A Solution to the Case Study	71
3.6	What We've Learned	82
3.6.1	The Iterative Steps of CRC Modeling	83
3.7	References	85

Contents

$\boxed{xvii}$

Chapter 4
Ensuring User Requirements Are Correct:
Use-Case Scenario Testing   87

4.1   Use-Case Scenario Testing   91

 4.1.1 Pros and Cons of Use-Case Scenario Testing   94

4.2   Creating "Testing" Use-Case Scenarios   95

4.3   Acting Out Scenarios   97

 4.3.1 Acting Out a Scenario—An Example   100

 4.3.2 Note-Taking by the Scribe—An Example   104

4.4   Use-Case Scenarios for the Bank Case Study   105

 4.4.1 How Our CRC Model Should Have Been Affected   107

4.5   What We've Learned   111

 4.5.1 Interesting Testing Facts   111

 4.5.2 Steps of Use-Case Scenario Testing   111

 4.5.3 Advantages of Use-Case Scenario Testing   112

 4.5.4 Disadvantages of Use-Case Scenario Testing   112

4.6   References   113

Chapter 5
Understanding the Basics: OO Concepts   115

5.1   OO Concepts from a Structured Point of View   117

5.2   Objects and Classes   120

 5.2.1 How to Name Classes   121

 5.2.2 Instantiation   122

5.3   Attributes and Methods   122

 5.3.1 Class Definitions Include the Definitions
   of Attributes and Methods   123

 5.3.2 Methods Do One of Two Things   123

Contents

5.4	Abstraction, Encapsulation, and Information Hiding	125
	5.4.1 Abstraction	125
	5.4.2 Encapsulation	125
	5.4.3 Information Hiding	126
5.5	Inheritance	128
	5.5.1 Single Versus Multiple Inheritance	129
5.6	Persistence	133
	5.6.1 Persistence Tips	133
	5.6.2 Persistent Memory	134
	5.6.3 Object-0riented Databases (OODBs)	135
5.7	Instance Relationships	135
	5.7.1 Recursive Instance Relationships	138
	5.7.2 How Instance Relationships Are Implemented	139
5.8	Aggregation	139
	5.8.1 Aggregation Tips	141
5.9	Collaboration	142
	5.9.1 Messages	143
	5.9.2 Two Types of Collaboration	143
	5.9.3 Collaboration Tips	143
5.10	Persistent Versus Transitory Instance Relationships	145
	5.10.1 Persistent Instance Relationships	146
	5.10.2 Transitory Instance Relationships	146
5.11	Coupling and Cohesion	148
	5.11.1 Coupling	149
	5.11.2 Cohesion	150
5.12	Polymorphism	152
	5.12.1 A Partial OO Design for the Big Card Game	154

Contents

$\lfloor xix \rfloor$

5.12.2 Polymorphism in the University	155
5.12.3 Why Polymorphism Is Important	156
5.13 Structured Versus Object-Oriented Applications	156
5.13.1 Structured Applications	157
5.13.2 Object-Oriented Applications	157
5.14 What We've Learned	160
5.15 References	160

Chapter 6
Developing a Better Understanding of the
System: Class Modeling

	161
6.1 Steps of Class Modeling	162
6.1.1 Finding Classes, Attributes, and Methods	164
6.1.2 Finding Object Relationships	166
6.1.3 Defining Inheritance	171
6.1.4 Defining Aggregation	175
6.1.5 Defining Collaborations	178
6.2 Documenting Class Models	181
6.2.1 How to Document a Class	181
6.2.2 Documenting Design Trade-Offs	183
6.3 Class Modeling Tips and Techniques	184
6.3.1 Class Modeling Pointers	184
6.3.2 How to Recognize Coupling in a Class Model	186
6.3.3 Sources of OO Coupling	186
6.4 Class Modeling Case Study: Part I	188
6.4.1 The ABC Case Study	188
6.4.2 An Answer to the Case Study	190

Contents

$$\boxed{xx}$$

6.5	Class Modeling Case Study: Part II	204
	6.5.1 The ABC Case Study: Part II	204
	6.5.2 An Answer to the Case Study	205
6.6	What We've Learned	207
	6.6.1 Class Modeling	208

Chapter 7
Putting It All Together: OO in Practice **211**

7.1	A New Development Strategy	214
	7.1.1 The Steps of Object-Oriented Development	215
	7.1.2 What's So Different About OO Development?	216
	7.1.3 The Pinball SDLC (v2.0)	217
	7.1.4 The Steps of the Pinball SDLC	220
7.2	Where to Go from Here	223
	7.2.1 Advice for Overcoming the OO Learning Curve	223
	7.2.2 OO Career Choices	225
7.3	What We've Learned	227
7.4	Parting Words	227

Further Reading	229
Appendix A A Visual Glossary	233
Appendix B Notation Summary and the Pinball SDLC	239
Index	243

> *Developers are good at building systems right.*
>
> *What we're not good at is building the right system.*

Chapter 1

Introduction

What the object-oriented paradigm is all about.

How object-oriented development is different from procedural/structural development.

As a student of object orientation you need to read this introductory chapter and the one that follows to understand why you should consider embracing object-oriented techniques. To do this, you first need to understand the difficulties that the Information Technology (IT) industry currently faces and how the OO paradigm addresses them.

1.1 Object-Orientation: A New Development Paradigm

DEFINITION

Paradigm—A paradigm (pronounced para-dime) can best be described as an overall strategy or approach to doing things. Many people consider a paradigm to be a specific mind-set.

This book describes the object-oriented (OO) paradigm, a development strategy that is based on the concept that systems should be built from a collection of reusable components called objects. Instead of separating data and functionality as is done in the structured paradigm, objects actually encompass both. Although the object-oriented paradigm sounds similar to the structured paradigm, as we'll see in this book it is actually quite different.

1.1.1 The Structured Paradigm versus the Object-Oriented Paradigm

The structured paradigm is a development strategy based on the concept that a system should be separated into two parts: data (modeled by a data model) and functionality (modeled by a process model). In short, using the structured approach we develop applications in which data is separate from behavior in both the design model and in the system implementation (i.e., the program).

On the other hand, as we see in Figure 1.1 the main concept behind the *object-oriented paradigm* is that instead of defining systems as two separate parts (data and functionality), we now define systems as a collection of interacting objects. *Objects* do things (i.e., they have functionality) and they know things (i.e., they have data). Although this sounds similar to the structured paradigm, it's actually quite different. So let's look at an example.

Consider the design of an information system for a university. Taking the structured approach we would define the layout of a database and the design of a program to access that data. In the database there would be information about students, courses, rooms, and professors. The program would allow us to enroll students in courses, assign professors to teach courses, schedule courses in certain rooms, and so on. The program would access and update the database, in effect supporting the day-to-day business of the school.

Now let's consider the university information system from an object-oriented perspective. In the real world we have students, professors, rooms, and courses. All of these things would be considered

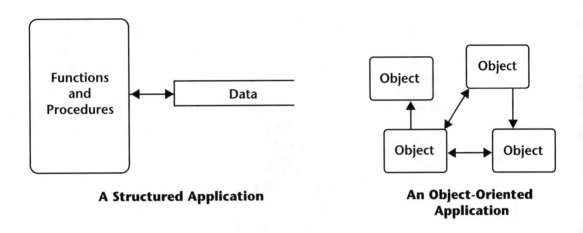

A Structured Application

An Object-Oriented Application

objects. In the real world students know things (they have names, addresses, birth dates, phone numbers) and they do things (enroll in courses, drop courses, drive cars). Professors also know things (the courses they teach, their names) and they do things (input marks, make schedule requests). From a systems perspective, rooms know things (the building they're in and their room number) and should be able to do things too (like tell you when they are available and allow you to reserve them for a certain period of time). Courses also know things (their title, description, who's taking them) and should be able to do things (like allow students to enroll in them or drop them).

To implement this system, we would define a collection of classes (a class is a generic representation of similar objects) that interact with each other. For example, we would have "Course," "Student," "Professor," and "Room" classes. The collection of these classes would make up our application, which would include both the functionality (the program) and the data.

As you can see, the OO approach results in a completely different view of what an application is all about. Rather than having a program that accesses a database, instead we have an application that exists in what we'll call an *object space*. The object space is where both the program and the data for the application reside. We'll discuss this concept in further detail in chapter 5, but for now think of the object space as virtual memory.

Figure 1.1.
The structured paradigm versus the object-oriented paradigm.

DEFINITIONS

The object-oriented paradigm—A development strategy based on the concept of building systems from (one hopes) reusable components called objects.

Object—A person, place, thing, concept, or event that is applicable to the system at hand. Objects both know things (i.e., they have data) and they do things (i.e., they have functionality).

Class—A collection of similar objects. Although in the real world John Smith, Sam Louie, Sally Jones, and Jane Doe are all "student objects," we would model the class "Student" instead.

Object space—When it boils down, this is a fancy term for virtual memory. As far as our applications are concerned, objects exist and interact with one another within the object space. In a pure object-oriented environment, the object space (and hence all objects) are automatically saved to storage (usually some form of database).

OO—This is an acronym that is used interchangeably for two terms: Object-oriented and object-orientation. For example, when we say OO programming, we really mean object-oriented programming. When we say that this is a book that describes OO, we really mean that it is a book that describes object-orientation.

> *For individuals, OO is a whole new way to think.*
>
> *For organizations, OO requires a complete change in their system development culture.*

Chapter 2

Object-Orientation: A New Development- Strategy Paradigm

What We'll Learn in This Chapter

The difficulties encountered with traditional methods.

The advantages of OO.

The disadvantages of OO.

Structured development techniques came out of the late 1960s and early 1970s, an era in which computing meant batch jobs running on large centralized mainframes. Although structured development techniques appeared to serve us well, toward the end of the 1980s serious problems became apparent: the application backlog, the productivity paradox, and the high failure rate of some projects. To add to these problems, in the 1990s users demand applications that have complex intuitive graphical user interfaces (GUIs)—not to mention applications that are on-line and decentralized. It is clear that developers need a new set of tools and techniques to meet the demands of today.

Enter object-orientation.

2.1 Potential Benefits of Object-Orientation

Object-orientation offers the potential to solve (or at least lessen) many of the problems currently faced by the IT industry. OO became popularized in the corporate world in the late 1980s, and has been growing in usage ever since. Some of the benefits follow.

1. **Reusability.** The OO paradigm provides opportunities for reuse through the concepts of inheritance, polymorphism, encapsulation, modularity, coupling, and cohesion. Although we won't discuss them here, we'll see in chapter 5 that these are all fairly straightforward concepts that lead to better design. When it gets right down to it, good design is the only thing that gives us increased reusability.

Good design leads to increased reusability!

2. **Extensibility.** Because classes have both data and functionality, to add new features to the system we only need to make changes in one place—the applicable class. This is much different than in the structured world, where a change in business rules could effect many programs. For example, say we have four structured programs that access the student data table in our university database. Now we add the attribute "Guardian name" to the table. All four programs need to be modified to work with this new data. Now say we've developed an OO university system. As we'll see later in this book, all of the data and functionality for students are encapsulated (contained) in the class "Student." To add "Guardian name" we merely have to modify the definition and source code of the class "Student." What's easier—making the change in four places or in one?

As a second example, say we need to modify our existing system to keep track of university administrators. A university administrator is just like a professor, except that in addition to teaching courses administrators also schedule them. In our structured application, we would need to add a new data table for administrators, and a new program module to handle administrative functions. That's a lot of work. In our OO system, we would define the class "Administrator," which would inherit from "Professor." Granted, we'd still need to write the code to schedule courses, but we wouldn't have to worry about all of the data and functionality already defined for professors.

The preceding two examples show how it is easy to extend existing OO applications in two different ways: First, existing classes are easily changed because both the functionality and data reside in one place. Second, through the use of inheritance new classes are created by taking advantage of the work already done on existing classes—no more reinventing the wheel!

The more extensible a system is the easier it is to change.

3. **Improved quality.** Quality systems are on time, on budget, and meet or exceed the expectations of their users. Improved quality comes from increased participation of users in systems development. As we'll see, OO systems development techniques provide greater opportunity for users to participate in the development process (for example, in the next chapter we'll discuss CRC modeling, a technique in which users do the bulk of systems analysis, and a portion of systems design).

4. **Financial (bottom-line) benefits.** Reusability, extensibility, and improved quality are all technical benefits. Although they all sound like good things (and they are), the reason why they are important is because they lead to the business benefits of OO. From the point of view of our users (remember them, the people who pay the bills), the real benefits are that we can build systems:

Increased user involvement in system development results in improved quality.

- *B*ETTER
- *F*ASTER
- *C*HEAPER

Although most OO books like to concentrate on the technical benefits, the only ones that count are the business ones. Throughout the book we'll refer to these ones as the *BFC* (better, faster, cheaper) benefits. Not only are the BFC benefits applicable to project development, they also apply to maintenance and operations as well. Systems with high rates of reusability have less code to maintain than systems with low rates of reusability (that's because instead of reusing common code, the same code appears over and over again).

The more code, obviously the more effort it takes to maintain it. Furthermore, by definition a system that is easily extensible is easy to maintain. Finally, a system that meets the needs of its users will receive fewer change requests and fewer support calls than a system that doesn't meet their needs.

It is important to note that the benefits of object-orientation are achieved throughout the entire life cycle. We use inheritance during analysis, design, and programming. That means we can reuse our analysis and design efforts, as well as our code. To add new features or to modify existing features in a system, we must first update our analysis and design models, and then modify our code. Therefore both our models and our code must be extensible (and they are). An indispensable way to effectively improve the quality of systems is to increase the involvement of users throughout the entire development process. That's exactly what OO does. Therefore, because the technical benefits are realized throughout the entire development life cycle, the BFC ones are too (remember, the BFC benefits are the direct result of the technical benefits).

The benefits of OO are realized throughout the entire development life cycle, not just during the programming phase.

In the 1990s developers are faced with several serious problems: Applications are becoming more complex, there is a very high rate of project failure, applications take long even to get started, and we spend disproportionate amounts of money on maintenance. Object-orientation specifically addresses these issues, and offers the potential to

- increase the chance of project success,

- reduce the maintenance burden,

- reduce the application backlog,

- deal with complexity.

2.1.1 OO Increases the Chance of Project Success

This isn't what you want to hear, but developers traditionally have not done a very good job at delivering affordable systems in a timely manner that meet the needs of our users. We need to find a way to develop high-quality systems quickly and cheaply, and object-orientation is one potential solution to our problems.

By this definition, almost every single systems development project has failed! Although at first glance the definition may appear harsh, it is actually quite fair. To convince yourself of this, consider the following scenario.

> **SCENARIO** You and your spouse have decided to take the plunge
> and have a house custom-built for your family. You go to a house
> developer, describe your needs and your budget, and tell the
> developer to draw up a plan. At your next meeting, the
> developer shows you something he or she calls a prototype,
> which is a scale model of your house that is made out of
> styrofoam. Because it isn't quite what you want, you tell the
> developer about a few changes that need to be made. After a
> few meetings in which you evaluate the prototype and suggest
> changes, you finally have a house design that you like. The developer has architectural plans drawn up, and at the next meeting
> gets you to sign off on them. You're not an architect so you really
> don't understand the drawings, but they seem fairly complicated
> so they must be right. You and the developer finally settle on a
> price of $200,000 and a moving date of June 14th (right now it's
> the middle of March).
>
> Time goes by, and every second week you receive a progress
> report from the developer. Although he or she keeps telling you
> that everything is going well, you begin to suspect that
> something is wrong. Then, during the last week of May, your
> worst fears are confirmed, you get a call from the developer:
> "Gee, it seems we're a little behind schedule. Due to unforeseen
> complications we've had to tear down and rebuild a few sections
> of the house, so it won't be ready until July 30th." You stand there
> in disbelief—your house is going to be 7 weeks late, a time
> slippage of 50%! Where are you going to live? To make things
> worse, the developer tells you "Oh by the way, we're also a little
> over budget, now that we've actually started building the house
> we have a better idea of what it will really cost: $400,000." As you
> try not to faint, you realize that $400,000 is double the original
> estimate. You aren't happy about the situation, but you've already
> invested a lot of money, so you tell the developer to continue.
>
> August 14th roles around and you are finally able to move into
> your house (the schedule slipped an additional 2 weeks). You
> don't mind as much, because the final bill came in at only

DEFINITION

Project success—A
project is considered
a success when it
meets all of the
following criteria:

- It is on time

- It is on budget

- It meets the needs
  of its users

> $385,000. You walk through the front door, and trying to flip on the lights you realize that there's no light switch. You turn to the developer, and ask how to turn on the lights. "You wanted lights in your house? You never told me that!" exclaims the developer. Angrily, you say "Of course I wanted lights you fool! Hey, where are the wall plugs? Isn't there any electricity in this house?"
>
> "There wasn't any electrical wiring in the architectural plans or in the prototype, didn't you notice? You signed off on them, this is the house that you've paid for, so you better get used to it." replies the developer. Unbelievably, you shout "This isn't right! You're incompetent! You'll never work in this town again! Get out of my house!" The developer exits quickly, and begins walking away, muttering all the while, "That's the problem with people, they don't know what they want. And then when I can't read their minds they blame me. Boy are they ever stupid!"

Sound familiar? How happy would you be if this had really happened to you? How do you think that your users feel when the systems that you develop are late, over budget, and/or don't meet their needs?

In our scenario the house developer didn't get the right specifications from the clients. Although prototyping was a very effective technique for understanding the basic needs of the clients, it didn't provide the developer with the full details that were needed in order to produce a complete design for the house. Sure, forgetting to put electricity in a house seems like a fairly obvious problem. However, systems developers often miss features that seem basic and obvious to our users. The reasons why developers miss "obvious" features isn't because we're incompetent, it's because WE DON'T KNOW THE BUSINESS WELL ENOUGH TO ASK THE RIGHT QUESTIONS.

The house developer showed the clients drawings (models) that they didn't really understand, but still had to sign off on anyway. The fundamental problem is that the developer didn't have a medium that he or she could use to effectively communicate the design to the clients. What was needed was a model that was simple to understand but still showed the details necessary to make an educated decision about the design of the house. The prototype was simple yet lacked the required details, whereas the architectural plans were too complicated. Just like the house developer, as a system developer you must have a way to communicate your design to your users in a way that they can understand.

The developer then went away and built a house that didn't meet the needs of its eventual owners. Had the buyer been more involved with the development of the house, he or she might have realized that the house needed to be wired for electricity! This is a fundamental flaw in the way that systems are currently developed using structured techniques: Although we know that the chance of project success increases as users become more involved in development, users are typically only involved during analysis and user acceptance testing, but not during design and development. We need to find a way to involve our users more in the development process (in chapters 3 and 4 we'll see that CRC modeling and use-case scenario testing can be used to do just that).

Furthermore, the developer delivered the house late and over budget. The main cause for this is that the developer didn't have a handle on how much it would really cost and how long it would really take before he or she started building. Had the developer drawn up better design plans he or she would not have wasted as much time and materials when rebuilding sections of the house. Furthermore, had he or she made use of reusable components (prebuilt walls, kitchens, bathrooms) both the time and cost to build the house could have been reduced.

System developers face the same sort of issues: When we don't spend adequate time designing an application, we end up scrapping and rewriting large sections of code. Even when we do spend enough time designing the system, we produce a large mound of documentation that the user doesn't understand, and probably doesn't have time to read. We could just as well write our design in Latin for all the good that it will do our users. Instead of producing incomprehensible documents, we should instead find ways to inexpensively communicate our design before we begin construction. Wouldn't it have been nice to find out the light switches were missing before the house was finished?

Furthermore, we are constantly reinventing the wheel by programming the same things over and over (how many times have you programmed the logic to go to the next/previous screen)? By using reusable code (and even reusable designs) we can dramatically reduce the time and cost of systems development.

It is possible for all projects to be successful. As developers we must use techniques that allow us to work with our users to a greater extent, and to communicate our designs to them in a way that they understand. We must also invest in reusable components to a greater extent to reduce development time and cost. As we'll see, object-orientation allows us to do all of these things, and more.

Meanwhile, Back in Reality
Don't get me wrong here, I'm not saying that this is all our fault. It's really difficult to convince users that they need to invest the time that it takes to get proper user requirements. It also doesn't help that users are constantly changing their minds about what they want (often their needs have changed, but that's another story). Not to mention the fact that users want systems yesterday, often pushing for unreasonable deadlines.

2.1.2 OO Reduces the Maintenance Burden

We currently spend too much money keeping existing projects going, and because of the long waiting list of work to be done, it takes us too long to get new projects started. These two problems are, respectively, called "The Maintenance Burden" and "The Application Backlog," and object-orientation can help us to deal with these problems.

Figure 2.1 describes one of the most pressing problems facing developers today. Most of the IS (information system) department's budget is spent on supporting and maintaining existing "legacy" systems. In fact, some organizations spend upwards of 95% of their IS budgets on maintenance and support-related activities! However your IS budget is proportioned, the fact is that very little of it is spent developing new systems. This phenomenon is called the "maintenance burden."

Some of the reasons for the existence of the maintenance burden follow.

1. **There were a lot of systems developed in the past that we're still using.** Some organizations have been developing systems for over 30 years, and it has begun to add up! Just like you need to occasionally spend money on maintaining your

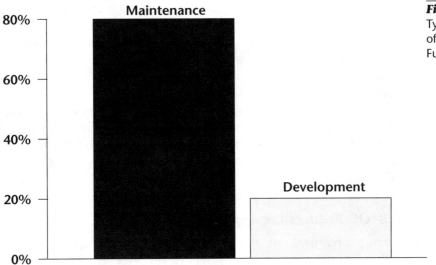

Figure 2.1.
Typical Allocation
of IS Department
Funds

car to keep it going, occasionally you need to spend money to keep a computer system going. This is the most common excuse given by developers, and for the most part it is true. It doesn't explain why we spend SO MUCH MONEY on maintenance, however, although the next two reasons do.

2. **System documentation is very poor, if it exists at all.** We don't like to document our systems, nor do we like to keep documentation up to date. As a result, system documentation is almost always out of date. In fact, it is common to have systems that are completely undocumented. The main problem is that lack of documentation dramatically increases the cost of maintenance. Instead of being able to look at the documentation and determine what's wrong, maintenance programmers need to spend days, and sometimes even weeks or months looking at the code. That's expensive.

3. **Compared to the standards of today, legacy systems are poorly built.** In the past we didn't know that the techniques we were using would lead to systems that are difficult to maintain. We didn't fully realize the importance of simple strategies like internal documentation, use of white space, intelligent

variable naming, loose coupling, and high cohesion. Many of the concepts and techniques of OO specifically address the need to build systems that are easy to maintain. We know what we need to do, now we just need to do it.

Meanwhile, Back in Reality

It's a lot easier to criticize than it is to do. I'm guilty of all of these problems, as probably are you. We can finger point all that we want, but it really isn't going to get us there. The best attitude to take, I think, is to recognize that these problems exist and that we need to deal with them.

2.1.3 OO Reduces the Application Backlog

In many organizations there is currently a 2–5-year "application backlog." Application backlog refers to the average amount of time that it takes for the systems department to get going on the development of a system, as measured from the time that the idea for the project was first conceived.

A list of some of the interesting facts concerning application backlog follows.

    1. **The application backlog directly affects the time that it takes to implement a system.** In Figure 2.2 we see that the

Figure 2.2. How the application backlog affects the total implementation time of a system.

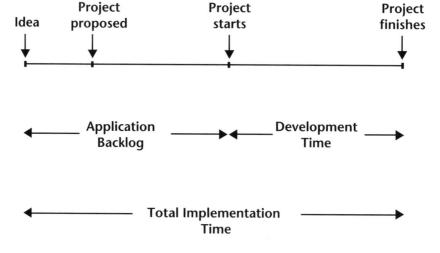

total implementation time for a system is made up of two parts: The time it takes to actually get going (the application backlog) on the project and the time it takes to build it. This implies that if we can reduce the application backlog we can get systems out the door faster.

2. **The application backlog grew during the recession.** During the recession many organizations put off development projects in an effort to reduce short-term expenses. By putting more projects in the queue, the application backlog naturally increased. The recession can't be used to explain the entire application backlog; however, we had a serious backlog long before the recession (although the recession did help to increase it).

3. **The application backlog might not be as bad as we think.** If a project has been waiting to get started for 5 years, chances are it never will. Most organizations take on new projects in priority order, shoving lower priority projects to the back of the line. Therefore, projects that have been waiting a long time might never actually happen! Projects like this should be removed from the queue, and no longer counted as part of the application backlog. Although this will definitely help to reduce the backlog, there is still a serious wait for many projects to get started in most organizations.

4. **OO can help to reduce the application backlog.** The main reason why we have an application backlog is because we simply can't get around to working on those projects. Because OO techniques are more productive than structured techniques (we can develop applications faster and spend less effort maintaining them) we are able to free up resources sooner to tackle new projects. In the long run, this will help to reduce the application backlog.

OO techniques are more productive than structured analysis is.

Meanwhile, Back in Reality

The application backlog is never going to go away. Every time you deliver a new application feature, chances are your users are going to ask for two more. Although this can be very frustrating, it's human nature. I like to look at it like this—I'd rather have my users asking me to continue working on a project than to have them let me go because there isn't any more work for me to do.

2.1.4 OO Deals with Complexity

The applications that we are being asked to develop are becoming more and more complex. When the structured paradigm was introduced in the 1960s and 1970s, we were developing large, batch, mainframe-based transaction-processing systems. Although these systems were often huge, they we fairly straightforward—you get the data, you crunch the data, then you output the data. In the 1990s, systems are much more complex. Applications are now online and real-time, developed for client/server and peer-to-peer architectures. They use complicated, graphical user interfaces, and support a complex and swiftly changing business environment. In short, the development needs of the 1990s are orders of magnitude more complex than what structured approaches were designed to handle. A list of some of the development trends used in the 1990s follows.

1. **Personal computers.** Personal computers (PCs) are now being used for mission-critical information systems. The problem is that many of the tools and techniques that we used to develop mainframe systems are no longer applicable for PC-based systems. Personal computer applications are far more complex to develop, support, and maintain than mainframe-based systems. Think of it like this—instead of developing systems in a centralized, heterogeneous, standard mainframe environment we're now developing systems to run on tens, hundreds, or perhaps thousands of desktop machines, all of which are configured differently. That's not easy.

2. **Graphical user interfaces.** Graphical user interfaces (GUIs), such as MicroSoft Windows, the Apple Macintosh interface, and OS/2 have also become extremely popular. Command line, text-based systems are no longer acceptable to our users. If it doesn't have icons, windows, and a mouse, forget it. Although GUIs look nice, they are actually quite difficult to program from scratch. Just think how much code it would take to write a simple window. Windows can be resized, moved, expanded, and shrunk. When a window changes either its shape or location, the area of screen that was behind it must be redrawn. I don't know about you, but I wouldn't want to have to write the code for that!

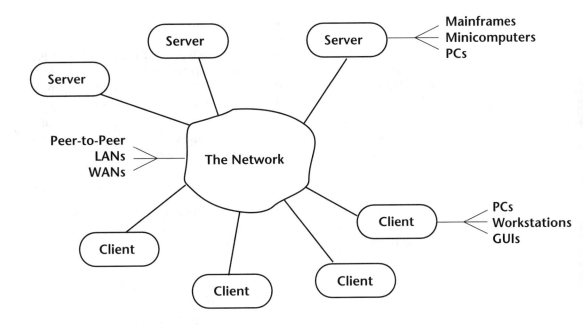

3. **Networking.** As shown in Figure 2.3, networks allow us to connect computers so that we can share data with other people. The combination of personal computers and networking technology has led to both client/server and peer-to-peer development in which the functionality and data of a system are spread out among multiple machines. The sheer complexity of managing and supporting a networked application requires that we discover tools and techniques to deal with that complexity.

4. **Changing business needs.** The only constant is change. The business rules and requirements that our systems support are constantly changing, therefore our systems must change with them. This wouldn't be too bad, if it wasn't for the fact that most business rules are very complicated. We need to be able to develop systems that support both the current and the changing business demands.

5. **End-user computing.** Users want to be able to develop their own systems and/or modify existing systems to meet their needs. Users might develop anything from a simple spreadsheet, to a new type of report, to their own database system.

Figure 2.3.
Systems in the 1990s.

They might also want to add their own, personal features onto an existing system, or just change the way that it looks. Although our users typically aren't programmers, it is our job to create an environment in which they can do these kinds of things. This means that we need to be able to make it simple for our users to do their own development. In other words, we need to be able to take something that is inherently complex, systems development, and make it simple. In short, we need to hide the complexity of systems development from our users.

Now that we appreciate some of the development trends we face, we can focus on what we need to do to develop better systems. A list of some basic principles follows.

1. **Build software from reusable objects.** Consider the way that computer hardware is built: You take a collection of industry standard chips, plug them into a motherboard, and put it in a plastic case. The advantage of this approach is that the chip designers dealt with the complexity of whatever the chip does once. The people who use the chip in their computers don't need to worry about the details of the chip, they only need to know how to use it properly. Think of it like this—it's much easier to build a computer using chips than it is using transistors.

   Wouldn't it be nice to be able to build computer software like this too? Well, that's one of the main benefits of object-orientation. We can create applications from reusable components called objects. Somebody deals with the complexity of part of the application by creating an object that deals with it. Then other developers use the object as part of their application. This allows them to create complex systems out of a few simple components (objects). Chapters 5 and 6 will show us how to build systems out of reusable objects.

2. **Expect that systems will need to change.** If we recognize the fact that our systems will need to change over time, sometimes on very short notice, we can take that into account when we initially design them. In this book we'll see that

when object-oriented concepts are applied correctly they lead to systems that are easy to modify and maintain.

3. **Develop systems faster.** Business needs change quickly, and we need to be able to react quickly to those changes. That means we need to be able to develop new systems quickly, and modify existing ones even quicker. Gone are the days of the 2-year, 3-year, or even 5-year projects. We need to be able to build systems in months, and sometimes even weeks. By implementing complicated concepts and business rules in objects, we are able to build complex systems quicker.

2.2 Potential Drawbacks of OO

Nothing is perfect, including object-orientation. Although there are many exciting benefits to OO, they come at a price.

1. **OO requires a greater concentration on analysis and design, the user community and upper management must accept this fact.** Actually, so did structured techniques, but we ignored this issue to our dismay. We can't build a system that meets the needs of our users if we don't know what those needs are (i.e., we need to do analysis). We can't start building a system unless we know how it all fits together (i.e., we need to design). Both our users and our organization's upper management often underestimate or don't realize the importance of analysis and design, so we must be prepared to deal with this issue.

2. **Developers must work closely with users.** Many (but luckily not all) developers must completely change their view of the user community. Users are the experts, they are the clients. It makes sense to include these people in the development of a system. At the same time, both users and upper management must understand this as well and support the fact that we need to increase user involvement in systems development. This is easier said than done, and will take months and probably even years to attain.

3. **OO requires a complete change in mind-set on the part of individuals.** Systems are now made up of a bunch of interacting objects that have both functionality and data. This is completely different from the structured approach, which separates functionality and data. Don't underestimate the huge difference between these two approaches.

4. **OO requires changes in the development culture of your IS department.** The change in the mind-set of individual developers will actually reflect an overall change in your development culture. Individual developers will be using a new paradigm, do more analysis and design (and hence significantly less programming), and work with your users more. If these things aren't already happening in your organization, you'll need to undergo a significant culture change when you introduce OO techniques into your IS department.

5. **OO is more than just programming.** Part of the process of changing your development culture is the realization that there is more to system development than just programming. Don't forget—the benefits of OO are achieved throughout the entire system development life cycle. This means that you can't just go out and buy a C++ compiler and get the benefits of OO. You actually have to learn how to do OO right. This isn't easy, and it isn't cheap.

6. **OO benefits are all long term.** Although increased reusability and extensibility will help to reduce development time and cost, it is during maintenance that your really get a lot of bang for your buck. That means you may have to wait several years before you begin to truly benefit from OO.

7. **OO demands up-front investments in training, education, and tools.** You need to train your people. You need to buy OO development tools. These things require up-front investment. The short-term need for investment coupled with the long-term payback may mean that upper management will think twice about OO.

8. **OO techniques don't guarantee that you'll build the right system.** While OO offers the potential for increasing the probability of project success, it still depends on the ability of the people involved. Everybody—developers, users, and man-

agers—must be committed to working together to create an atmosphere in which the OO paradigm can flourish.

9. **OO is just part of the solution to our problems.** Object-orientation isn't a silver bullet. We still need to use CASE (computer aided system engineering) tools to help us do our modeling, we still need to do quality assurance to ensure that

---

**TABLE 2.1. The Benefits and Potential Drawbacks
of Object-Orientation**

The Benefits of OO	The Potential Drawbacks of OO
• Reusability	• OO requires a greater concentration on analysis and design, and the user community and upper management must accept this fact
• Extensibility	
• Improved quality	
• Financial (bottom-line) benefits allow us to build systems:	• OO requires developers to work closely with their users
• Better	• OO requires a complete change in mind-set
• Faster	• OO requires that the development culture of your IS department change
• Cheaper	
	• OO is more than just programming
	• OO benefits are all long term
	• OO demands up-front investments in training, education, and tools.
	• OO techniques don't guarantee that you'll build the right system
	• OO is just part of the solution to our problems

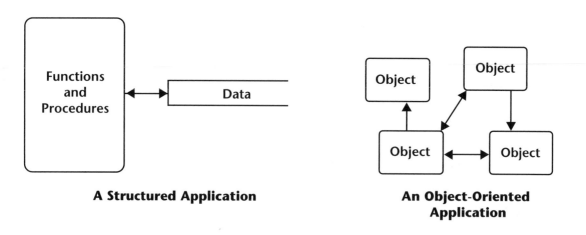

A Structured Application

An Object-Oriented Application

Figure 2.4.
The structured paradigm versus the object-oriented paradigm.

a system meets the needs of its users, and we still need to produce usable interfaces so that our users can work with systems effectively. In short, OO isn't a panacea. It is, however, part of the solution.

2.3 What We've Learned

The object-oriented paradigm is a development strategy based on the concept of building systems from reusable components called objects. Object-orientation offers the potential to solve many of the problems facing the systems industry today.

"User" is a four-letter word, but that isn't such a bad thing.

2.3.1 The Object-Oriented Paradigm

The main concept behind the *object-oriented paradigm* is that instead of defining systems as two separate parts (data and functionality), we now define systems as a collection of interacting objects (see Figure 2.4). *Objects* do things (i.e., they have functionality) and they know things (i.e., they have data). Object-orientation allows us to meet the demands of our users more effectively (see Table 2.2).

Now that we have a basic understanding of the object-oriented paradigm, it is important to clarify what is meant by OO. *OO* is an acronym that is used interchangeably for two terms: object-oriented and object-orientation. For example, when we say OO programming, we really mean object-oriented programming. When we say that this

---

Table 2.2. How to Deal with the Demands of Our Users

Our users	So we should
• Want less money spent on maintenance	• Use OO techniques to reduce the the maintenance burden
• Don't want to wait for applications	• Use OO techniques to reduce the application backlog
• Want systems that meet their needs	• Make sure we understand what our users want
• Want systems on time and on budget	• Spend more time on design and get it right before construction
• Are the experts, not us	• Involve our users in systems development
• Pay the bills	• Realize they can get rid of (outsource) you

---

is a book that describes OO, we really mean that it is a book that describes object-orientation. The list that follows clarifies some of the things that make OO so different from other development strategies.

- OO requires that we work with our users more.
- OO puts a greater emphasis on analysis and design.
- OO benefits are achieved throughout the entire development life cycle.
- OO development requires a new mind-set on the part of everyone.
- OO development requires a culture change within IS departments.
- OO development is iterative in nature, not serial.

Adopting the OO paradigm will change the way that you interact with your users, with management, and with your fellow developers.

> *Work with your users, not against them.*

Chapter 3

Gathering User Requirements: CRC Modeling

How to effectively gather user requirements.

How to find classes.

How to find responsibilities.

How to define collaborations.

How to combine CRC (class responsibility collaborator) modeling and prototyping.

How to prototype screens and reports.

How to effectively arrange CRC cards.

How to perform CRC modeling

How to put together a CRC modeling team.

How to take advantage of CRC modeling tips.

How to benefit from the advantages of CRC modeling.

How to avoid and/or deal with the disadvantages of CRC modeling.

The more you work <u>with</u> your users the greater the chance of project success. CRC modeling is the best way to work with your users to gather requirements.

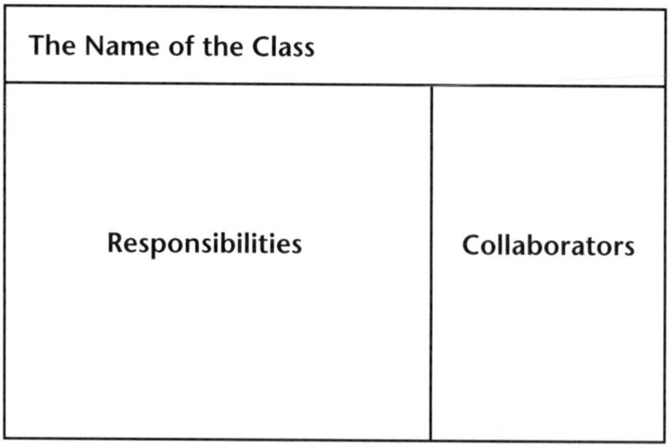

Figure 3.1.
CRC card layout.

The Name of the Class	
Responsibilities	Collaborators

The first step of systems development is to gather user requirements. You can't build a system if you don't know what it should do. CRC (class responsibility collaborator) modeling provides a simple yet effective technique for working with your users to determine their needs.

A CRC model (Jacobson, 1992; Wirfs-Brock, Brick, Wilkerson, & Wiener, 1990) is a collection of standard index cards (see Figure 3.1) that have been divided into three sections.

The steps that follow exemplify CRC modeling in a nutshell.

1. Put together the CRC modeling team, and get them into a room.

2. Do some brainstorming, asking questions like:
   - What should this system do?
   - What shouldn't it do?
   - What will it likely have to do in the future?

3. Explain the CRC modeling technique.

4. Have the business domain experts stand around a table.

5. Iteratively perform the following modeling steps:
   - Find classes
   - Find responsibilities
   - Define collaborators

DEFINITION

Class—A class represents a collection of similar objects. An object is a person, place, thing, event, or concept that is relevant to the system at hand. For example, in a university system there would be students, professors, and course classes. The name of the class appears across the top of the card.

Responsibility—A responsibility is anything that a class knows or does. For example, students have names, addresses, and phone numbers. These are the things that a student knows. Students also enroll in seminars (I realize that the term "class" is more common than "seminar," but because we are already using the term "class" to mean something else, "seminar" is more appropriate), drop seminars, and request transcripts. These are the things that a student does. The things that a class knows and does constitute its responsibilities. Important: A class is able to change the values of the things that it knows, but it is not able to change the values of what other classes know. In other words, classes update their own attributes, and nobody else's.

Collaborator—Sometimes a class will have a responsibility to fulfill, but will not have enough information to do it. For example, we see in Figure 3.2 that students sign up for seminars. To do this, a student needs to know if there is a spot available in the seminar, and if so he or she then needs to be added to the seminar. Students only have information about themselves (their name), and not about seminars, however. What the student needs to do is collaborate (work with) the card labeled "Seminar" in order to sign up for the seminar. Collaboration will take on one of two forms: A request for information (in this case the card "Student" requests an indication from the card "Seminar" whether or not there is a space available) or a request to do something (in this case "Student" will then request to be added to the "Seminar" if there is a seat available).

- Define use cases
- Move the cards around
- Prototype

6. When you are finished CRC modeling, perform use-case scenario testing (chapter 4) on your CRC model.

NOTE: CRC modeling is an iterative process. That means you can find some of the classes, then some responsibilities, then some more

Figure 3.2.
An example of
a CRC card.

Student	
Student number Name Address Phone Enroll in a seminar Drop a seminar Request transcripts	Seminar

classes, and so on. In short, you don't have to perform the steps in order (although you can if you want to).

Although CRC cards were originally introduced (Beck and Cunningham, 1989) as a technique to teach object-oriented concepts, they have been successfully used by both developers and users to understand an OO application throughout its entire system development life cycle. It is my experience that CRC cards are an incredibly effective tool for gathering user requirements, and that's the context in which we'll discuss them. The main point to be made here is that you should use CRC cards wherever you feel that they are appropriate. I like to use them to gather user requirements, but that's just me!

3.1 Putting the CRC Team Together

For CRC modeling to be a success, you need to get the right people into the room. When you are using CRC cards to gather user requirements, that means you must get the right business domain experts (BDEs), a good facilitator, and good scribes. The following list describes the roles taken in CRC modeling sessions. A summary of the qualities needed for each of these roles is provided on the following page.

Business Domain Experts—These are the real users of the system. Users do the work day in and day out—They have the business domain knowledge, not the systems staff. There are typically four or five BDEs involved in CRC modeling. If you have less than four you'll find that

---

**Desirable Qualities for
CRC Modeling Team Members**

Business Domain Experts
Know the business
Think logically
Can communicate well
Are willing to invest the time in systems development
Often, but not always, come from the user community

Facilitators
Have good meeting skills
Understand the CRC modeling process
Can ask valid, intelligent questions

Scribes
Listen well
Have good written communication skills
Have good oral communication skills
Have an ear for business logic

---

you won't get a wide-enough range of knowledge and experience, but once you get beyond five or six people you'll find that there are too many people involved and that they're getting in each others way.

Facilitator—This is the person who runs the session. The main role of the facilitator is to communicate what CRC modeling is all about, make sure that the cards are filled out properly, ask pertinent questions during modeling, and to recognize when prototyping needs to be done and to lead the prototyping effort. Facilitators need good communication skills and should also be technologically adept. The facilitator is often the project leader or a trained meeting facilitator.

Scribe(s)—You should have one or two scribes in the room. Scribes take down the detailed business logic that isn't captured on the cards. For example, on the student card we've recorded that students enroll in courses. What we haven't recorded is the process that they have to go through to actually enroll. This is the type of information that scribes record. Scribes do not actively participate in the session, although they may ask questions to confirm the business rules or processing logic that they are recording.

Observers—For training purposes, you may wish to have one or more people sit in on the modeling session as observers. These people sit at the back of the room and do not participate in the session at all.

Good business domain experts have the following qualities:

1. **They know the business.** That's the definition of a BDE.

2. **They think logically.** Not only do BDEs need to understand the business, they must also be able to think logically. They should be able to describe what they do step-by-step in a logical manner. As a general rule of thumb (note, this isn't always true), someone who finds computers easy to learn and use most likely is able to think logically.

3. **They can communicate well.** The BDEs will be working as a team to create the CRC model. That means they must have good people and communication skills.

4. **They are willing to invest the time in systems analysis and design.** BDEs have better things to do than work on a CRC model. It is the job of the project manager to convince the BDEs that it is worth their while to invest their time in working on the CRC modeling team. Users who have had bad experiences in the past with broken promises from the systems department may be very unwilling to take the time out of their busy schedule to do CRC modeling.

5. **Most, but not all of the BDEs will come from the user community.** When choosing BDEs it is important that one or two of them come from outside the user community. Although you MUST have real users of the system who know the business, it is also a very good idea to have relative "outsiders" who have a vision of the future for your application. These people could be business analysts, system architects, or simply users from a different part of the company.

Good facilitators have the following qualities:

1. **They have good meeting skills.** A CRC modeling session is basically a special kind of meeting. Therefore, because the facilitator runs the session, he or she needs to have top-notch meeting skills. There are several very good meeting books, so pick one up.

2. **They understand the CRC modeling process.** Facilitators should understand the entire OO development process (see chapter 7), including CRC modeling.

3. **They can ask valid, intelligent questions.** One important function of the facilitator is to help the BDEs explore the various aspects of the system being analyzed; therefore facilitators need to be able to ask pertinent questions in order to follow cause-and-effect issues.

Good scribes have the following qualities:

1. **They listen well.** Scribes are there to listen and record business logic and rules; therefore, they need good listening skills.

2. **They have good written communication skills.** Scribes are there to write down the business logic.

3. **They have good oral communication skills.** Scribes will often need to ask questions to determine exactly what the BDEs mean. This implies that they need good oral communication skills.

4. **They have an ear for business logic.** Scribes need to be able to recognize business logic when they hear it if they are going to be able to write it down.

Meanwhile, Back in Reality
Putting together a CRC modeling team is often the toughest part of the entire process. In some organizations it is very difficult to convince users that they need to be involved in gathering requirements—they want to leave it up to the developers. At the other end of the scale, some developers find that everyone and their mother may want to be involved in the definition of user requirements. Instead of fighting to get users into the CRC modeling session,

they're fighting to get them out of it. Rumor has it that there are some organizations in which it is very easy to find just the right number of people for CRC modeling sessions, although rumor also has it that there's a pot of gold at the end of the rainbow too!

3.1.1 How to Become a Facilitator

Facilitators are made, not born. Well, perhaps they're born, I'm not too sure. My experience is that you if you want to become a facilitator, you'll need to do some training first.

1. **If possible, attend another CRC modeling session as an observer.** If your organization is not currently doing CRC modeling, consider bringing in a consultant who has experience as a CRC facilitator to run your first modeling session.

2. **Take a facilitator course.** Meeting facilitation courses are quite common, as are JAD (Joint Application Design) facilitation courses. I suspect that leading-edge training companies will soon start offering courses in facilitating CRC modeling sessions, so keep your eye out for them.

3. **Try it.** Remember, experience is the best teacher.

3.2 Running a CRC Session

I believe that the best CRC-modeling sessions are a lot like JAD sessions—they are facilitated, structured meetings. The most important thing to remember is that the BDEs are the ones that do the modeling, and not JUST the techies. BDEs are the people who have the business domain knowledge, therefore it makes sense that they should be the ones who document the system requirements. The role of the other people in a CRC modeling session is to facilitate and document the results, that's it. The following list supplies the steps needed to run a CRC.

1. **Organize the room.** The meeting room must be set up so as to accommodate the needs of the CRC modeling team. The following page describes this issue in detail.

2. **Brainstorm.** To get everyone warmed up and on the same wavelength, do some brainstorming. To get the brainstorming going, the facilitator should ask questions like "What is the business problem?," "Where is the business going?," "What should the system do?," "What shouldn't the system do?," "Who uses the system?," and "What will the system need to do in the future?" Brainstorming is a proven technique that helps groups of people to quickly and effectively generate ideas.

3. **Explain the CRC modeling technique.** Once brainstorming is finished, the facilitator should describe the technique of CRC modeling. This usually takes between 10 and 15 minutes, and will often include the creation of several example CRC cards. Because people learn best by doing, it is a very good idea for the facilitator to lead the BDEs through the creation of the example CRC cards.

4. **The BDEs follow the CRC modeling steps.** The group of BDEs stand and/or sit around a large table and fill out the CRC cards. Although they'll spend most of their time sitting and discussing the system, BDEs will often stand up to get a bird's eye view of their model, allowing them to get a better feel for the overall system. The steps of CRC modeling (which we'll discuss in detail in following sections) are

   - find classes,
   - find responsibilities,
   - define collaborators,
   - define use cases,
   - arrange the cards on the table,
   - prototype.

5. **Perform use-case scenario testing.** To verify that our CRC model is correct and complete, use-case scenario testing (Greenbaum & Kyng, 1991; Jacobson, 1992) should be performed on it by the team. Although we'll use use cases to help us create our CRC model, use-case scenario testing is a technique that can potentially reduce the cost of finding and fixing analysis errors by five orders of magnitude. Although

TIPS

Steps of CRC Modeling

• Organize the room

• Brainstorm

• Explain the CRC modeling technique

• Create the CRC model

• Perform use-case scenario testing

this technique is covered in great detail in the next chapter, it is done immediately following CRC modeling and should actually be considered just one extra step.

3.2.1 Organizing the CRC Modeling Room

In Figure 3.3 we see the suggested layout for a CRC modeling session. There are several considerations that must be taken into account when you are organizing the CRC modeling room. A list of these considerations follows.

1. **Reserve a meeting room that has something to write on.** You need a flip chart and/or a whiteboard to write on to do brainstorming and prototyping. Flip charts are great because you can tape your sketches on the wall. Whiteboards are great for drawing quick pictures that you might have to edit. My advice—the more whiteboard space the better.

2. **Bring CRC modeling supplies.** You'll need a couple of packages of index cards and some whiteboard markers. If you're going to do use-case scenario testing (and you should!) you'll also need a soft, spongy ball.

3. **Have a modeling table.** There should be a large table for people to CRC model on.

4. **Have chairs and desks for the scribe(s).** Basically, the scribes need something to write on. Put them in the back or sides of the room where they are out of the way but can still see what is going on.

5. **Have chairs for the BDEs.** People will want to sit down during the session, so make sure you have enough chairs.

6. **Have chairs for the observers.** If there are observers, put them in the back of the room. Observers aren't there to participate, so it is valid to put them toward the back of the room.

3.2.2 Do Some Initial Brainstorming

To get the business domain experts thinking on the same wavelength, the facilitator should lead them through a brainstorming ses-

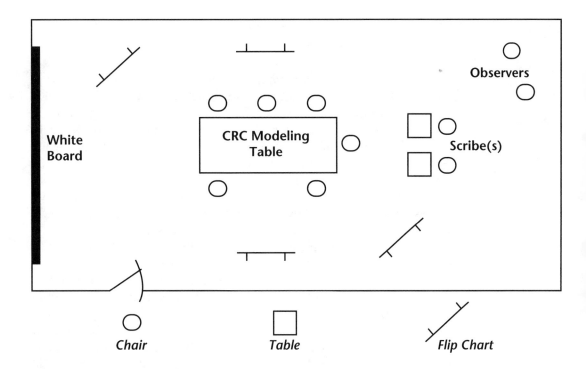

Figure 3.3.
Room layout for
a CRC modeling
session.

sion at the beginning of the CRC modeling session. The main idea is that you want to explore the business objectives for the system that you are developing.

Brainstorming is a technique in which a group of people discuss a topic, and say anything that comes into their minds about it. The rules are simple:

- All ideas are good—they aren't judged by the group.

- All ideas are owned by the group, not the individual.

- All ideas immediately become public property; anybody is allowed to expand on them.

The basic idea is that the facilitator leads the group through brainstorming. The facilitator starts by explaining the rules, and explaining what issues are to be discussed (see the following page). When a BDE suggests an idea, it should be immediately recorded by a scribe

TIP

Give everyone a personal copy of the brainstorming rules before the CRC modeling session so that he or she is aware of them.

onto flip-chart paper. The flip-chart paper should be taped onto the wall so that everyone can see the ideas.

3.2.2.1 Facilitating a Brainstorming Session

The facilitator is responsible for drawing ideas out of the BDEs, and for ensuring that everyone follows the rules. Ideas can be drawn out by asking for examples or anecdotes to an idea, asking for the complete opposite to an idea, or asking for details about an idea. Because it is easy for the group to go off on tangents following an idea, the facilitator will occasionally revisit ideas that have not yet been explored. Brainstorming is an iterative process that doesn't follow a specific path, so facilitators need to be willing to lead the group down multiple avenues of discussion.

To run a brainstorming session effectively, the facilitator should have a fairly good idea what the system, and the business needs that it is supporting, are all about. In other words, the facilitator must be prepared before the CRC modeling session. This is often done while he or she is putting the CRC modeling team together. To find good BDEs you must interview them (either in person or over the phone) and determine what they know about the business. During the interviews the facilitator will pick up valuable knowledge that he or she will use during CRC modeling.

3.2.2.2 Issues to Be Discussed

During the brainstorming session, you want to explore the business objectives for the system. Systems are often developed, or redeveloped, because of changing business needs, it is critical that you understand the business process that the system will support. In their series of reengineering books, Michael Hammer and James Champy (1993; Champy, 1995) discuss several interesting issues that need to be explored during the reengineering process. The boxed text that follows lists several of the issues that you may wish to explore during a CRC brainstorming session.

3.2.3 Finding Classes

An object is any person, place, thing, event, concept, screen, or report that is applicable to your system. A class represents a collection of similar objects. For example, although "Gary Mitchell," "Benjamin Finney," and "Janice Lester" are all examples of airline passengers, we

---

Potential Brainstorming Issues to Be Discussed

- Who is this system for?
- What will they do with the system?
- Why do we do this?
- Why do we do this the way that we do?
- What business needs does this system support?
- What do/will our customers want/demand from us?
- How is the business changing?
- What is our competition doing? Why? How can we do it better?
- Do we even need to do this?
- If we were starting from scratch, how would we do this?
- Just because we were successful in the past doing this, will we be successful in the future?
- Can we combine several jobs into one? Do we want to?
- How will people's jobs be affected? Are we empowering or disempowering them?
- What information will people need to do their jobs?
- Is work being performed where it makes the most sense?
- Are there any trivial tasks that we can automate?
- Are people performing only the complex tasks that the system can't handle?
- Will the system pay for itself?
- Does the system support teamwork, or does it hinder it?
- Do our users have the skills/education necessary to use this system? What training will they need?
- What are our organization's strategic goals and objectives? Does this system support them?
- How can we do this faster?
- How can we do this cheaper?
- How can we do this better?

> **TIP**
> Photocopy this boxed information and distribute it to your BDEs!

---

model the class "Passenger," and not each individual person. Finding classes is fundamentally an analysis task, because it deals with identifying the building blocks for your application. The following list enumerates ways to find classes.

1. Look for anything that interacts with the system, or that is part of the system. If it's a real-world person, place, thing, event, concept, screen or report then chances are it's a class!

2. **Ask yourself if there is a customer.** Ninety-nine times out of 100 there will be some sort of customer card. Universities have students, banks have clients, network operating systems have users, and airlines have passengers. Students, clients, users, and passengers are all examples of customers.

3. **Follow the money.** Ask yourself where the money comes from (usually customers), how it is earned (through the sale of products or services), and what it is spent on? By following the money, you can identify many of the core classes for the system (the customer(s), the products and/or services being sold, and the components that make up the product/service being sold.

4. **A report is a class.** Any report generated by the system is a class. Reports request information from other classes (i.e., they collaborate), process the information, and then output it. In a university information system examples of reports would include student transcripts, class lists, and professor class schedules.

5. **A screen is a class.** Each screen should also be modeled as a class. Interactive systems require input from users. A university system might have a screen to input student information and a screen for professors to input seminar marks. A flight reservation system would have a screen that shows available flights, then a screen that shows available seats on a flight, as well as a screen to input passenger information.

Once the classes have been identified one needs to know what to do with them. The following list gives advice on how to proceed.

1. **Look for the 3–5 main classes right away.** These are the core of the system. If you can't describe the core, then you probably don't understand the business. For example, "Passenger," "Flight," "Staff," and "Airport" would be the main classes for an airline reservation system. "Student," "Professor," "Course," "Seminar," and "Room" would be the main classes for a university information system.

2. **When you think you've identified a class, create a new card for it immediately.** We're using a stack of standard index cards that are available for $1 or $2 per hundred. Go wild and spend the penny or two and use up a card. At the end of the modeling session, you'll find that you've either identified some responsibilities for that card (therefore it's a valid class) or you haven't (so throw it away). Think of it like this—the time that you spend trying to determine whether or not you've identified a class costs far more than the cost of the card.

3. **There are four types of classes that you should be interested in: actor classes, interface classes, report classes, and business classes.** We'll talk about these different types of classes in the next section.

4. **Use one or two words for the class name.** Class names should be simple and should be singular. For example, which name is better: "Student" or "Person who takes seminars"? We use singular names because each class represents a generalized version of a singular object. Although there may be the student "Miles O'Brien," we will model the class "Student". The information about a student describes a single person, not a group of people. Therefore, it makes sense to use the name "Student" and not "Students".

In Figure 3.4 we see several of the classes that would be identified during the analysis of a university information system. There are several "real-world" classes, such as "Professor," "Student," "Course," "Seminar," and "Room." There are also several interface classes, such as "Marks Entry Screen," "Student Editing Screen," and "Student Transcript."

In a real CRC modeling session, our users would have talked about each one of these classes, probably in the context of "what is this system all about?" If they hadn't realized that they had identified a new class, then the facilitator should have piped in with something like "Hey, it sounds like 'Professor' should be a class, what do you think?" The point to be made here is that the users are the ones doing the analysis, not the facilitator. The facilitator provides input and makes sure things run smoothly.

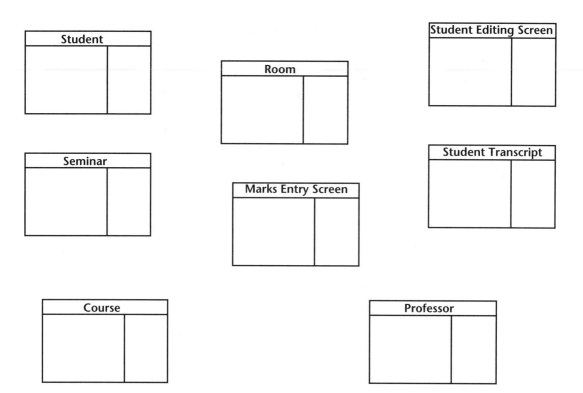

Figure 3.4.
Some of the CRC cards for a university information system.

3.2.3.1 Different Types of Classes

There are four different types of classes: actor classes, interface classes, report classes, and business classes (see Figure 3.5). Although we do not need to distinguish between these classes in our CRC model, it is good to understand that we really need to be looking for several types of classes. The text that follows identifies these four class types.

1. **Actor classes.** Actors are people and/or organizations in the real world that interact with the system. Examples of people who interact with a university information system include students and professors. For example, students enroll in courses and professors input student marks. An example of an organization that interacts with a system would be a bank. A university would process student payments and loans with a local bank, and would probably need to create summary reports for the bank.

An important point to make is that we are interested in keeping track of actors. For example, we want to keep track of students (they're our customers) and professors (their names appear on transcripts and in the university course calendar). We aren't interested in keeping track of registrars, however. Although they work with the system (they are the people who actually enroll students in courses) we wouldn't create a CRC card for them. The reason for this is simple. Although we are interested in the fact that students enroll in courses, we really don't care which individual registrar enrolls them in the course, as long as they get enrolled. On the other hand, if payroll was part of the system that we were building, we might in fact have a "Registrar" card because we need to pay them. In summary, it boils down to the context of the application: Only include the classes that are pertinent to the system at hand.

2. **Business classes.** Business classes are places, things, concepts, and events that describe what the business is all about. For example, "Course," "Seminar," and "Room" are all examples of business classes. A course is a concept (well, I suppose you could argue that it's a thing), a seminar is an event, and a room is a place.

3. **Interface classes.** Interface classes are the screens and menus that make up the user interface of the system. Examples would include a student-editing screen, a seminar-enrollment screen, and a marks-input screen. Additionally, there would also be one or more menus, or front-ends, tying all of these screens together into one application. For example, there may be "Registrar Workbench" and a "Professor Workbench" classes that tie together all of the registrar interface classes (the student-editing screen, the seminar-enrollment screen) and the professor interface classes (the marks-input screen, the course-description screen), respectively.

The reason why we have a class for each screen is that there is often a lot of functionality associated with each type of screen (for example, the seminar-enrollment screen works with information from "Student," "Seminar," and "Course"). Additionally, as we'll soon see we'll be creating rough sketches (prototypes) of each screen. By having a CRC card representing the screen, we'll have a one-to-one mapping of prototypes to interface CRC cards. Furthermore, by putting all the functionality for any given screen in one class, we can change the implementation of that class (add new features or modify existing features) in one place and one place only—the appropriate interface class. This helps to reduce the maintenance burden.

Please note that the use of the term "interface class" may not be ideal. Many developers use the term interface class for classes that are used to access, or interface with, other applications outside the current system. From the viewpoint of these developers, "I/O class" would potentially be a better term to describe screen/report classes. From the point of view of our users, however, "interface class" is perhaps a little more obvious. Actually, you could even argue that "screen/report class" is a good way to go as well, but I wanted to keep it to one word that covers both screens and reports, hence "interface class" was the way that I went. Moral of the story: I can't stop you from calling "interface classes" whatever you want, so use the term with which you are most comfortable!

Figure 3.5.
The four kinds
of classes.

Interface Classes
• Screens
• Menus

Actor Classes
• People
• Organizations

Report Classes:
• Printed
• Electronic

Business Classes:
• Places
• Things
• Concepts
• Events

4. **Report classes.** Report classes are created for any printed or electronic reports or pieces of output. For example, both "Transcript" and "SeminarList" would be considered report classes. A transcript is basically a printed report card. A seminar list is a printed report showing the names and student IDs of all people who are enrolled in the course. We want to create report classes for the same sorts of reasons that we create interface classes: There is a lot of functionality associated with each report, we prototype reports, and we want to be able to change the implementation of a report easily.

The text that follows offers some important tips to remember concerning actor classes and report classes.

1. **Actor classes often do things that don't get implemented.** Actor classes such as "Student" and "Professor" often do things in the real world that we don't implement in code. For example, students purchase monthly passes for the university parking lot. Although this is an important source of revenue to the university, it potentially isn't something that we will include in our system. Perhaps another team will develop a parking lot management system some time in the future.

2. **Report classes only do three things: get data, process data, and output data.** Reports need to get information from other classes (this is called collaboration, which we'll talk about later in the chapter), process it, and then output it. That means you'll end up with a bunch of "Get XXX," "Calculate YYY," and "Output YYY" responsibilities.

Style Issue
Depending on their style, some people like to differentiate from the real-world actor and the object in the system representing them. As a result, to model students they'll create two cards, one called "Student (real world)" and "Student (system)." There's absolutely nothing wrong with this approach. The advantage of having two cards is that you can indicate the use cases associated with the actor on the "real-world" card, while you indicate the stuff that you will actually implement for students on the "system" card. My personal style, which is the one we'll take in this book, is to use one card for actors. The main advan-

Let your BDEs choose whether or not they'll create one or two cards for actors.

tage is that you end up dealing with fewer cards, which can be an issue for large systems, although it can be a little confusing for the BDEs.

3.2.4 Finding Responsibilities

The responsibilities of a class are the things that it knows and does. Finding responsibilities is basically an analysis task, because it deals with defining what a class is all about, without going into how to do it. Remember how the OO paradigm is based on combining data and functionality in the form of a class? Well, the things that a class knows are its data, whereas the things that it does are its functionality. Identifying classes and their responsibilities are a big part of what object-orientation is all about. In the list that follows we identify how to find responsibilities.

1. **Ask yourself what the class knows.** In other words, ask yourself what information must be stored about each class. This is straightforward for real-world classes, but can prove interesting for interface classes. For example, consider the real-world class "Student": We'll want to keep track of their names, addresses, student numbers, and phone numbers. Now consider the interface class "Seminar List": Although we know that we'll need temporary variables to print out the seminar list, I wouldn't record them. The reason for this is simple—our users aren't programmers, therefore the concept of a temporary variable is probably beyond the scope of their experience, so you don't want to be talking about them. This leads to a more generalized concept that systems professionals will find valuable throughout their career—there is no value in confusing users with technical concepts and/or terms, you'll only turn them off and hamper the analysis process. The moral of the story is this: There's a fine line between technical issues that users may not understand and business issues that they do. Only through experience can you learn where that line is.

2. **Ask yourself what the class does.** In other words, ask yourself what functionality the class must perform. Once again this is straightforward for real-world classes but might not be for interface classes. For example, consider the "Student" class again. Students enroll in courses, drop courses, and drive to

school. Now consider the class "Seminar List." It needs to collaborate with the class "Student" to get the person's name, and with the class "Course" to get the name of the course, and with the class "Professor" to get the professor's name. It must then output all of this information to the printer. This means that "Seminar List" would have responsibilities like "Get course name," "Get professor name," "Get student names," and "Print seminar list."

3. **If you've identified a responsibility, ask yourself what class it "belongs" to.** Sometimes you find a responsibility and you're not sure what class it belongs to. This means you're in one of two situations: either the class it belongs to has already been identified, or it hasn't. If the group of BDEs is having problems deciding where the responsibility belongs, the facilitator should mention that perhaps they have overlooked a class. Another possibility is that the responsibility is shared by many classes (i.e., they collaborate). In this situation, ask yourself what class would initiate the process—that's where to put the responsibility. You'll then need to determine what classes it must collaborate with to fulfill the responsibility, and how that collaboration works (which we'll cover in the next section).

Now that we have an understanding of finding responsibilities, we have to consider some additional points. The two items that follow give some advise on responsibilities and collaborations.

1. **Sometimes we get responsibilities that we won't implement.** For example, we identified that students drive to school. Although this is something that they do, we won't be implementing this feature (we still want to record this information, because we may need to develop a system to sell parking passes). It is common for actor classes to have responsibilities that won't be implemented.

2. **Classes will collaborate to fulfill many of their responsibilities.** It is quite common to find that a class is not able to fulfill a responsibility by itself. In other words, it will have to collaborate. Note, when a class needs to collaborate with

Student	
Student number Name Address Phone number Enroll in seminar Drop seminar Drive car	

Seminar List	
Get student names Get professor name Get course name Output	

Professor	
Name Address Phone number Submit marks Teach seminar Request seminar list	

Seminar	
Course# Date/Time Room# List of students Student marks # seats available Waiting list	

Course	
Name Description Prerequisite	

Figure 3.6.
CRC cards
with the initial
responsibilities
added.

another class, that means the second class now has the responsibility to fulfill that collaboration. In other words, as we find responsibilities we'll need to define collaborations, and as we define collaborations we'll often find new responsibilities. This is one of the things that makes CRC modeling an iterative process.

Figure 3.6 shows five CRC cards for the university information system with the initial responsibilities filled in. The reason why these are only the "initial" responsibilities is because when we define collaborations in more detail (in the next section) we'll identify new responsibilities (remember, the "collaboratee" has the responsibility to fulfill the collaboration).

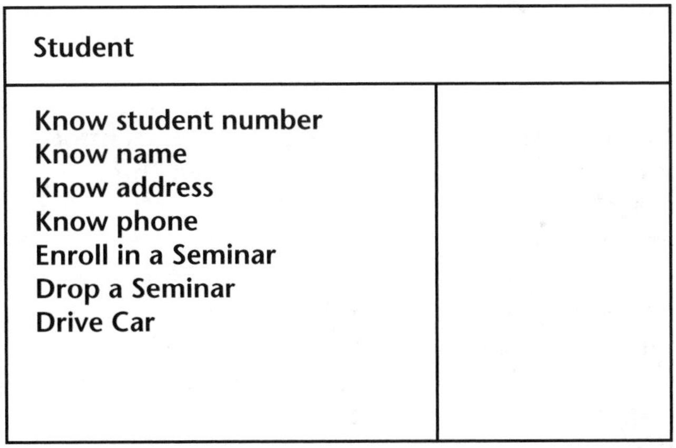

Student	
Know student number Know name Know address Know phone Enroll in a Seminar Drop a Seminar Drive Car	

Figure 3.7.
An alternative approach to documenting the responsibilities of "Student."

Another interesting point to be made concerning Figure 3.6 is that we used user terminology to describe the system. Note for example the use of the term "Submit grades." This is a user term. A techie term would have been something like "Enter grades." Although we know that in the end we'll end up creating some sort of editing screen that will allow professors to enter student marks into the system, they call this submitting marks. Therefore, "Submit marks" is the proper name for that responsibility. In fact, we should have probably used the class name "Marks Submission Screen" as opposed to "Marks Entry Screen."

Style Issue
Finally, throughout the book we'll show data responsibilities as nouns, and functional responsibilities as verbs. As shown in Figure 3.7, many people will document everything as verbs, for example, the responsibility "Name" in student would read "Know Name," the main idea is that everything is named consistently. Both approaches to documenting responsibilities are valid, and I'm not convinced that either is better than the other. My advice is to do whatever you feel most comfortable with.

> **TIP**
> Use the terminology of your users in all of your models. The purpose of analysis is to understand the world of your users, not to foist your artificial, technical terms on them. Remember, they are the experts, not you.

3.2.5 Defining Collaborators

Sometimes classes do not have enough information to fulfill their responsibilities. As a result, they need to collaborate (work) with other classes to get the job done. Collaboration will be in one of two forms: A request for information, or a request to perform a task. The following text indicates how collaborations are defined.

1. **Collaboration occurs when a class needs information that it doesn't have.** Each class has certain things that it knows, and that's it. Very often, a class needs information that it doesn't know. That means that it needs to request the information from another class. For example, when a student wants to sign up for a seminar, he or she needs to find out if there is any room left for them in the class. This means that the card "Student" must collaborate with the card "Seminar." ("Student" will ask for the number of seats still available in the "Seminar.")

   This is a completely different mind-set than in structured development. In the object-oriented world you have to be polite and ask for information, whereas in the structured world if you want information you just take it. For example, in structured development in order to determine if there was a space available in a class, the student program module would take a pass at the "Seminar" data table and count the number of seats left. In other words, it would take the information from the "Seminar" table. Although this approach is very straightforward, it leads to code that is hard to maintain. When the structure of the "Seminar" table changes, any program that accesses it will be affected. In an OO program, if the structure of a class changes, the effects of that change will be localized to the definition of only that class. Nothing else is affected.

2. **Collaboration occurs when a class needs to modify information that it doesn't have.** Each class can update only the information that it knows. This implies that if it needs to have information updated in another class, then it must ask that class to update it. For example, if there is room for a student in the seminar, then he or she needs to be signed up for the seminar. A seminar maintains a list of students who are enrolled in it—this means that only the class "Seminar" can modify it. Therefore, a student must ask the seminar to be enrolled in it. Remember, only a class can change its own

data. To enroll a student he or she needs to be added to the list of students for the seminar, which means that the student list changes. Therefore, to enroll in a course, the "Student" card must collaborate with the "Seminar" card.

The following list supplies additional advice on responsibilities and collaboration.

1. **There will always be at least one initiator of any given collaboration.** In other words, a collaboration starts somewhere, and you need to identify that place!

2. **Sometimes the collaborator does the bulk of the work.** Just because a class initiates a collaboration, it doesn't mean it's going to do a lot of work. For example, consider enrolling a student in a seminar. "Student" collaborates with "Seminar" to see if there are any seats left, and if so then asks to be added to the seminar list. "Seminar" is doing all the work! "Seminar" has to determine how many seats are left, as well as update the list of students in the given seminar. On the other hand, "Student" merely manages (directs) the entire process.

3. **Don't pass the buck.** In order to fulfill a collaboration, a class may have to collaborate with other classes. If this is the case, then the class should do something of value to the process. If class A collaborates with class B, who then passes the buck to C, consider cutting out the middleman (class B) and have A collaborate directly with C. This is usually more efficient.

4. **New responsibilities may be created to fulfill the collaboration.** If a class is asked for information or asked to do anything, then that means it now has the responsibility to fulfill that collaboration! For example, "Student" asks "Seminar" how many seats are left. That means "Seminar" now has the responsibility to fulfill this collaboration.

Note how in Figure 3.8 we've only listed a collaborator once for each class, and not once for each collaboration. For example, "Student"

Student	
Student number Name Address Phone number Enroll in seminar Drop seminar Drive car Give name Seminars enrolled in	Seminar

Seminar List	
Get student list Get student names Get professor name Get course name Output	Seminar Student Professor Course

Professor	
Name Address Phone number Submit marks Teach seminar Request seminar list Give name Drive car	Marks Entry Screen Seminar List

Seminar	
Course# Date/Time Room# List of students Student marks # seats available Waiting list Indicate # seats left Get prerequisites Add/drop student Give student list	Course

Course	
Name Description Prerequisites Give name Give prerequisites	

Figure 3.8.
CRC cards with collaborators and new responsibilities added.

needs to collaborate with "Seminar" several times: Once to determine if there is an available seat in a seminar, once to enroll, and once to drop. Although "Student" collaborates with "Seminar" three separate times, "Seminar" is only listed once as a collaborator (because we don't want to clutter up the card listing the same information over and over).

Student	
Student number Name Address Phone Enroll in a Seminar Drop a Seminar Drive Car	Seminar Seminar

Figure 3.9.
An alternative approach to documenting the collaborators of "Student."

Because the scribe(s) record the business logic of each responsibility, we've recorded the fact that "Student" collaborates with "Seminar" several times. Furthermore, notice how we've added new responsibilities to the cards (such as "Give Name" and "Add/Drop Student"). These new responsibilities were created as the result of collaboration. Remember, if class A collaborates with class B, class B has the responsibility to fulfill that collaboration.

Sometimes the set of collaborations between two classes is two-way, and some times it is only one-way. For example, the collaboration between "Student" and "Seminar" is a one-way street. "Student" requests information from "Seminar," and asks "Seminar" to do things as well. "Seminar" asks nothing of "Student," however. Therefore, we list "Seminar" as a collaborator of "Student," but "Student" isn't shown as a collaborator of "Seminar." The general rule is *Class B is listed as a collaborator of class A if and only if B does something for A.* On the other hand, the collaboration between "Seminar List" and "Professor" is a two-way street. The class "Professor" asks the class "Seminar List" to print itself out, whereas "Seminar List" asks "Professor" for its name (the name of any professor who is involved in teaching a seminar is always included at the top of the seminar list). Therefore, "Seminar List" is shown as a collaborator of "Professor," and "Professor" is shown as a collaborator of "Seminar List."

> **TIP**
> Class B is listed a collaborator of Class A if and only if B does something for A.

Style Issue

The way that we've documented collaborators is the style in which Beck and Cunningham (1989) originally suggested. As shown in

Figure 3.9, a second way (Wirfs-Brock et al., 1990) is to list the collaborators for each responsibility beside it on the card, the end result being that the same collaborator may be listed several times on one card. The advantage of this approach is that BDEs find this easier to understand. The main disadvantage is that your CRC cards become a little more cluttered.

3.2.6 Defining Use Cases

A use case, or use-case scenario, describes a situation that the system may or may not be able to handle. Use cases are ways in which real-world actors interact with the system. By identifying use cases and describing use cases, BDEs are able to find new classes, responsibilities, and collaborations within the system.

A use-case scenario is a description of a potential business situation that may be faced by the users of a system. For example, the following would be considered use-case scenarios for a university information system:

- A student wishes to enroll in a course, but he or she doesn't have the prerequisites for it.

- A professor requests a seminar list for every course that he or she teaches.

- A student wants to drop a seminar the day before the drop date.

Figure 3.10.
The layout of a use-case scenario card.

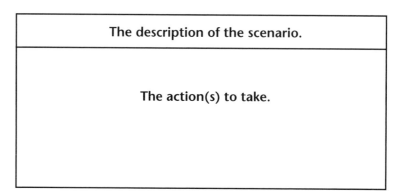

- A student requests a printed copy of his or her transcript so that he or she may include copies of it with a resume.

In short, a use-case describes a way in which a real-world actor interacts with the system. For now, a use-case scenario is usually described with a sentence or two (we'll see in chapter 4 that our scribes will need to document each scenario much more thoroughly). Our approach will be to write each scenario on its own index card using the following format shown in Figure 3.10.

The description of the scenario should be written across the top of the card, and a general summary of the action(s) to be taken are written in the body of the card. Using this format, Figure 3.11 shows the two lines of thought as to how use-case scenarios should be described.

1. **Write a generic use-case scenario, and describe each alternative action.** For example, when a student enrolls in a course, the student is automatically allowed to enroll if he or she meet the prerequisites. If the student does not, a form must be filled out explaining why he or she wants to take the seminar. This form is sent to the professor who teaches the seminar, who makes the decision whether or not to allow the student to take the course. This means I would write one use-case scenario for a student who wants to enroll in a course, with the body of the card describing both alternatives. Another option is given in the text below.

2. **Write specific use-case scenarios, one for each alternative action relating to the scenario.** For the above example you would write two use-case scenarios, one for a student with the prerequisites, one for a student without the prerequisites.

Although we're using index cards to record the use-case scenarios, these are not CRC cards! Remember, a CRC card describes a class, whereas a use-case scenario card describes a business situation. These are two completely different things.

Jacobson (1992) suggests that use-case scenarios be summarized as we have done before, and then expanded on using structured-English

A student wants to enroll in
a seminar.

1. If he or she has the correct prerequisites for the course, enroll
   the student.
2. If he or she does not have the
   proper prerequisites, have him or
   her fill out a special enrollment
   form and take it to the professor
   to get it signed.

A student with the correct prerequisites wishes to enroll in
a seminar.

Enroll them.

A student without the correct
prerequisites wishes to enroll in
a seminar.

Have the student fill out a special
enrollment form and take it to the
professor to get it signed.

Figure 3.11.
The two different
options available
when filling out
use-case scenario
cards.

or pseudo-code to describe the scenario further. We'll see in chapter 4 that the scribes will in fact do exactly this while the BDEs perform use-case scenario testing.

So Who Cares?

Use-case scenarios are important for two reasons: First, by describing how people interact with the system we are developing the use-case scenarios help us to better understand it. Second, they help us to identify new classes, responsibilities, and collaborations. For example, the scenarios in Figure 3.11 describe how students need to get special enrollment forms signed by professors. At the present time this is being done manually, but who is to say we can't do it electronically. The implication being that perhaps we need to identify the need for a "special enrollment" screen used by professors. Or perhaps an email message should be automatically generated and sent to the appropriate professor. Either way, it's obvious that we've just identified the need for new responsibilities, and maybe even a new class or two.

We now appreciate the importance of use-case scenarios. In the text that follows we will learn how to create them.

1. **The BDEs will identify use-case scenarios as the responsibilities of actors (that's because they are!).** Although the BDEs are identifying the responsibilities of actor classes, they will discuss the way in which the real-world actor interacts with the system. That's the definition of a use case. The implication is that the facilitator wants to keep an ear out and make sure that the use case gets documented at the time it is identified. The use cases will be employed later on in the user-requirements gathering process as input into use-case scenario testing.

2. **Go through your brainstorming notes.** During the initial brainstorming process described previously many use-case scenarios will have been identified. Take advantage of this fact by going through your notes and pull out any appropriate use cases.

3. **Transcribe the scenarios onto cards.** Once a scenario is identified, create a scenario card for it (be a big spender and invest the entire penny on a new card). Using either style, it doesn't really matter, record the scenario and describe the appropriate actions to take.

3.2.7 Arranging the CRC Cards

CRC modeling is done by a group of business domain experts around a large desk. As the CRC cards are created, they are placed on the desk so that everyone can see them. To improve everyone's understanding of the system, the cards should be placed on the table in an intelligent manner. Basically, two cards that collaborate with one another should be placed close together on the table, whereas two cards that do not collaborate should be placed far apart.

3.2.7.1 How to Move Cards Around

1. **Cards that collaborate with each other should be close to one another on the desk.** By having cards that collaborate with one another close together, it makes it easier to understand the relationships between classes. For example, the "Student" card collaborates with the "Seminar" card. There is a business relationship between these two cards—students take seminars. Because they work together to fulfill common responsibilities (that of enrolling students in seminars and dropping them out of seminars) it makes a lot of sense to have them close together.

    Think of it like this—in the real world the more you work with someone else, generally the easier that work becomes when you are close together. The main advantage is that when you look at the cards from above (which is exactly the viewpoint your BDEs have standing around the table) you can get an overall view of the system, seeing how each class interacts with the others. Furthermore, you can concentrate on any given section of the system, and know that you'll have all of the cards involved with that section right there in front of you.

2. **The more that two cards collaborate, the closer that they should be on the desk.** When you follow this rule in addition to the first one, not only will you have an understanding of what classes are related to each other, you'll also get a feel for how much they are related.

We now have an idea as to how to place the cards. The following points offer some additional advice.

1. **Expect to be moving the cards around a lot at the beginning.** Typically, at the beginning of a CRC modeling session you will quickly identify several cards. As you define the initial responsibilities and collaborators for each card, you will be moving them around a lot. However, because people have a tendency to identify the most obvious responsibilities first, and because these responsibilities tend to lead to the main

collaborations, you'll find that you will be able to determine the "right" position for your cards fairly quickly.

2. **Put "busy" cards towards the center of the table.** The busiest cards are often the core of the system, so it makes sense to have the core at the center. One really good rule of thumb is to put the customer at or near the center of the table (the customer often has the most important responsibilities within the system, and is usually involved in initiating many collaborations).

3. **Actually move them around.** The benefits of intelligently moving the cards around on the desk are very subtle, yet still important. There is a tendency for people to fill the cards out and then put them down on the table wherever there is room. CRC facilitators must keep an eye on the BDEs/users and make sure that they move the cards around intelligently. Don't underestimate the modeling value of moving the cards around.

4. **People will identify business relationships between classes as they move the cards around.** Typically one person will pick up a card and say that he or she wants to put it beside another because they collaborate. Somebody else will then pipe up and say it should go somewhere else because it is related to another card. The scribe should listen closely to this conversation, and record any business rules that come out of it.

To simplify the example, the CRC model shown in Figure 3.12 below does not include the responsibilities for the classes (to move cards around, you are only concerned with the collaborators). Notice how the classes "Seminar" and "Seminar List" now collaborate with the class "Room." The example we used when we discussed how to define collaborators did not include a card for rooms, so we didn't show "Room" as a collaborator. Both classes need to collaborate with "Room" to obtain certain room information, such as where it is, how many seats are available, the type of equipment it has, and so on.

Although the class "Marks Entry Screen" collaborates with "Course," we weren't able to get it anywhere close to the "Course" card. "Course" collaborates with many cards, and sometimes we just can't arrange the cards so that all of the collaborators are close

Figure 3.12.
CRC cards
after being
arranged on
the table.

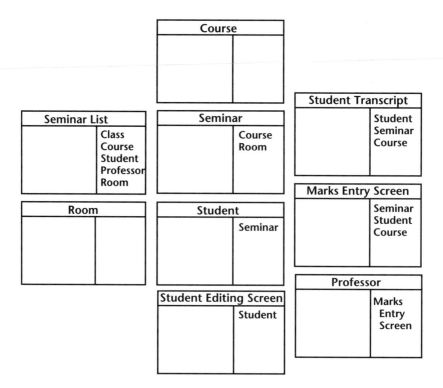

together. This happens. Moving the "Course" card into the center would help, but then we'd get the same sort of problem with either the "Student" or "Seminar" cards.

The advantage to following these strategies for moving cards around is that we can quickly look at any CRC model and get a good understanding of what it is all about. In other words, our model becomes more readable, which makes modeling that much easier.

Another big advantage is that when we convert our CRC model into a class model (class modeling is the topic of chapter 6) the cards on the table are in reasonably good positions for transcribing them onto corresponding positions on the class model. Just take my word on this for now (it'll become obvious when we cover class modeling).

3.2.8 Prototyping

CRC modeling and prototyping go hand-in-hand. In fact, because they work so well together from now on we will consider prototyping as one of the steps of CRC modeling. For the purposes of a CRC modeling session, we will perform only the very rough prototyping of screens and reports in the form of hand-drawn sketches. In this section we will discuss this form of prototyping, as well as prototyping in general.

1. **Do it right away.** As soon as the business domain experts identify the need for a new screen or report, prototype it. It's on their minds right then, so start sketching it right away.

2. **Tape the prototypes on the wall for everyone to see.** Draw the prototype on a piece of flip-chart paper, label it, and then tape it to the wall (with masking tape) so that it is visible to all of the BDEs. That way people can look at the prototype sketches that have been made while they are working on the CRC model.

3. **Ask yourself what functionality the prototype represents.** When the prototype is finished, as a group determine what functionality the system needs to support that screen or report. This is important because we need to identify the responsibilities for the class (card) associated with the prototype. For example, consider the prototype for a university transcript (see Figure 3.13). From the sketch we can immediately see that it has to be able to print out the student name, number, and address at the top of the page, as well as the date the transcript was printed. Furthermore, it has to be able to list all of the seminars the student has taken, who taught it, and what mark they got in the seminar. Finally it needs to be able to calculate and output the overall average mark that the student has earned. From this list of things that need to be done to print a transcript, I think it should be fairly obvious that we've just identified the main responsibilities of the "University Transcript" class.

3.2.8.1 Prototyping in General

In the systems world, the term "prototyping" normally refers to the creation of a mock set of screens and reports that displays the interface of a system, but not its functionality. What I mean by this is that a prototype looks like the application that you are developing, but it doesn't really do anything. Although our rough sketches can be considered prototypes, developers normally use a prototyping tool that

Figure 3.13.
The prototype
of a transcript
report.

University Transcript

Miles O'Brien
Student #123 456 789
1234 Main Street
Metropolis, NY
10000-1234   Printed: Jan. 7, 1996

Course	Professor	Mark
CSC 100 – OO Concepts	Kirk	A++
CSC 110 – Intro C++	Picard	A
CSC 120 – Intro. Smalltalk	LaForge	A–
CSC 200 – OO Modeling	Troi	A+
CSC 300 – OO Testing	Riker	A+
CSC 220 – Conv.Klingon	Worf	B+

Average: A

Figure 3.13.
The prototype
of a transcript
report.

creates an actual program. Prototyping tools will always have some sort of screen painting functionality, allowing us to create menus, editing screens, and dialog boxes. Additionally, it is becoming more common to see these tools include features like report definition and code generation.

3.2.8.2 Prototyping Steps

1. **Do some analysis.** You first must determine what your users need. To do this, you can conduct some interviews, observe your users, hold focus-group sessions, or perform CRC modeling.

2. **Build the prototype.** Create the prototype using a prototyping tool or high-level language.

3. **Evaluate the prototype.** Get together with your users and have them evaluate the prototype. There are three questions that they should be trying to answer:

   • What's good about the prototype?

TIP

When evaluating a prototype, ask: What's good, what's bad, and what's missing. Clint Eastwood, eat your heart out!

- What's bad about the prototype?

- What's missing from the prototype?

4. **Iterate.** If you aren't finished, go back to step 1. You're finished when you aren't getting a lot of changes anymore, and your users are satisfied with the prototype.

3.2.8.3 Prototyping Advice

We now have an understanding of prototypes and prototyping. The following list supplies some additional advice.

1. **Explain what a prototype is.** The biggest complaint that developers have about prototyping is that their users say "That's great, install it this afternoon." Basically, this happens because users don't realize that there is still a few months of work left to do on the system. The reason why this happens is simple: From the users point of view, a fully functional application is a bunch of screens and reports tied together by a menu. Unfortunately, that's exactly what a prototype looks like. To avoid this problem, point out that your prototype is like a styrofoam model that architects build to describe the design of a house. Nobody would expect to live in a styrofoam model, so why would anyone expect to use a system prototype to get the job done?

2. **Work with the real users.** The people who should evaluate the prototype are the people who will be actually using the system. These are the people who will have to work with the system for years to come, it only makes sense that they should be the ones who evaluate the prototype.

3. **Let your users work with it.** Showing users the prototype isn't good enough, they have to work with it. Just like you need to take a car for a test drive to get a feel for it, your users need to take the system for a test drive. Looking at pictures doesn't cut it.

4. **Only show features that you can actually build.** Christmas wish lists are for kids. If you can't deliver the functionality, don't prototype it.

5. **Use a prototyping tool.** There are a lot of good prototyping tools out there that can save you significant amounts of time. Use them.

6. **Get an interface expert to help you design it.** Interface experts understand how to develop easy-to-use interfaces, whereas you probably don't. General rule of thumb: If you've never taken a course in human factors, you don't know what you're doing.

3.3 CRC Modeling Tips

The actions of the facilitator will make or break your CRC modeling session. The facilitator can increase the chances for a successful modeling session by following the advice given below.

1. **Send ahead an agenda a few days before the modeling session.** So that people know what to expect, you should send ahead an agenda for the CRC modeling session. The agenda should include: (1) a description of the system that is being analyzed; (2) a one- or two-paragraph description of why they are attending (after all, they are expert about one or more aspects of the business); (3) a description of anything that they are asked to bring (for example copies of reports or screens currently in use, procedure manuals, etc.); (4) a description of the CRC modeling process (I'd give them a photocopy of the first section in this chapter); and (5) a list of names of the people who will be attending, including contact information so that everyone knows how to reach the others if they need to. By sending an agenda ahead, you give the BDEs time to prepare for the CRC modeling session. Although it takes some time to create an agenda, it helps to dramatically increase the productivity within the modeling session. In short, there's a lot of bang for your buck here.

2. **Prominently display the CRC definitions.** As you explain the CRC modeling process to the BDEs, on a piece of flipchart paper create a summary of what CRC cards are all about. At the top include a picture of the layout of a CRC card, and at the bottom include a one-sentence description for the terms "Class," "Responsibility," and "Collaborator."

3. Work with the "outsider" to put together the modeling team. Like we said earlier, one or two of the BDEs might be an "outsider," who is usually a systems analyst who knows the business really well. This person will have a good idea of what the system is all about, and will be able to provide guidance as to what types of people you need on the modeling team. For example, for a university system you would probably want to have a professor, a student, and a registrar on the team.

We have just reviewed some general tips on CRC modeling . The list that follows offers additional advice.

1. Use their terminology. Don't force artificial, technical jargon onto your BDEs. They are the ones doing the modeling, they are the ones the system is being built for, therefore it is their terminology that you should use to model the system.

2. Keep it low tech. CRC modeling is inherently a low-tech method, which is one of the reasons it works so well. Keep it that way.

3. Keep it fun. System analysis and design do not have to be arduous tasks. In fact, you can always have fun doing it. Tell a few jokes, and keep the CRC session light. People will have a better time and will be more productive in a "fun" environment.

4. Expect to prototype. CRC modeling and prototyping go hand-in-hand. At least, expect to draw some rough sketches of what reports and screens will look like.

5. Expect to take a few days. CRC modeling will take at least one, if not several days. If you find that you are spending more than a week CRC modeling, then chances are you're in trouble. Either you aren't doing CRC modeling right, or the system that you are attempting is too large (remember, large systems take a lot of time to develop and because user's needs change quickly, you won't be able to develop a system that meets their needs,

TIPS

CRC Modeling Advice Summary

- Send an agenda ahead a few days before the modeling session.

- Prominently display the CRC definitions.

- Work with the "outsider" to put together the modeling team.

- Use their terminology.

- Keep it low tech.

- Keep it fun.

- Expect to prototype.

- Expect to take a few days.

- Get management support.

- Include CRC modeling in your system development life cycle.

guaranteeing that your project will fail). If this is the case, break your large system up into smaller subsystems and create a CRC model for each one.

We now have a grasp of the processes involved in CRC modeling. The text that follows provides some good organizational advice to help with your CRC modeling session.

1. **Get management support.** CRC modeling offers a dramatic change in the way that analysis is performed—users are now doing analysis, not developers. When you stop to think about it, this is basically a change in the development culture of your organization. As with any culture change, without the support of upper management you just can't do it. You'll need support from both the managers within your information system department and within the user area. CRC modeling changes the roles of both developers and users, therefore management from both sides must support CRC modeling.

2. **Include CRC modeling in your system development life cycle.** CRC modeling is a big part of the OO analysis process, therefore it should appear as a step in your system development life cycle. The same thing can be said about use-case scenario testing (which is actually part of CRC modeling, although we'll treat is as a separate topic just to confuse you!) covered in chapter 4. Object-oriented system development life cycles are discussed in chapter 7.

3.4 Advantages and Disadvantages of CRC Modeling

CRC modeling is an exciting new analysis technique. As with anything, there are certain advantages and disadvantages. On the one hand, CRC modeling leads to improved analysis quality. This is because for the most part, CRC modeling is done by users (who are the experts), not by technical staff. On the other hand, many systems professionals find CRC modeling threatening because it represents a completely different analysis mind-set. Systems people fear losing control of the analysis process. As a result, many developers are leery of trying a new method—even when their existing techniques don't work. We will first examine some of the advantages of CRC modeling.

1. **The experts perform the analysis.** The people who understand the business are the ones defining the requirements. Although this is completely different than the current approach taken by many systems departments, if you stop to think about it having the real experts model the system makes a lot of sense.

   I have always believed that it is inappropriate for systems people to do analysis. First, unless the person can sit down and do the job of their users, then he or she obviously doesn't know the business as well as the person who does that job. Second, while techies often have technical skills that are second to none, they might not have the communication skills that are necessary to obtain user requirements effectively. Hey, not everyone can be perfect! Third, and most important, when techies are interviewing users, they're usually thinking about how they're going to build the system, not what the system needs to do. I know that whenever I'm interviewing a user I constantly find myself thinking about how I'm going to design the database, or about how the class structure is going to look. I can't help it, and I'm sure it happens to a lot of other systems professionals too.

2. **User participation in system development is increased.** Study after study has shown that the more users are involved in the development of a system the greater the chance of success. CRC modeling increases the participation of users in systems development by having them do the bulk of the analysis.

   Although having users perform analysis is a radical idea for many organizations, it is an idea whose time has come

3. **CRC modeling helps to break down the communications barriers between users and developers.** By providing users with a technique that actively involves them in system analysis, you increase the opportunities for improving the communication between developers and users. Remember, it doesn't matter how proficient you are technically, you can't build a system that will meet the needs of your users if you don't know what those needs are.

4. **CRC cards are easy and inexpensive to prepare.** As you've seen, CRC modeling is very straightforward. Furthermore, the cost of materials to perform CRC modeling is trivial: A few dollars for a package of index cards.

5. **CRC modeling is nonthreatening to users.** In short, nobody is afraid of losing their job to a stack of cards. When people are afraid of losing their jobs, they are not very willing to work with systems. By using a nonthreatening analysis technique, you lessen the probability of having to deal with recalcitrant users.

6. **CRC cards are quick and portable.** You simply throw a package of index cards and a pen in your briefcase and go.

7. **CRC modeling goes hand-in-hand with prototyping.** Both CRC modeling and prototyping are iterative analysis methods. During an analysis session you'll find the group will transparently move back and forth between CRC modeling and prototyping in the effort of recording the requirements for the system.

8. **CRC modeling gives you a good overview of a system.** Users transfer their knowledge of the business onto the CRC cards and into the prototype sketches of the screens and reports.

9. **CRC modeling leads directly into class modeling.** As we'll see in chapter 5, CRC modeling is an excellent start to class modeling. Although the CRC model may not be optimal from a design point of view, it is still pretty darn close to what you want. Class models are the mainstay of OO analysis and design.

10. **CRC modeling is an effective way to gather user requirements.** What more can I say?

11. **CRC modeling allows you to deal with system complexity one class at a time.** One of the first things that people ask is "With a 'real' system, wouldn't you get lots of cards?" Yes! That's because systems are complex. One of the advantages of CRC modeling is that you can concentrate on the system one card at a time, which means you don't get bogged down worrying about everything at once. Think of

Table 3.3. The Advantages and Disadvantages of CRC Modeling

Advantages	Disadvantages
• The experts do the analysis	• CRC modeling threatens developers
• User participation increased	• It's hard to get users together
• Breaks down communication barriers	• CRC cards are limited
• It's simple and straightforward	• Class modeling is still needed
• Nonthreatening to users	• Management support is still needed
• Inexpensive and portable	
• Goes hand-in-hand with prototyping	
• Provides a good system overview	
• Leads directly into class modeling	
• An effective method to gather requirements	
• Allows you to deal with system complexity one class at a time	

it like this—if you think dealing with 50 or 60 cards is hard, it's orders of magnitude easier than trying to handle that much detail all at once.

We have just run through many of the advantages of the CRC modeling process. We must now examine some of the disadvantages of CRC modeling. A listing of the major advantages and disadvantages is shown in Table 3.3.

TIP

If you've read ahead in the book, you'll have come across concepts like aggregation and inheritance. Pretty confusing at first, weren't they? Your users don't need to be burdened with these issues during CRC modeling, so don't mention them. CRC modeling works because it is simple and straight-forward—don't make it complicated.

1. **CRC modeling is threatening to systems developers.** This is true because CRC modeling involves something completely different. Users doing analysis? Preposterous! Developers have always performed analysis, not users! It would never work!

2. **It can be very difficult to get users together.** Users have their own jobs to do. Although user involvement is key to systems development, still one of the hardest tasks facing a CRC modeling facilitator is that of convincing users it is worth their while to be involved in the modeling process. It's not that they aren't interested, it's just that the past performance of systems developers doesn't exactly motivate users to get involved anymore. Why should users spend their valuable time working with systems developers just to have a system delivered to them that isn't what they need, that is late, and that is over budget?

3. **CRC cards are limited.** We can't record detailed business logic on CRC cards (that's what the scribe is there for). We can't record screen/report designs on the cards (that's why we have flip charts to draw on). As we'll see in chapter 5, there are several OO concepts (such as inheritance, aggregation, and object relationships) that we really can't model using CRC cards. However, CRC cards are effective because they are simple.

4. **You still need to perform class modeling.** You can't hand a stack of index cards to your manager and claim that it represents your analysis, your manager just won't go for that. We need to take our completed CRC model and convert it into a class model. We can then use the class model for our system documentation. Class models are a more traditional form of model—they show a bunch of bubbles connected by lines.

5. **You need management support.** If both information systems management and user management don't fully support CRC modeling you're finished.

Meanwhile, Back in Reality
Although "inheritance" is a pretty big word, in a way it's a straight-forward concept. If you haven't read ahead, the main idea is that inheritance is a mechanism that allows you to model similarities

between classes. The bottom line is that people aren't stupid. Whenever there are similarities between cards, the BDEs will be tempted to write something like "all the stuff on XYZ plus." Great! The main point here is that the BDEs should come up with this "quasi-inheritance" on their own, and shouldn't be forced into it by the facilitator.

3.5 CRC Modeling Case Study

To gain a better understanding of what CRC modeling is all about, please read through the following case study.

> **SCENARIO** The Archon Bank of Cardassia (ABC) would like to develop an information system for handling accounts. The following is a summary of interviews with employees and customers of the bank.
>
> The bank has many different types of accounts. The basic type of account is called a savings account. Savings account customers do not get a monthly account statement. Instead, they have a passbook that gets updated when they come in. Each passbook page has enough room to hold up to ten transactions, and every time the book is updated the next transaction immediately after the last update printed in the book. The bank already has the passbook printers and printing software in place (we bought it from a third-party vendor).
>
> Customers are able to open and close accounts. They can withdraw or deposit money, or get the current balance. The current balance is displayed on an account update screen that will be part of the teller's information system. This screen displays the account number, the customer's name, and the current balance of the account. An account is associated with a specific branch. Although we now support multi-branch banking, every account is still assumed to have a "home" branch.
>
> A checking account is just like a savings account, except customers can also write checks on it. We sell checks for $30 for a box of 100. Once a customer uses 75 checks, or check #90 comes in (sometimes people make mistakes and rip checks up)

we send them a notice in the mail asking them if they want to purchase more checks. Account statements are sent out every month. Checking accounts do not have passbooks, and savings accounts do not have account statements.

We charge $1,200 a year for Private Banking Accounts (PBAs). PBAs are just like checking accounts, but they entitle customers to investment counselling services, as well as other services not available to other clients. A PBA account can be held by only one customer (they're not joint), although a customer may have more than one PBA account. This is exactly as it is for savings accounts. Checking accounts, however, can be joint. This means that a checking account can be accessed by one or more customers (perhaps a husband and wife).

A current account is for our corporate customers. It works like a checking account, with a few extra features. For example, there is a quarterly account statement (which is exactly the same as a monthly account statement, except it is done for an entire quarter) that is sent out in addition to the regular monthly statements. The quarterly statement is sent in the same envelope as the statement for that month. Corporate customers also get to choose the number of checks they are sent (100, 250, 500, or 1000) at a time. Current accounts are not joint, nor can they be accessed through an automatic teller machine (ATM). Furthermore, because of the different service needs of our corporate customers, we deal with them at special branches called "Corporate Branches." Corporate branches serve only corporate customers, and do not serve our retail (normal) customers. Corporate customers can be served at "Retail Branches," although they rarely do because the tellers in a retail branch do not have the necessary background to meet their special needs.

There can be more than one account accessible from a bank card. We currently give cards out to any customer who wants them. Customers access their accounts using two different methods—at an automated teller machine or at a bank branch. ATMs allow customers to deposit, withdraw, and get balances from their accounts. They can also pay bills (this is basically a withdrawal) and transfer money between accounts (this is basically withdrawing from one account and depositing into another).

Everything that can be done at a bank machine can also be done by a real-live teller in a branch. The teller will have an information system that provides the screens to perform all of these functions. Additionally, tellers can also help customers to open and close their accounts, as well as print out account statements for the customer. The account statements are just like the monthly/quarterly statements, except they can be for any time period. For example, a customer could request a statement from the 15th of August to the 23rd of September, and we should be able to print that out on the spot.

Monthly and quarterly account statements are normally printed out on the first Saturday of the following month. This is done by an automated batch job.

Because we have started to put ATMs into variety stores and restaurants (in the past we only had ATMs in branches) we now consider each and every ATM, including those in our "brick-and-mortar" branches, to be a branch as well. That means that ATMs have branch IDs and addresses, just like a normal branch does.

To manage the bank effectively, we split it up into collections of branches called "areas." An area is a group of between 10 and 30 branches. A branch is part of only one area, and all branches are in an area. Each area has a unique name, and is managed by an "area manager." Area managers receive weekly transaction summary reports every Monday morning before 9 A.M. This report summarizes the number and total amounts of all withdrawals, deposits, and bill payment performed at each branch (including ATMs) for the previous week. For brick-and-mortar branches, there is also an indication of how many accounts in total were at that branch at the beginning of the week, how many accounts were opened during the week, and how many accounts were closed during the week, and how many accounts there are now. Finally, all of these figures are summarized and output for the entire area.

3.5.1 A Solution to the Case Study

This section presents a solution to the ABC case study (see Figure 3.14). It is by no means definitive. I purposely made a few mistakes in

Figure 3.14.
A possible
solution to the
case study.

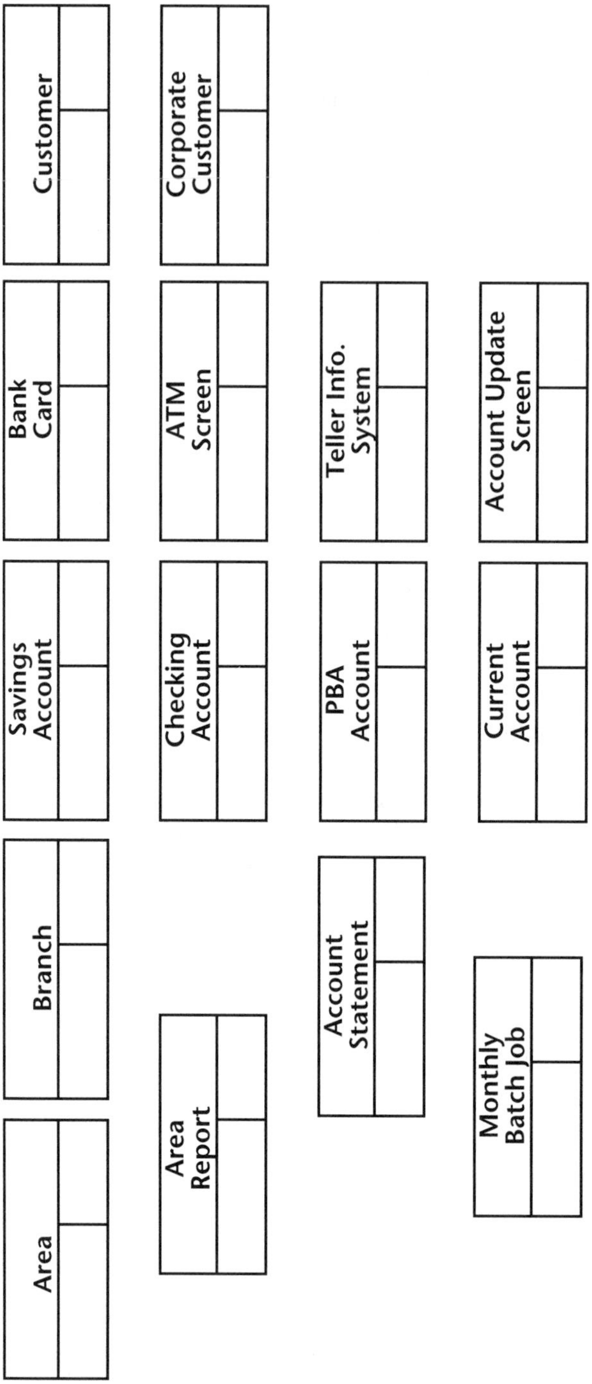

Customer

Corporate Customer

Bank Card

ATM Screen

Teller Info. System

Account Update Screen

Savings Account

Checking Account

PBA Account

Current Account

Branch

Account Statement

Area Report

Monthly Batch Job

Area

this model (in the next chapter we'll discuss how to find these mistakes).

3.5.1.1 An Overview of the Solution

The following text provides a description of all the cards (as shown in Figure 3.14) needed to examine the bank's requirements.

Account statement—Account statements are reports sent to customers that summarize the activity that has occurred on an account over a given period of time.

Account update screen—This screen displays information about an account, such as its current balance and the name and address of the account holder.

Area—A group of branches that are geographically close to one another.

Area report—A report summarizing the activity that has occurred in the area's branches over a period of time.

ATM screen—The screen(s) displayed to customers at an automated teller machine.

Bank card—Customers use bank cards to access their accounts through bank machines.

Branch—Customers interact with the bank at our branches, which include ATMs.

Checking account—An account held by customers on which they are able to write checks.

Corporate Customer—A customer that is a business, not a person.

Current Account—A checking account that is held only by a corporate customer.

Customer—A person who does business with the bank.

Monthly batch job—Prints out the monthly account statements for each account.

Private banking account—A specialized account for wealthy individuals who need a higher level of service.

Savings account—An account that supports only the basic banking services.

Teller Information Screen—The "main" screen displayed to tellers that provides access to all of the account processing functions.

What follows is a list of initial comments. These comments as needed to understand the processes that will help us fulfill the bank's requirements.

1. **There are more details to come.** On the following pages we'll discuss the solution to the case study in detail, a few cards at a time.

2. **There is always more than one answer.** If you don't completely agree with this solution, that's OK! There is always more than one answer to any given problem.

3. **This solution is not complete.** I've left a few things out, so that in the next chapter (use-case scenario testing) we'll learn a simple yet effective technique for discovering missing information.

4. **There is no "Passbook" card.** I made the assumption that the passbook printers are reasonably smart and could figure out what line to start printing on. If the printers don't have this ability, then you would need to keep track of which line to print on next. This would either be done via a "Passbook" card, or via a "Next Line To Print On" responsibility on the savings account card.

5. **There is no "Passbook Printer" card.** It would be very valid to model a passbook printer, but I chose not to because we were told that the printers were already purchased, therefore it was of no use to model them. Had we been in a position to buy/build whatever printers we wanted, then we would prob-

Customer	

Name, Address,
    Accessible accounts
Open account,
    close account
Withdraw from account
Deposit to account
Transfer between
    accounts
Request balance
Write checks, Pay bills
Request statements
Give name
Give address	

Corporate Customer	

Name, Address,
    Accessible accounts
Open account,
    close account
Withdraw from account
Deposit to account
Transfer between
    accounts
Request balance
Write checks, Pay bills
Request statements
Choose # of checks in
    shipment
Give name, Give address	

ably want to model the printer. This would allow us to gain a better understanding of what features we need and perhaps even desire from a printing unit.

Figure 3.15.
The CRC cards representing the two types of customers.

3.5.1.2 Customers and Accounts

Customers and accounts are the core classes of our model. We need to understand these classes if we want to fully understand what the bank is all about. A list of comments that will aid our understanding of the classes follows.

1. **There are two types of customers.** Because the bank deals with corporate customers differently than they do with normal customers (generally called "retail customers"), we need to have two different cards (see Figure 3.15). For example, we allow retail customers to have a wider range of account selection than do corporate customers, whereas corporate customers have a choice as to how many checks they can order in a shipment. Furthermore, we actually serve them in different branches!

2. **There are cards for each type of account.** There are four account cards: "Savings Account," "Checking Account," "Current Account," and "PBA Account" (see Figure 3.16). These are four separate kinds of accounts, all of which have different features. Therefore, we must have a card for each type of account. Many developers would be tempted to create

Savings Account	
AccountID, BranchID Balance, Transactions Customer who accesses account Deposit, Withdraw Open, Close Give transactions Update passbook	

Private Banking Account	
AccountID, BranchID Balance, Transactions Customer who accesses account Annual Fee Deposit, Withdraw Open, Close Give transactions Counseling services	

Checking Account	

AccountID, BranchID
Balance, Transactions
Customers who access
  account
Last check# processed
#checks process since
  last bundle
Deposit, Withdraw
Open, Close
Give transactions
Process check	

Current Account	

AccountID, BranchID
Balance, Transactions
Customers who access
  account
Last check# processed
#checks processed since
  last bundle
#checks in shipment
Deposit, Withdraw
Open, Close
Give transactions
Process check	

Figure 3.16.
The CRC cards representing the four different kinds of accounts.

a generic card called "Account" that would be able to handle all the features of each account type. Although this strategy sounds simple, because "Account" would not be very cohesive this strategy would actually lead to very complicated code (we'll discuss issues like this in detail in chapter 5).

For example, consider the different types of accounts. A checking account has to be able to process checks, whereas a savings account doesn't. That means we need a separate card. Current accounts are very similar to checking accounts, but they are treated differently: Only corporate customers can have current accounts, and current accounts have a quarterly statement. (Note: It would be valid to have one card called "Checking Account" with the responsibility "Account Type," which would indicate if it is a checking or current account. After all, the differences between these two classes are really small. In chapters 5 and 6, however, we'll learn a really slick concept called inheritance that will allow us to take advantage of all of these similarities.) Finally, there is a PBA account card because of the different fee structure for it and the investment counseling services that it includes.

> **TIP**
>
> The way to tell when you should use multiple cards is this: If two potential classes perform different functions, then have separate cards. If your users treat the two potential classes in a significantly different manner, then have separate cards. Otherwise, have one card.

3. **There is no "Check" card.** We weren't told whether or not we need to keep track of processed checks, so I left it out. Don't let this disturb you, we would at least have a transaction recorded for every check cashed so that we know it was processed. As an aside, many banks are currently in the process of implementing (or have already implemented) a system where a scanned image of each check is stored online. If this were the case at ABC, then we would need to have a "Check" card because we would be keeping track of each individual check.

4. **Current accounts keep track of check shipment size.** Although the size of the check shipment is defined by the corporate customer, it is really an attribute that is applicable to the account, because it describes the number of checks in the shipment for that account. Depending on the way that shipments of checks are produced, we probably should have had a "Check Shipment" class that would take care of that functionality.

3.5.1.3 Areas, Branches, and Reports

Areas are a collection of branches (see Figure 3.17), and branches are where customers physically go to do business with the bank (perhaps in the future ABC will offer banking via modem and/or telephone). The monthly batch job loops through all of the accounts and prints the statement for them. Area reports are used by area managers to help them manage the branches for which they are responsible, and account statements are sent to customer to summarize the activity that has occurred on their account over a given period of time (usually 1 month).

Areas are organizational units based on a collection of geographically close areas. Areas provide information for the area report,

Area	
AreaID Area name Area manager Office address Branches in area Give area name Give address Give branch list	

Branch	

BranchID
Branch name
Address
Branch type
Give branch name
Calculate stats for
  area report
	Savings
	  account
	Checking
	  account
	Current
	  account
	Private
	  banking
	  account

Figure 3.17.
The CRC cards representing areas and branches.

which we will discuss in detail. Branches are either "normal" brick-and-mortar branches where customers are served by tellers or ATMs where customers serve themselves. Although an ATM might be in a brick-and-mortar branch, we consider it a branch on its own. This is due to the fact that some bank machines are freestanding, perhaps in hotels, office buildings, or variety stores.

The Monthly Batch Job
The monthly batch job basically loops through all of the checking, current, and private banking accounts and prints the statement for them (see Figure 3.18).

In the text that follows we will consider some comments concerning the account statement and area reports. Figure 3.19 provides a visual example of the cards needed for these items.

1. **There is only one account statement.** The only difference between a monthly account statement and a quarterly account statement is the period of time that it concerns. Therefore, we only need one account statement card!

2. **Area reports require a lot of collaboration.** The logic for the area report is spread out among several classes. The area report card basically manages the printing process, with the bulk of the work being done by "Branch." The first thing an area report does is get a list of the branches within the area. It then requests each branch to calculate it's weekly transaction statistics. To do this the branch gathers the transactions for the week and summarizes them.

Monthly Batch Job	
Print statement for each account	Account statement

Figure 3.18.
(left) The CRC card representing the monthly batch job.

Figure 3.19.
(below) The CRC cards representing the area report and account statement

Area Report	
Get area info Output area info Get list of branches Get branch stats Output branch info Summarize branch stats Output summary	Area Branch

Account Statement	

Get customer info
Output customer info
Get & output account ID
Calculate & output
  opening balance
Get & output transactions
Output closing balance
	Customer
	Corporate
	  customer
	Checking
	  account
	Current
	  account
	Private
	  banking
	  account

The advantage of this strategy is that if your operating system supports multitasking you can have several branches calculating their totals at once, significantly reducing the time it takes to generate this report. The disadvantage is that the logic for area reports is spread out among multiple classes, making them less cohesive (for example, "Branch" implements both branch things and area report things). As always, there are design tradeoffs!

3.5.1.4 Screens and Bank Cards
The ATM screen card represents the interface presented to customers at automated teller machines. Similarly, the teller information screen card represents the interface presented to tellers. The account update screen

displays the current balance of an account, as well as the name and address of the customer. Figure 3.20 provides examples of these three screen cards. A list of comments concerning the screen cards follows.

1. **Not all the screens are shown here.** We weren't given any details as to how the teller information system and an ATM works. Obviously we need screens to open accounts, close accounts, make deposits and so on.

2. **There are several ways to build the interface for this system.** As with any computer system, there is almost always

ATM Screen	

Branch ID
Accept & verify PIN
Perform deposit
Perform withdrawal
Accept payment
Display balance
	Customer
	Corporate
	  customer
	Savings
	  account
	Checking
	  account
	Current
	  account
	Private
	  banking
	  account
	Bank
	  card

Teller Information Screen	

BranchID
Accept & verify PIN
Perform deposit
Perform withdrawal
Open account, Close
  account
Accept payment
Display balance
Print statement
Display update screen
	Customer
	Corporate
	  customer
	Savings
	  account
	Checking
	  account
	Current
	  account
	Private
	  banking
	  account
	Account
	  statement

Account Update Screen	

Get customer name
Get customer address
Get accountID
Get account balance
Display
	Customer
	Corporate
	  customer
	Savings
	  account
	Checking
	  account
	Current
	  account
	Private
	  banking
	  account

Figure 3.20.
The CRC cards representing the screens in the system.

more than one way to build it, and OO applications are no exception. We have two main strategies to choose from:

a. **Have a menu class that controls the interaction between several screen classes.** This is the strategy that we've already taken in our model. The teller information screen class would effectively be the main menu, and the account update screen would be one of the many screens that it would call. The advantage is that it is easy to identify each screen (it's a class), and it would be easy to maintain (if we want to change a screen, we only have to change one class).

b. **Have an information system class that does everything.** We could create one class that handles the teller screens, and one class that handles ATM screens. Although all of the interface functionality would be in one place, these classes would be very large and cumbersome, and likely very difficult to maintain.

The main purpose of "Bank Card" is to verify that customers using physical bank cards in the real world to access their accounts are who they say they are (see Figure 3.21). They store the personal identification number (PIN) for the card and verify that the right PIN has been typed in at the ATM. Once the PIN is verified, they inform the ATM (and the teller information screen) what accounts the person has access to.

Although these comments deal with implementation issues, they deal with issues that are often confusingly brought into the user requirements definition process.

Bank Card	
Card# PIN Customer who uses card Accessible accounts Verify PIN Indicate accessible accounts	

Figure 3.21. The CRC card representing physical bank cards.

1. **We haven't dealt with normalization issues (yet).** For all of you database experts out there, these classes aren't normalized yet. Don't worry, this is an advanced design issue that will be discussed in a subsequent book for SIGS by the present author. Object-oriented normalization techniques deal with the issue of ensuring that both data and functionality are stored/performed in one place and one place only.

2. **There aren't any foreign keys listed.** In the database world, a foreign key (if X is an attribute in entity A, and X is also the key (unique identifier) of entity B, within entity A the attribute X is considered a foreign key) is used to maintain relationships between entities. For example, to maintain the fact that a customer can access certain accounts, we would include a list of account IDs as attributes in the definition of a customer (yes, I realize this isn't normalized). Account ID is the unique identifier of an account, therefore it would be considered a foreign key as an attribute of customer. Although the concepts of foreign keys work very well in the relational database world, we don't need them in the object world. For now, we can assume that we can maintain these relationships between objects (if worse comes to worse we use foreign keys). The end result of all of this is that on our CRC cards we only need to identify that an account keeps track of who can access it. Think of it like this—foreign keys are a techie thing, not a user thing. Therefore, trying to use them in a CRC model will only confuse the issue.

Here is an additional piece of advice. Try creating a CRC model for a system that you've worked on in the past. Remember, the more you try something the better you'll get at it.

3.6 What We've Learned

CRC modeling is an iterative systems analysis technique that can be performed by the business experts, namely the users of the system. CRC modeling is straightforward, using nonthreatening tools (standard index cards) and techniques. CRC modeling helps to increase the quality of a system by increasing the participation of users in its development. A CRC model is a collection of CRC cards. Figure 3.22

shows the layout used for CRC cards. A CRC card is a standard index card that has been divided into the following three sections.

Class—A class is collection of similar objects. An object is a person, place, thing, event, or concept that is relevant to the system at hand. For example, in a university system, there would be student, professor, and course classes. The name of the class appears across the top of the card.

Responsibility—A responsibility is anything that a class knows or does.

Collaborator—Sometimes a class will have a responsibility to fulfill, but will not have enough information to do it.

3.6.1 The Iterative Steps of CRC Modeling

3.6.1.1 Finding Classes

- Look for anything that interacts with the system, or is part of the system.

- Ask yourself "Is there a customer?"

- Follow the money.

- Look for reports generated by the system.

- Look for any screens used in the system.

- Immediately prototype interface and report classes.

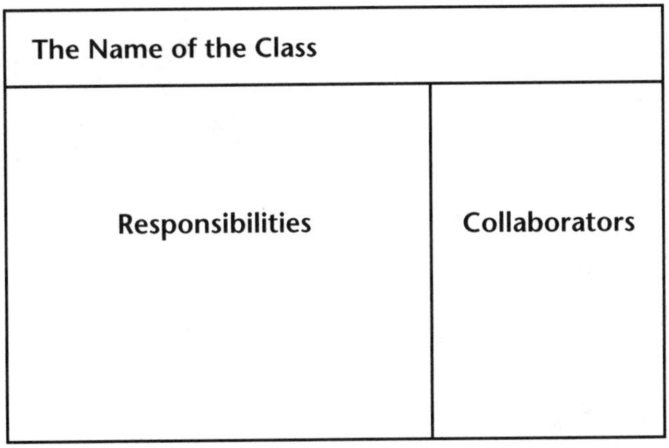

The Name of the Class	
Responsibilities	**Collaborators**

Figure 3.22.
The CRC card layout.

- Look for the three to five main classes right away.

- Create a new card for a class immediately.

- Use one or two words to describe the class.

- Class names are singular.

3.6.1.2 Finding Responsibilities

- Ask yourself what the class knows.

- Ask yourself what the class does.

- If you've identified a responsibility, ask yourself what class it "belongs" to.

- You'll sometimes get responsibilities that we won't implement, and that's OK.

- Classes will collaborate to fulfill many of their responsibilities.

3.6.1.3 Defining Collaborators

- Collaboration occurs when a class needs information that it doesn't have.

- Collaboration occurs when a class needs to modify information that it doesn't have.

- There will always be at least one initiator of any given collaboration.

- Sometimes the collaborator does the bulk of the work.

- Don't pass the buck.

- New responsibilities may be created to fulfill the collaboration.

3.6.1.4 Defining Use Cases

- The BDEs will identify them as responsibilities of actor classes.

- Do some brainstorming.

- Transcribe the scenarios onto cards.

3.6.1.5 *Moving the Cards Around*

- Cards that collaborate with each other should be close to one another on the desk.

- The more two cards collaborate, the closer that they should be on the desk.

- Expect to be moving the cards around a lot at the beginning.

- Put "busy" cards towards the center of the table.

- Actually move them around.

- People will identify business relationships between classes as they move them around.

3.6.1.6 *Prototyping*

- Do it right away.

- Tape the prototypes onto the wall for everyone to see.

- Ask yourself what functionality the prototype represents.

3.6.1.7 *Final Advice*

- Remember, it is your users that do the modeling, not you!

- Work with your users, not against them!

3.7 References

Beck, K., & Cunningham, W. "A laboratory for teaching object-oriented thinking." OOPSLA'89 Conference Proceedings, pp. 1–6.

Champy, J. (1995). *Reengineering Management.* New York: Harper-Collins.

Greenbaum, J., & Kyng, M. (1991). *Design at Work.* Hillsdale, NJ: Lawrence Erlebaum Associates.

Hammer, M., & Champy, J. (1993). *Reengineering the Corporation—A Manifesto for Business Revolution.* New York: HarperCollins.

Jacobson, I. (1992). *Object-Oriented Software Engineering.* Reading, MA: Addison-Wesley.

Wirfs-Brock, R., Wilkerson, B., & Wiener, L. (1990). *Designing Object-Oriented Software.* Englewood Cliffs, NJ: Prentice-Hall.

> *The errors that cost us most are the ones*
> *that we make during analysis.*

Chapter 4

Ensuring User Requirements Are Correct: Use-Case Scenario Testing

What We'll Learn in This Chapter

What use-case scenario testing is.

How to dramatically reduce the cost of testing.

How to dramatically increase system quality.

How to create scenarios.

How to act out scenarios.

As a student of object-orientation, you need to understand use-case scenario testing. You need to ready this chapter to foster that understanding. Use-case scenario testing is a simple yet effective method to find analysis errors when they're inexpensive to fix—during analysis. Furthermore, the scenarios that are developed are a very good start at your user acceptance test plan.

It isn't enough to gather user requirements, you also need to verify that they are correct. This is where systems professionals have always fallen down—until now. You can gather user requirements until you are blue in the face, but unless you can be sure they are correct what good are they? The most common errors made in the development of a system are analysis errors—user requirements that are either missing or misunderstood. Remember, although developers are good at building systems right, we're not that good at building the right system (because we make analysis errors). Use-case scenario testing is an extension of use-case scenarios (Greenbaum & Kyng, 1991; Jacobson, 1992), which is an effective technique used to find and fix analysis errors when they are the least expensive to fix—during analysis.

> **DEFINITION**
>
> *Analysis Errors*— An analysis error occurs when:
>
> • A user requirement is missing.
>
> • A user requirement is misunderstood.
>
> • An unnecessary requirement is included.

What's the implication of this definition for object-oriented development? We would be missing user requirements if we've missed a few responsibilities for a class, or even missed an entire class. A missing user requirement could also mean we missed one or more collaborations too. For example, if we missed a class, then we obviously missed all of the collaborations that it is involved with as well.

Misunderstood user requirements are also a serious issue. Requirements can be misunderstood in three ways: by the user, by the analyst, and/or by the designer. The most serious problem occurs when users misunderstand a requirement. This is why when we build our CRC modeling team we want business domain experts (BDEs) from a variety of backgrounds so that we reduce the chance of this sort of misunderstanding (the wider the range of user experience, the greater the chance that someone will understand a requirement). We can reduce the risk of both analysts and designers misunderstanding requirements by producing a requirements document that is simple and unambiguous. We've seen that CRC models are exactly that!

In the past, unnecessary requirements were often included in a requirements document, and this wouldn't be discovered until field testing. With use-case scenario testing, part of the process is to keep your eye out for unnecessary requirements so that they can be removed before the system is actually built. In the text that follows we will explore some interesting testing facts.

1. **The most significant mistakes are those made during analysis.** Errors made during analysis guarantee that the proj-

ect will fail. If you miss or misunderstand a user requirement, you automatically ensure that the system will not completely meet the needs of your users—either it is missing a feature or a feature is implemented wrong. Instant project failure.

2. **The cost of fixing errors increases the later they are detected in the development life cycle.** The cost of fixing an error snowballs the longer it takes to detect it (McConnell, 1993). If you make an analysis error and find it during analysis it is very inexpensive to fix—you merely change a portion of your analysis document. A change of this scope is on the order of $1(you do a little bit of retyping/remodeling).

   If you don't find it until the design stage it is more expensive to fix. Not only do you have to change your analysis, you also have to reevaluate and potentially modify the sections of your design based on the faulty analysis. This change is on the order of $10 (you do a little more retyping/remodeling). If you don't find the problem until programming you'll need to update your analysis, design, and potentially scrap portions of your code, all because of a missed or misunderstood user requirement. This error is on the order of $100, because of all the wasted development time based on the faulty require-ment. Furthermore, if you find the error during testing, where we typically start looking for errors, the error is on the order of $1,000 to fix (you need to update your documentation, scrap/rewrite large portions of code). Finally, if the error gets past you into production, you're looking at a repair cost on the order of more than $10,000 to fix (you need to send out update disks, fix the database, restore old data, rewrite/reprint manuals). Wouldn't it be wonderful if there was a way to find analysis errors when you make them, during the analysis phase?

3. **Developers don't like to test their systems.** Developers are programmers at heart, not testers. They want to write code, not test it. To put it bluntly, many programmers simply aren't interested in testing, they'd rather go on and start cod-ing on an other project. Furthermore, because testing is tra-ditionally left towards the end of the system development process, and because projects are often late, testing is com-monly cut short. The reason for this is simple—The vast

majority of programmers are optimists, and they know that the system will work. Besides, if it doesn't they can easily fix any problem that might arise. At least that's what they think.

4. **When left to the end of the life cycle, testing is often left out.** Projects are almost always late, and project managers are often desperate to get them back on schedule. As a result, they start looking for places to cut corners, and because testing and documentation are often the only things that need to be worked on, they are often cut back.

5. **We test systems the way we think they're supposed to work, not in the way they actually get used.** Users have a tendency to use systems in completely different ways than those that we originally intended. #$#@%! The problem with this is that we didn't think they'd try some of the things that they do, and as a result they put the system through situations that it simply can't handle.

As we can see in Figure 4.1, the snowballing cost of finding and fixing errors makes it clear that we need to deal with errors sooner

Figure 4.1.
The rising cost of fixing errors.

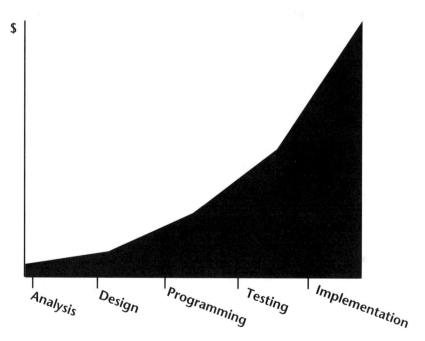

in the development life cycle—preferably when we make the errors.

I don't claim that we only make analysis mistakes. It is obvious that we also make mistakes during design and programming too. But, what I do claim is that developers are very good at dealing with technical issues, those that arise during design and programming (remember, we're good at building systems right). Because we are technically competent, we are usually able to find and deal with design and programming problems—that's what we're good at. What we're not good at is finding and fixing analysis errors.

To compound the problem, sometimes programmers aren't even allowed to talk to our users, even when they desperately want to. Because of the way information system departments are often organized, only the analysts talk with the users and not the coders. The end result is that coders often don't receive the information they need to build the system properly.

Recognizing that there is a problem, many firms have created the role of "Business Analyst." The job of a business analyst is to gather user requirements and convert them into system specifications that the developers can understand. Some firms are even experimenting with having users document their own requirements, usually in the form of a CRC model (see Chapter 3). Although both of these techniques are an improvement over having technical people gathering and documenting user requirements, one fact still remains—there will always be errors in your analysis. This means that we need a technique to find those errors as early as possible, which is what use-case scenario testing is all about.

4.1 Use-Case Scenario Testing

Use-case scenario testing is an integral part of the object-oriented development life cycle. It is performed immediately after CRC modeling by the same group of people who created the CRC model. In fact, many people consider use-case scenario testing as simply an extension of CRC modeling. Basically, use-case scenario testing is a technique that helps to ensure that your analysis, in this case your CRC model, accurately reflects the aspect of your business that you are modeling. The following steps indicate how to perform use-case scenario testing.

1. **Perform CRC modeling.** For an understanding of CRC modeling, see Chapter 3. Use-case scenario testing is performed as either a part of CRC modeling (this is usually the way to go) or is performed as a separate task immediately following CRC modeling (you could then argue that it is still part of the CRC modeling process—holy semantics, Batman!)

2. **Create the use-case scenarios.** A use-case scenario describes a particular situation that your system may or may not be expected to handle. Although many scenarios were created during CRC modeling, we'll see in the next section that you'll still need to create some new ones. You'll typically start by having the business domain experts brainstorm some scenarios. The scenarios are then transcribed onto index cards. We'll discuss this process in greater detail in the next section.

3. **Distribute the CRC cards among the BDEs.** The CRC cards need to be distributed evenly among the BDEs. Each BDE should have roughly the same amount of processing in his or her hands. This means that some BDEs will have one or two busy cards, whereas others may have numerous not-so-busy cards. The main goal here is to spread the functionality of the system evenly among the BDEs. Additionally, it is very important that you DO NOT give two cards that collaborate to the same person. The reason for this will become apparent when we discuss acting out the scenarios.

4. **Describe how to act out a scenario.** The majority of effort in use-case scenario testing is the acting out of scenarios. Just like you needed to explain CRC modeling to your BDEs, you must also describe how to act out scenarios. The best way to do this is to first describe the process, and then to walk through one or two scenarios with them.

5. **Act the scenarios out.** As a group, the facilitator leads the BDEs through the process of acting out the scenarios. The basic idea is that the BDEs take on the roles of the cards that they were given, describing the business logic of the responsibilities that support each use-case scenario. To indicate which card is currently doing "processing," a soft, spongy ball is held by the person with that card. Whenever a card has to collaborate with another one, the user holding the card

throws the ball to the holder of the second card. The ball helps the group to keep track of who is currently describing the business logic, and also helps to make the entire process a little more interesting. We want to act the scenarios out so that we gain a better understanding of the business rules/logic of the system (the scribes write this information down as the BDEs describe it), and find missing or misunderstood responsibilities and classes.

6. **Update the CRC model.** As the BDEs are working through the scenarios, they'll discover that they are missing some responsibilities, and sometimes even some classes. Great, that's why we're acting out the scenarios in the first place! When the group discovers that the CRC model is missing some information, the model should be updated immediately. As a result, once all of the scenarios have been acted out the group ends up with a fairly bullet-proof model. There is very little chance of missing information (assuming you generated a complete set of use-case scenarios) and there is very little chance of misunderstood information (the group has acted out the scenarios, describing the exact business logic in detail).

7. **Save the scenarios.** Don't throw the scenarios away once you are finished acting them out. The stack of scenario cards is a really good start at your user acceptance test plan, so keep them. This is another subject that will be discussed in greater detail in a follow-up volume.

We now appreciate the need for use-case scenario testing. In the text that follows we will learn how use-case scenario testing helps to improve the quality of our analysis.

1. **The scenario itself helps to define how people interact with the system.** Interface designers talk about the human–computer interaction (HCI) boundary (see Figure 4.2), which basically defines how and when people interact with the system. Use-case scenarios help us to flesh out the HCI boundary, and hence the interface and report classes of the system. The HCI boundary is represented on a CRC model

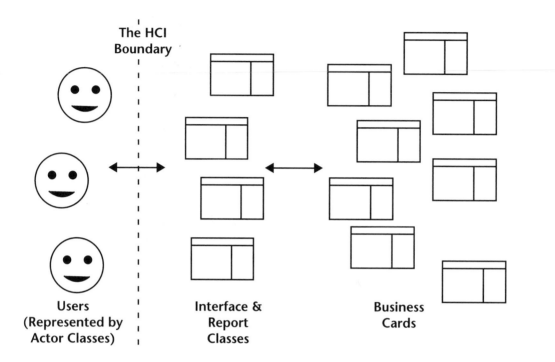

The HCI Boundary

Users
(Represented by
Actor Classes)

Interface &
Report
Classes

Business
Cards

Figure 4.2.
How the HCI
boundary relates
to CRC cards.

as the collection of interactions between actor classes and interface/report classes.

2. **Acting out the scenarios helps to flesh out the application.** Basically, acting out the scenarios forces us to think about the business rules/logic of the system, which allows us to accurately fill out the CRC model. During use-case scenario testing it is common to discover that you are either missing classes, responsibilities, and/or collaborations. Conversely, you may also find that you've identified some classes, responsibilities, and/or collaborations that never get used.

4.1.1 Pros and Cons of Use-Case Scenario Testing

As with everything else, there are advantages and disadvantages to use-case scenario testing. Although many of the advantages are concrete, the disadvantages aren't. The implication of this is that you "only" have to do a sales job to the troops to bring use-case scenario testing into your organization.

4.1.1.1 Advantages of Use-Case Scenario Testing

1. **It helps you to inexpensively find and fix analysis errors.** Let's find and fix problems, when we make them during analysis, and not after the fact when it's usually too late to deal with them.

2. **It provides you with a detailed description of the business logic of the system.** Acting through each scenario provides the scribes with enough information to fully describe the business logic of the system.

3. **It's simple and it works.** Use-case scenario testing is low tech, making it easy to understand. Furthermore, it gives us a detailed and correct description of our system, exactly what we're looking for.

4.1.1.2 Disadvantages of Use-Case Scenario Testing

1. **Your BDEs (users) must make the time to do the testing.** As we've mentioned previously with CRC modeling, one of the hardest parts of the entire process is to get the people together to do it. This is easier said than done.

2. **Managers often feel that "real" work isn't being accomplished.** A bunch of people gathered together in a room throwing a ball back and forth to one another? You call that systems development? Some people just aren't happy unless you go though a complex, time-consuming process that generates mounds of documentation that no one ever reads. Go figure.

3. **Because it's low tech systems professionals are often skeptical.** This is related to the issue above. Use-case scenario testing looks too simple. Throwing a ball around will help you to test an electronic information system? My reply to this is that the proof is always in the pudding—give it a try, you'll probably like it.

> **TIP**
>
> Use-case scenario testing should be performed immediately after CRC modeling. The best way to think about it is that CRC modeling and use-case scenario testing are really one process, not two.

Use-case scenario testing is part of CRC modeling.

4.2 Creating "Testing" Use-Case Scenarios

During CRC modeling we will have already identified and described many use-case scenarios. Although this is a very good start, we still need to create a few more "testing" use cases that help us to explore important business rules and possible identify requirements that are out of scope.

In chapter 3 we saw that use-case scenarios are an important part of identifying classes, responsibilities, and collaborations. We also saw that during CRC modeling the BDEs will identify use-case scenarios that describe the way that actors interact with the system. Although these scenarios are an effective way to gather user requirements, they may not be sufficient to verify that the requirements fully describe the system. The main issue here is that although the current collection of use cases may handle "common" scenarios, we most likely have missed a few unusual ones.

For example, consider enrolling a student in a seminar. We've probably identified scenarios such as a student trying to enroll in a seminar that still has seats available and one that doesn't. Although on the surface these scenarios appear adequate, they probably aren't. What happens when the seminar is full, but has nobody on the waiting list yet (i.e., there are 30 students enrolled in a seminar that has 30 spots available in it)? Is the thirty-first student put on a waiting list? Is there a waiting list? How long is it? Or is student #31 enrolled into the course with the knowledge that one or two people will likely drop out of it, therefore opening up a spot for #31? What happens with student #32, or #33? At what point do we start putting them on the waiting list?

The point to be made here is that these are all interesting issues that need to be explored BEFORE we start building the system. We don't want to get into the position where we're just about to deliver the system and one of our users says "Oh, by the way, does the system handle this . . . ?" and not be able to answer "Yes, and this is how it does it."

We now understand the need for use-case scenario testing. In the text that follows some points of advice are given.

TIP

A good user requirements definition describes both what is in and out of scope.

1. **Create scenarios that the system should and shouldn't be able to handle.** Remember, our good user requirements definition describes both what is in and what is out of scope. This means that not only do you want to identify scenarios the system should be able to handle, but also ones that it shouldn't. Identifying what the system won't do helps to prevent creeping featuritis. When you identify a scenario that the system shouldn't handle, or perhaps will handle in a future ver-

sion, you want to document your reasons why (so you can cover your a**).

2. **Explore business rules.** If your users have told you about a business rule, create a scenario for it. For example, if students can take a maximum of five courses, create a scenario for someone trying to enroll in six! By doing this, you'll bring into question the validity of existing business rules that may or may not make sense anymore. Perhaps the reason why people are only allowed to enroll in five courses per term is because that's how much room was on the paper form when it was originally designed in the 1960s. Do we still want our system to conform to this business rule?

3. **Do some more brainstorming.** To create "testing" use-case scenarios, the facilitator should make the BDEs aware of the issues described previously, and then lead them through another short brainstorming session.

Meanwhile, Back in Reality
It's pretty rare to find that you're missing more than one or two "testing" use-case scenarios. The fact is that your BDEs will have probably identified and included pertinent business rules in the existing scenarios, and will have identified scenarios that they later decided the system wasn't going to handle after all.

4.3 Acting Out Scenarios

Once all of the use-case scenarios have been defined, you want to ensure that your system has the ability to deal with them. As shown in Figure 4.3, the business domain experts must act out each scenario one at a time, updating the CRC cards as they go along. During use-case scenario testing the BDEs will throw a foam ball around. The ball identifies the card that currently has control of the processing, and passing the ball between people represents the passing of control between cards (i.e., they're collaborating). We will now examine how to act out the scenarios.

1. **Call out a new scenario.** Both the description of the scenario and the action(s) to be taken are called out by the facilitator.

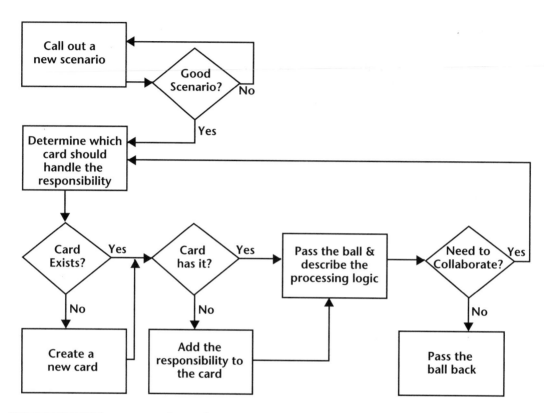

Figure 4.3.
A flow chart
describing how
to act out
scenarios.

Once this is complete, the group must decide if this scenario is reasonable (remember, the system can't handle some scenarios) and if it is, which card is initially responsible for handling the scenario. The facilitator starts out with the ball, and throws it to the person holding that card. When the scenario is completely acted out the ball will be thrown back to the facilitator.

2. **Determine which card should handle the responsibility.** When a scenario has been described, or when the need for collaboration has been identified, the group should decide what CRC card should handle the responsibility. Very often there will already be a card that has the responsibility already identified. If this isn't the case, update the cards. Once the update is complete (if need be), whoever has the ball should throw it to the person with the card that has the responsibility.

3. **Update the cards whenever necessary.** If a card needs to be updated, one of two situations has arisen: The responsibility

TIP

Photocopy Figure 4.3 and distribute it to your BDEs when you explain use-case scenario testing.

needs to be added to an existing card, or a new card needs to be created with that responsibility. If a responsibility needs to be added to an existing card, then ask yourself which card logically should have it, and then have the BDE with that card update it. If a new card needs to be created, the facilitator should hand a blank CRC card to one of the BDEs and ask him or her to fill it out. At the same time, you may also find that you need to update your prototype drawings as well (if an interface or report class changes, then the prototype may need to change as well).

4. **Describe the processing logic.** When the ball is thrown to someone, he or she should describe the business logic for the responsibility step-by-step. Think of it like this: The BDEs are effectively describing pseudo-code (high level program code) for the responsibility. This is often the most difficult part of use-case scenario testing, as some of your BDEs might not be used to documenting processes step-by-step. If this is the case with some of your BDEs, then the facilitator needs to help them through the logic. You'll find that after running through the first few scenarios the BDE's will quickly get the hang of describing processing logic. As the BDE describes the processing logic, the scribe should be writing it down (remember, the job of the scribe is to record the business logic/rules for the system, which is exactly what the BDE is currently describing.)

5. **Collaborate if necessary.** As the BDE describes the business logic of the responsibility, he or she will often describe a step in which collaboration with another card is needed to complete the step. That's great—that's what use-case scenario testing is all about. If this is the case, go back to step 2.

6. **Pass the ball back when done.** Eventually the BDE will finish describing the responsibility. When this happens, he or she should throw the ball back to whoever it was who originally threw it to him or her. This will be another BDE (remember, every time you need to collaborate you throw the ball to the person holding the card that you need to collaborate with) or to the facilitator (remember, the facilitator starts with the ball and throws it to the person holding the card that initially handles the scenario).

The thing to note is that the role of the facilitator is to ensure that the processing logic is being described thoroughly, that the BDEs update the cards, and that they throw the ball whenever they need to collaborate. The ball is important because it indicates who currently has "processing control" (who's doing something).

In the next section we'll walk through in detail the acting out of a simple use-case scenario. You should pay attention to how the facilitator keeps things flowing smoothly, while at the same time the facilitator has the BDEs describe the business logic in exacting detail.

4.3.1 Acting out a Scenario—An Example

The following dialog should help give you a better idea of what it is like to act out a scenario.

> **SCENARIO** The facilitator, Dixon Hill, says "OK, here's the next scenario: A student wants to enroll in a seminar and has the correct prerequisites. What card should handle this?"
>
> Madeline, one of the BDEs says: "Well, to enroll in a course the student needs to go to the registrar's office and hand in the appropriate forms. The registrar would check the form to verify that it was filled in correctly, and then input the information into the system. I guess that means that the registrar's screen needs to be able to handle that feature. I think that Felix has that card."

TIPS

1. It's often tempting to use a tape or video recorder to take down the business logic. The cost of transcription (between 2 and 6 hours for every hour of recording) plus the fact that people don't like to be recorded should make you think twice about this alternative.

2. Keep your eye out for classes or responsibilities that you have never used, as it is a sure sign that something is wrong. Either you have identified "useless" classes and/or responsibilities, or you've missed some scenarios that would test those classes/responsibilities.

3. Expect to occasionally identify new scenarios when you are working through another one. Acting out scenarios often gets the "intellectual juices" flowing and gets people thinking about new potential scenarios.

"Wait a minute!" cries Jessica. "I don't get it. Isn't it the person, the registrar, who enrolls students in courses, not the system?"

"Yes, the registrar uses the system to do this," says Dixon. "However, we're modeling the system and not the person, so even though it is the registrar who the student goes to, for the purpose of this model, the only thing that we're interested in here is the system that they use to do their job. Although, there isn't anything stopping us from creating a new card representing the registrar to represent their role in the registration process."

Felix says, "Hey, I have the registrar's screen card, and I have the responsibility to enroll students in seminars." The facilitator throws the ball to Felix.

"This is an easy one for me," states Felix. "I display an input dialog box to enter the student's name. I have that card too. Once it's entered, the student editing screen is displayed, which includes a list of all of the courses that the student had either taken or is currently in. Who has that card?"

"I do," says Cyrus, "throw me the ball." Felix does, and Cyrus continues on. "I display myself and wait for the registrar to hit a function key. If he presses the "Enroll" key the seminar enrollment dialog is displayed. Madeline has that card." Cyrus throws the ball to Madeline.

Speaking quickly, Madeline blurts out, "The enrollment screen basically allows the registrar to input up to seven course numbers that the student wants to enroll in. When the number is input, the name of the course should be displayed to the right of the input field. In addition to the course number, the registrar must also input the section number of the specific seminar that the student wants. Many of our courses have more than one seminar of them running in a term. When the section number is input, the date, time, and room number for the seminar is also displayed on the screen. Once all of the course numbers are input, the registrar presses the enter key and the student is enrolled in all of the courses. I'm done, here's the ball back Cyrus."

"Hey, hold on!" exclaims the facilitator. "I think you've missed a few details!"

"Like what?"

"Well, first of all, Madeline, how do you get the name of the course, as well as the date, time, and room number?"

"Oh that's easy, I get the course name from the course card, and the date, time, and room number from the seminar card. Does that mean I need to throw the ball to the people with those cards?"

"Yes it does," replies the facilitator. "Whenever you need to get information from another card, or have another card do something for you, you need to collaborate with it. In order to collaborate, you have to throw the ball to the person holding that card."

"Okay. I guess that means to get the name of the course I need to throw the ball to the person with the course card. Who has it?"

"I do, Madeline," says Cyrus. Madeline throws the ball to Cyrus, and Cyrus says that he already has the responsibility to give the name of the course to whoever asks. He says that he does it, and then asks "OK I've given Madeline the name of the course, so what do I do with this stupid ball?"

"Madeline was the person who initially threw it to you, so give it back to her," says the facilitator. Cyrus does so.

"OK, I display the name, then I collaborate with the 'Seminar' card to get the date, time, and room." Madeline throws the ball to Jessica, who holds the seminar card.

"OK, I know the date, time, and room number. I'll just give them to Madeline," exclaims Jessica.

"Hold on! Jessica, do you have the responsibilities to give the date, time, and room number?" asks the facilitator.

"No I don't. I guess I had better add them to the card." Jessica does so and throws the ball back to Madeline.

"OK, all the information is displayed on the screen, the registrar presses the 'Enter' key, and the student gets enrolled. I'm finally done!"

"No you're not!" says the facilitator. "What happens when the student doesn't have the prerequisites for the course?"

"But that would never happen," says Madeline, "the registrar wouldn't enter the course number if the student didn't have the prerequisites."

"Yes they would! Registrars are always enrolling students in courses accidentally. Eventually we figure it out, but often it's too late. It seems to me that the system should be able to figure out whether or not a student should be allowed in a course." says Cyrus.

Thinking about it, Madeline responds, "I guess that's right. I guess the system could display a screen that says that the student doesn't have the correct prerequisites. It could ask if the student wanted to go through the special enrollment process where the professor teaching the course has to sign-off on letting the student in. Hey, we could even email the professor and cut out having the student to fill out a form and then submit it."

"That's a great idea Madeline. I guess that means we need to add a new CRC card to represent this new screen. Jessica, could you handle that?" says the facilitator. "We're going to have to proto-type both the screen and how to implement this email message thing. For now though, let's finish off this scenario and then we'll discuss these new changes immediately afterward. Let's assume the student has all of the prerequisites."

"OK, I guess that means that I need to collaborate with the 'Sem-inar' card to add the student to the seminars," says Madeline as she throws the ball to Jessica, who has the seminar card. Jessica says she knows how to enroll the student, describes how to do it, and throws the ball back to Madeline.

"I'm done, so I guess I finally throw the ball back to Cyrus now," says Madeline, doing so. Cyrus says that he's done, so he throws the ball back to Felix, who originally threw him the ball. Felix is also finished, so he throws the ball back to the facilitator.

"OK, that worked out well. We identified a few missing responsibilities, as well as a missing class," says the facilitator. "Now let's do a scenario where a students tries to sign up for a seminar that he doesn't have the prerequisites for."

4.3.2 Note-Taking by the Scribe—An Example

Although the BDEs act out the scenarios, the scribe(s) should be writing down a detailed explanation of each scenario in some sort of pseudo-code. An example follows.

A scenario for enrolling a student with the correct prerequisites into a seminar:

1. The student goes to the registrar's office and hands in the necessary forms.

2. The registrar verifies the forms are filled-in properly and uses the enrollment screen to input the information into the system.

3. The student search dialog is displayed and is used by the registrar to find the student's information.

4. The student information screen for this person is displayed, and the registrar presses the "Enroll" key to add the student to a seminar.

5. The registrar inputs the course number into the enrollment screen, as well as the section number for the seminar that the student wants.

6. The course name is retrieved for the appropriate course and displayed on the screen. Likewise, room, date, time, and loca-

tion information is obtained from the appropriate seminar and displayed on the screen.

7. If there is room in the seminar, the student is enrolled in it. If not, the system displays a list of other sections the student may wish to enroll in instead.

Style Issue
Although we covered this in Chapter 3, it's worth repeating: Some people like to create one use-case scenario for each alternative, whereas others like to create one really big scenario. For example, when a student enrolls in a seminar, he or she may or may not have the prerequisites for it, and there may or may not be room in the seminar for the student. Some people would create four (two times two) simple scenarios (one in which the student has the prerequisites and there's room, one in which the student has the prerequisites but there's no room, etc.). Other people would create one scenario, which describes "if-logic" for each alternative, as we see in step 7. Both styles work well, you just need to pick the one that is best for you.

4.4 Use-Case Scenarios for the Bank Case Study

The following list briefly describes some possible scenarios for the bank (see chapter 3, section 3.5), and then discusses what may have happened in a real use-case scenario session.

1. A customer wants to deposit $20 into her account at an ATM.

2. A customer wants to withdraw from an account, and has enough money to do it.

3. A customer requests that an account statement be printed out for the time period from the middle of last month until today.

4. A customer reports that he has lost his current bank card, and would like a new one issued.

5. A corporate customer requests a bank card to access a current account.

6. A customer wants to withdraw from an account that does not have enough funds in it.

7. A customer transfers money from one account to another.

8. A grandmother wants to deposit $50 into her grandson's account for his birthday.

9. An existing customer wants to open a new savings account, and make it accessible to his or her bank card.

10. Someone who is currently not a customer wants to open a PBA account and get a bank card for it.

11. Someone who is currently not a customer wants to open a PBA account, but does not want a bank card.

12. Someone who already has a PBA account wants to open a second one.

13. Somebody walks into a branch and sticks it up.

14. An area manager requests a report that is similar to the weekly one that she already receives, but instead of listing data for each of her branches, she wants the summary information for each area within the bank so that she can compare her area with the other ones.

We have just seen some possible scenarios for the bank case study. We can now appreciate what should have happened as pointed out in the text that follows.

1. **It's hard to do use-case scenario testing without real users.** The scenarios listed above are very reasonable, but unless you know the business inside and out, it is almost impossible to work through them. That's why in the real world BDEs are the ones who should be acting through the use-case scenarios! If the BDEs don't know the exact business logic for a scenario, take you best guess if you can't get the answer quickly, and move on.

2. **Some of the scenarios were out of scope.** This is reasonable. Remember, the process of analysis includes the definition of

both what is in and out of scope. It is important to define exactly what a system will do, and what it won't do. If you only define what a system should do, then you've left yourself open to creeping featuritis. This is a phenomena in which your users keep adding on new features throughout the development of your project, increasing both its costs and the time it takes to develop the system.

3. **Some of the simplest scenarios can identify important functionality.** Consider, for example, the case of the grandmother making a deposit into her grandson's account. This is a very straightforward scenario, or is it? What would happen if she didn't know the account number? Should she still be able to do it? If so, then you'll need to add some sort of customer name search screen to the teller information system. What about the bank robbery? Should the teller information system have some sort of alarm function key, or could the system detect if there was a robbery in progress? Perhaps this isn't a responsibility of the system, or at least the current version of the system

4. **Scenarios should explore existing business rules.** For example, corporate customers can't have bank cards. Is this a reasonable business rule? Why does it exist? Should we consider revising it? (We could probably charge corporate customers for the service, hmmmm.)

> **MODELING TIP**
>
> If you make an assumption, get it verified by your users. Nine times out of ten you'll make the right guess, but that one time in ten quickly adds up. You can easily make hundreds or even thousands of assumptions during the development of a system. No matter how small or how obvious they seem, get them verified. If you don't, you are only inviting the project to fail.
>
> *Verify your assumptions!*

4.4.1 How Our CRC Model Should Have Been Affected

When we perform use-case scenario testing, we almost always find that we are missing responsibilities, and sometimes even CRC cards. Our CRC model was missing at least one class, called "Transaction." Not only do we need to add all of the responsibilities for "Transaction," but we also need to add responsibilities for the classes that are involved in collaborations with "Transaction."

4.4.1.1 How Transaction Would Be Found

We would have found "Transaction" either through acting out an "open account," "make deposit," "make withdrawal," "make transfer,"

TIP

Many current business rules are the result of decisions made years, and sometimes even decades, ago. Because the business environment is constantly changing, you want to be constantly questioning whether or not a business rule is still valid. So create a scenario for it and see what your BDEs do with it!

Sometimes you need to question existing business rules.

"close account" scenario (somebody would have recognized the fact that we need to keep track of transactions. We could have also found "Transaction" when somebody realized that we need to print them out as part of an account statement. Transactions are very complicated (as we can see in Figure 4.4) and should be their own card, and not just a responsibility of accounts.

Meanwhile, Back in Reality

The group of BDEs may or may not have decided to make "Transaction" a separate class. They may have decided to have the tracking of transactions as a responsibility of an account, which would have been very reasonable to do. From a technical standpoint, we would "normalize" transaction out of accounts and create its own class, as we have suggested previously. Normalization is a database issue that we will discuss in detail in the previously mentioned upcoming book.

Let us now consider some comments concerning "Transaction."

1. **We need to post a transaction every time something happens.** A transaction is a recording of a single event that has happened to an account. For example, we post (record) an "open" transaction when an account is opened, a "deposit" transaction when a deposit is made into an account, and so on.

2. **Many responsibilities are straightforward.** We need to record the date and time the transaction was made, the type of transaction, the amount of the transaction, the branch it was made at, and the person who made it. Transactions also need to be able to post themselves. When a transaction posts itself, it would basically write itself out to some sort of transaction log.

3. **We need to be able to store the resulting balance of the transaction.** When an account statement is printed, one of the very first things that gets printed out is the opening balance for the period. The problem is that while accounts store their current balance, they don't keep track of their previous balances. Although we could back out all transactions in order to calculate the opening balance for the

Transaction	
Date/Time Transaction Type Amount Branch Customer ID Resulting Balance Post Give Resulting Balance Give Account Statement Info	

Figure 4.4.
The CRC card for "Transaction."

account, this is very costly and time-consuming. A better solution would be to store the resulting balance in each transaction, and then use the resulting balance of the first transaction previous to the reporting period to calculate the opening balance for the statement. For example, say we're printing the account statement for the period July 1st to July 31st. We made a deposit on June 28th, which brought the balance of our account to $100. The next transaction was made on July 5th. As you can see, because there was no action in our account after the deposit on the 28th, the opening balance must have been $100. Therefore, to calculate the opening balance for July 1st, the "account statement" would collaborate with the June 28th transaction and ask it for the resulting balance. This implies that "Transaction" needs to be able to know the resulting balance, and be able to give it account statements.

4. **We need to be able to give transaction information to print account statements.** The bulk of an account statement is the printing of all transactions for that period. Therefore a transaction must be able to give the information required by an account statement to print the transaction.

5. **Transactions don't collaborate.** A transaction has all the information it needs to post itself, so it doesn't need to collaborate.

4.4.1.2 *How the Addition of "Transaction" Affects Other Classes*

1. **Accounts post transactions.** The last step for opening accounts, closing accounts, depositing to accounts, and withdrawing from accounts would be the posting of a transaction to record what happened. Therefore each type of account (Savings, Checking) needs a "Post Transaction" responsibility, and would collaborate with "Transaction" to do so.

2. **Account statements request the resulting balance.** As we mentioned previously, account statements request the resulting balance of the first transaction previous to the start date for the statement so they can output the opening balance.

3. **Account statements print transactions.** Account statements need the information to print out each transaction for the period. Although you could have each transaction print itself out, I don't like to design reports that way. Basically, I have reports get the data, perform any calculations or formatting, and then output the data. By designing report classes like this, all of the logic for any given report is in one class only, instead of having it spread out among multiple classes. That way, if the format or layout of a report changes, I only need to make modifications to one class.

4.4.1.3 *Other Missing Features*

1. **Interface classes.** We were missing several interface classes (the menu and many of the screens to put together the teller system). We showed this as one class in our model "Teller Information Screen." We really should have shown this as several interface classes, one for opening an account, one for inputting a new customer, one for making a deposit, and so on. What we had as "Teller Information Screen" would probably get implemented as some sort of menu front end that would tie everything together. We would also want to do the same thing for the screens and menus displayed by automated teller machines.

2. **A batch job to print area reports.** We also need a weekly batch job to print area reports, just like the one that prints account statements.

4.5 What We've Learned

Use-case scenario testing is an inexpensive, simple, effective technique that helps us to find and fix analysis errors, which are missing or misunderstood user requirements. The basic idea is that the group of business domain experts creates (see Figure 4.5) and then acts out business situations that the system may or may not be able to handle. As they do this, they often identify missing responsibilities and/or classes in their CRC model, and at the same time define the exact business logic pertaining to each responsibility. The end result of a use-case scenario testing session is a bullet-proof CRC model that truly reflects the needs of your users. In this section we will reiterate some important points.

> **DEFINITION**
>
> ***Analysis Errors***—
> An analysis error
> occurs when:
>
> • A user requirement
>   is missing
>
> • A user requirement
>   is misunderstood
>
> • An unnecessary
>   requirement is
>   included.

4.5.1 InterestingTesting Facts

- The most significant mistakes are those made during analysis

- The cost of fixing errors increases the later they are detected in the development life cycle

- Developers don't like to test their systems

- When left to the end of the life cycle, testing is often left out

- We test systems the way we think they are supposed to be used, not the way they actually get used

4.5.2 Steps of Use-Case Scenario Testing

- Perform CRC modeling.

- Create the use-case scenarios.

    - Reuse existing scenarios created earlier during CRC modeling.

    - Do some brainstorming.

    - Create scenarios that the system should and shouldn't be able to handle.

    - Explore business rules.

Use-case scenario testing is an important part of CRC modeling!!!!!

- Distribute the CRC cards among the BDEs.

- Describe how to act out a scenario.

- Act the scenarios out.

  - Call out the scenario.

  - Determine which card should handle the responsibility.

  - Update the cards whenever necessary.

  - Describe the processing logic.

  - Collaborate if necessary.

  - Pass the ball back when done.

  - Save the scenarios for later testing.

4.5.3 Advantages of Use-Case Scenario Testing

- It helps you to inexpensively find and fix analysis errors.

- It provides you with a detail description of the business logic of the system.

- It's simple and it works.

Figure 4.5.
A use-case
scenario card
describing how
to enroll in a
seminar.

A student wants to enroll in a seminar

1. If he or she has the correct prerequisites for the course, enroll them.

2. If he or she does not have the proper prerequisites, have the student fill out a special enrollment form and take it to the professor to get it signed.

4.5.4 Disadvantages of Use-Case Scenario Testing

- Your BDEs (users) must make the time to do the testing.

- It's low tech—developers are often skeptical.

- Managers often feel "real" work isn't being accomplished.

References

Greenbaum, J., & Kyng, M. (1991). *Design at Work.* Hillsdale, NJ: Lawrence Erlebaum Associates, Publishers.

Jacobson, I. (1992). *Object-Oriented Software Engineering.* Reading, MA: Addison-Wesley.

McConnell, S. (1993). *Code Complete.* Redmond, WA: Microsoft Press.

TIPS

- Try it! Use-case scenario testing works. I realize that it's different and you've never tried anything like this before, but give it a shot anyway. There are too many potential cost savings and opportunities for improvement to pass up.

- Get the coffee cups off the tables. Don't forget, you're throwing a ball around!

- Close all windows and doors. Balls have a tendency to bounce!

- Save the cards. They're a great start at your user acceptance test plan.

Object-oriented concepts seem simple.

Don't be deceived.

Chapter 5

Understanding the Basics: OO Concepts

What We'll Learn in This Chapter

Object	*Cohesion*
Class	*Inheritance*
Method	*instance relationships*
Attribute	*Aggregation*
Abstraction	*Collaboration*
Encapsulation	*Messaging*
Information Hiding	*Polymorphism*
Coupling	*Persistence*

As a student of OO, you need to understand the underlying concepts of object-orientation. In this chapter we will explore these concepts as well as a notation to represent them. This will provide the foundation we need before we can discuss how to actually go about creating OO models.

We need to understand object-oriented concepts before we attempt to apply them to systems development. Because OO techniques grew in part out of the disciplines of software engineering and information modeling many OO concepts will seem familiar to you. Don't let this make you complacent—there are also several new concepts that we must understand before we can successfully develop systems using the OO paradigm.

Although we have discussed two object-oriented modeling techniques (CRC modeling and use-case scenario testing) in previous chapters, we didn't need to understand object-oriented concepts to do so. That's one of the strengths of those two techniques—you don't need a degree in software engineering to be able to work with your users. One of the many strengths of CRC modeling and use-case scenario testing is that they are based on a few, simple concepts. That's what allows your users to be involved in system development to such a great extent.

We didn't really know any OO concepts, yet we were still able to perform CRC modeling and use-case scenario testing.

The problem with CRC modeling and use-case scenario testing is that they aren't enough to completely describe an application. Although they are a fantastic start, we still need to do class modeling. And to do class modeling, we need to understand the basic underlying concepts of OO. This chapter discusses the concepts that make up the foundation of OO modeling techniques. Some of these concepts you will have seen before, and some of them you haven't. Many OO concepts, such as encapsulation, coupling, and cohesion, come from the world of software engineering. These concepts are important because they underpin good OO design. The main point to be made here is that you don't want to deceive yourself. Just because you've seen some of these concepts before, it doesn't mean you were doing OO, it just means you were doing good design. Although good design is a big part of object-orientation, there's still a lot more to it than that.

Although OO and good design go hand-in-hand, doing good design doesn't mean you're doing OO, and doing OO doesn't mean you're doing good design.

Meanwhile, Back in Reality

Don't get me wrong, you can still do good design using structural/procedural techniques.

OO concepts appear deceptively simple. Don't be fooled. The underlying concepts of structured techniques also seemed simple, yet we all know that structured development was actually quite difficult. For example, consider the following definition. *Top-Down Design*—When you have a problem that you can't easily deal with, break it down into small problems. Break those problems down, and so on, until you are finally left with a collection of small problems that you can deal with one at a time.

Sounds pretty simple doesn't it. I'm surprised that our users didn't just go out and develop systems all by themselves by using top-down design. Just like there was more to the structured paradigm than a few simple concepts, there's more to the OO paradigm too. Just like it took awhile to truly get good at structured development, it will take time to get good at OO development too.

To give you a taste for what this chapter is about, the concepts and the terms that we'll be discussing are briefly summarized on the next two pages.

5.1 OO Concepts from a Structured Point of View

Stick up your hand if you were overwhelmed by the above-presented lists. OK, everyone put down your hands. If you're studying for a test, I suppose those two lists will be useful to you. Most of us, however, are looking for a way to get into OO concepts easily. Before we get into detailed explanations, let's quickly describe the four basic OO concepts in language that is familiar to us—structured terminology.

Class—If you have database experience, start thinking of a class as a table. The definition of a table describes the layout of the records that are to be stored in it. The definition of a class describes the layout, including both the data and the functionality, of the objects that are going to be created from it. Notice how I said both data and functionality. Unlike a table, which defines only data, a class defines both data (attributes) and code (methods). For now, a good way to think about a class is that it is the combination of a table definition and the definition of the source code that accesses the data.

Object—If a class can be thought of as a table, an object can be thought of as a record occurrence. For example, consider customers. In a structured application, each customer would be represented as a record in the customer data table. In an object-oriented application, each customer would be represented as an object in memory. The main difference is that although customer records only have data, customer objects have both data (attributes) and functionality (methods). More on this later.

Object-Oriented Concepts and Terms—A Quick Summary

Abstract class	A class that does not have objects instantiated from it.
Abstraction	The definition of the interface of a class (what it knows and does).
Aggregation	Represents "is-part-of" relationships.
Attribute	Something a class (or object) knows (data/information).
Cardinality	A fancy word for "how many?"
Class	A collection of similar objects (what we actually model).
Class Hierarchy	A set of classes that are related through inheritance.
Cohesion	A measure of how much a method or class makes sense.
Collaboration	Classes work together (collaborate) to get things done.
Concrete class	A class that has objects instantiated from it.
Coupling	A measure of how connected two classes are.
Encapsulation	The definition of how to implement what a class knows or does.
Information hiding	The restriction of outside access to attributes.
Inheritance	Represents "is-a" and "is-like" relationships.
Instance	An object is an instance of a class.
Instantiate	We instantiate (create) objects from classes.
Message	A message is either a request for information or a request to do something.

Object-Oriented Concepts and Terms—A Quick Summary

Messaging	In order to collaborate, classes send messages to each other.
Method	Something a class (or object) does (similar to a function in structured programming).
Multiple inheritance	When a class inherits from more than one class.
Object	A person, place, thing, event, concept, screen, or report is an object.
Instance relationship	In the real world objects are associated with (related to) other objects.
Optionality	A fancy word for "do you have to do it?"
Override	Sometimes we need override (redefine) attributes and/or methods in subclasses The issue of how objects are permanently stored to disk.
Persistence	The issue of how objects are permanently stored to disk.
Persistent object	An object that is saved to permanent storage.
Persistent memory	Main memory plus all available storage space on the network.
Polymorphism	This means you can interact with objects without knowing their exact type.
Single Inheritance	When a class inherits from only one class.
Subclass	If class "B" inherits from class "A," then we say that "B" is a subclass of "A."
Superclass	If class "B" inherits from class "A," then we say that "A" is a superclass of "B."
Transitory object	An object that is not saved to permanent storage.

Attribute—An attribute is equivalent to a data element in a record. It also makes sense to think of an attribute as a variable.

Method—A method can be thought of as either a function or procedure. Methods access and modify the attributes of an object. Some methods return a value (like a function), whereas other methods don't (like a procedure).

While you are reading this book, you may find the need to come back to these definitions occasionally—Don't worry, that's normal. Object-orientation introduces several new concepts and terms that can easily overwhelm you. So take your time and reread this chapter a few times. That's the only way you're going to learn this stuff!

5.2 Objects and Classes

The OO paradigm is based on building systems from reusable components called classes. A class generalizes/represents a collection of similar objects. As has been mentioned, an object is any person, place, event, thing, screen, report, or concept that is applicable to the system. In a university system, Christopher Pike is a student object, he attends several class objects, and he is working on a degree object. In a banking system Pike is a customer object, and he has a checking account object from which he bounces rubber check objects. In an inventory control system every inventory item is an object, every delivery is an object, and every customer is an object.

In the real world, we have objects. Therefore we need the concept "object." In the real world, however, objects are often similar to other kinds of objects. Students share similar qualities (they do the same sort of things, they are described in the same sort of way), courses share similar qualities, inventory items share similar qualities, bank accounts share similar qualities, and so on. Although we could model *A class represents* (and program) each and every object, that's a lot of work. I would *a collection of* prefer to define what it is to be a student once, define course once, *similar objects.* define inventory item once, define bank account once, and so on. That's why we need the concept of a class.

Figure 5.1 shows how in the real world we have student objects, and how we model the class "Student." It also shows the notation

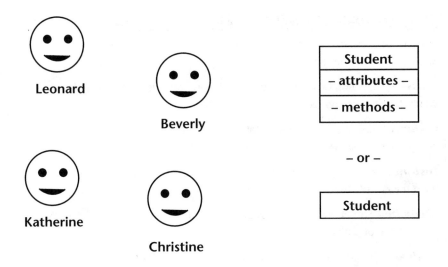

Figure 5.1.
Student objects in the real world and two ways to model the class "Student."

Some Student Objects **The Class "Student"**

that we use to model a class: Classes are modeled in one of two ways, as either a rectangle that lists its attributes and methods, or as just a rectangle. There are arguments for modeling classes both ways. On the one hand it's nice to list the attributes and methods because it allows readers of your class models to gain a better understanding of your design, whereas on the other hand listing the attributes and methods can clutter up your diagram. In this book we will use both techniques, listing the methods and attributes only where appropriate.

5.2.1 How to Name Classes

The name of a class should be one or two words, usually a noun, and should accurately describe the class. If you are having trouble naming the class, either you need to understand it better or it might actually be several classes that you have mistakenly combined. Furthermore, the name should be singular. We would model classes with names like "Student," "Professor," and "Course," not "Students," "Professors," and "Courses." Think of it like this: In the real world you would say "I am a student," not "I am a students."

Class names should be one or two words.

Class names are singular.

DEFINITIONS

Object—Any person, place, thing, event, screen, report, or concept that is applicable to the design of the system.

Class—A collection of similar objects. A class is effectively a template from which objects are created.

Instance—Just like we say that a data record is an occurrence of a data entity, we say that an object is an *instance* of a class.

Instantiate—When we create a student object, we say that we *instantiate* it from the class "Student."

Attribute—Something that a class or object knows. An attribute is basically a single piece of data or information.

Method—Something that a class or object does. A method is similar to a function or procedure in structured programming.

5.2.2 Instantiation

Objects are instances of a class

When an application is running, objects are *instantiated* (created/defined) from classes. We say that an object is an *instance* of a class, and that we *instantiate* objects from classes.

5.3 Attributes and Methods

Attributes and methods are the responsibilities of classes!

When we were CRC modeling, we saw that classes have responsibilities, the things that they know and do. Attributes are the things that classes know. Methods are the things that classes do. The object-oriented paradigm is based on the concept that systems should be built out of objects, and that objects have both data and functionality. Attributes define the data, while methods define the functionality.

In CRC modeling we found the responsibilities of a class: the things that it knows and that it does. When it gets right down to it, we were really looking for the attributes and the methods of the object of that class. The reason why we talked about finding responsibilities, instead of finding attributes and finding methods, is that attributes and methods are technical concepts, whereas responsibilities are fairly straightforward. Remember, when we are working with our users we want to use terminology that they are comfortable with, not technical jargon.

5.3.1 Class Definitions Include the Definitions of Attributes and Methods

When we define a class, we define the attributes that its objects have, as well as its methods. The definition of an attribute is straightforward. We define its name, perhaps its type (whether or not it is a number, or a string, or a date). Weakly typed languages like Smalltalk allow you to use attributes any way that you wish, and therefore do not require you to define their type. Strongly typed languages like C++, however, insist that you define the type of an attribute before you actually use it. The definition of a method is easy—we simply write the code for it, just as we would write the code for a function or a procedure.

5.3.2 Methods Do One of Two Things

1. **Some methods return a value.** Some methods are the equivalent of functions in the structured world. In other words they do something and then they provide a return value to whatever called them. It is quite common to see methods that simply return the value of a data attribute (although this sounds like unnecessary overhead, we'll see that this supports the concept of information hiding), although you'll also see methods that process some information and then provide a return value.

2. **Some methods do something, but don't return a value.** Some methods are just like procedures, in that they do something but they don't return a value.

Remember how in CRC modeling we said that collaborations are of one of two types, either a request for information or a request to do something? Also remember how whenever we defined a collaboration that the second class had a new responsibility to fulfill that collaboration? When we cover the concept of collaboration, we'll see that collaborations are fulfilled by methods.

In Figure 5.2 we have two different types of objects, a student and a seminar. Both objects know and do certain things, and we want to make sure that we record them. This record can be seen in Figure 5.3.

Please note the following comments.

1. **A class is divided into three sections.** The top section for its name, the middle section to list its attributes, and the bottom section to list its methods. In other words, we show the name of the class and its responsibilities (just like on a CRC card). However, we didn't list its collaborators (that's coming).

2. **We don't need to show the attributes and methods.** As we saw in the previous section, classes can also be shown as just a rectangle with the name of the class as its label. This is commonly done to "unclutter" complicated diagrams that have many classes. With this style, although you don't show the

Figure 5.2
Objects in the "real world."

I'm a student. I have a name, address, and phone number. I also enroll in courses, drop courses, pay tuition (@#$%^!), and request transcripts.

I'm a seminar. I keep track of who teaches me, what room I'm taught in, what course is being taught, and what students are enrolled in me. I have the ability to allow students either to enroll in me or drop me.

CSC 100 Sect. 3

Figure 5.3.
The class definitions for those objects.

Student
Name Address Phone Number
Enroll in Seminar Drop Seminar Pay Tuittion Request Transcript

Seminar
Course# Instructor(s) Room List of Students
Add Student to List Remove Student from List

attributes and methods within the "class bubble" you must still document them elsewhere.

5.4 Abstraction, Encapsulation, and Information Hiding

Instead of saying that we determined what a class knows and does, we say that we abstracted the class. Instead of saying that we designed how the class will accomplish these things, we say that we encapsulated them. Instead of saying that we designed the class well by restricting access to its attributes, we say that we've hidden the information.

5.4.1 Abstraction

The world is a complicated place. In order to deal with that complexity, we form generalizations, or abstractions of the things in it. For example consider the abstraction of a person. From a university's point of view the person's name, address, phone number, social security number, and his or her educational background is needed. From the point of view of the police, a person's name, address, phone number, weight, height, hair color, eye color, and so on is needed. It's still the same person, just a different abstraction depending on the application at hand.

   Abstraction is basically an analysis issue that deals with what a class knows or does. Our abstraction should include the features, attributes, and methods that are of interest to our application and ignore the rest. That's why the abstraction of a student would include his or her name and address, but probably not his or her height and weight. People often say that abstraction is the act of painting a clear box around something, or they say that abstraction is the act of defining the interface of something. Either way, you're defining what the class knows and does.

5.4.2 Encapsulation

Although the act of abstraction tells us that we need to store a students name and address, as well as be able to enroll students in seminars, it doesn't tell us how we are going to do this. Encapsulation deals with the issue of how we intend to modularize the feature of a system. In the object-oriented world, we modularize systems into classes, which in turn is modularized into the methods and attributes. We say that we *encapsulate* behavior into a class, or that we *encapsulate* functionality into a method.

Encapsulation is basically a design issue that deals with how functionality is compartmentalized within a system. You shouldn't have to know how something is implemented to be able to use it. The implication of encapsulation is that you can build anything any way you want, and then you can later change the implementation and it won't affect other components within the system (as long as the interface to that component didn't change).

People often say that encapsulation is the act of painting the box black. We're defining how something is going to be done, but we're not telling the rest of the world how we're going to do it. For example, consider your bank. How do they keep track of your account information? On a mainframe, a mini, or a personal computer (PC)? What database do they use? What operating system? It doesn't matter, because they've encapsulated the way in which they perform account services. You just walk up to a teller and do whatever transactions you wish. By hiding the details of the way they've implemented accounts, your bank is free to change that implementation at any time, and it shouldn't affect the way that services are provided to you.

5.4.3 Information Hiding

In order to support good design, we want to restrict access to data attributes and some methods. The basic idea is this: If one class wants information about another class, it should have to ask for it instead just taking it. When you think about it, this is exactly the way that the real world works. If you want to find out somebody's name, what would you do? Would you ask the person or would you steal the person's wallet and look at his or her ID? By restricting access to attributes, we prevent programmers from writing highly coupled code. When code is highly coupled, a change in one part of the code forces us to make a change in another, and then another, and so on. We'll discuss coupling in detail later in this chapter.

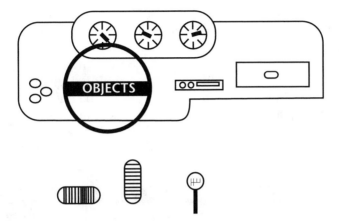

Figure 5.4.
The driver's
interface for
a car

An Example

In Figure 5.4, the abstraction is how we work with the wheel, pedals, and gear shift to drive a car. Encapsulation allows the different car makers to provide a consistent interface, even though each make of car is built differently. Information hiding is represented by the fact that although there is a certain amount of oil in the engine, the driver doesn't know what it is. In other words, information about the oil is hidden from the user.

Why this Stuff Is Important

Remember how we said that it was up to you how you implement things, and that you should be able to change the way that you implemented the thing at any time? This was called encapsulation. Encapsulation requires information hiding. For example, say that the programmer for the class "Student" knows that the attribute "ListOfStudents" in the class "Seminar" was implemented as an array. The programmer decides to just have "Student" add itself in the first available array element. A few months later, somebody else comes along and decides to reimplement the list of students as a linked list, in order to use memory more efficiently. This is a very reasonable and likely change. Unfortunately, the second programmer doesn't know that the first programmer was directly updating the array of students, and as a result the university information system crashes.

Had access to the attribute "ListOfStudents" been restricted, the programmer of "Student" would not have been able to directly update its value. As a result, the programmer would

Abstraction, encapsulation, and information hiding lead to more maintainable systems.

DEFINITIONS

Abstraction—The definition of the interface of a class (what it knows and does).

Encapsulation—The definition of how to implement what a class knows or does, without telling anyone how we did it.

Information Hiding —The restriction of access to attributes.

have had to have "Student" ask "Seminar" to add them to the seminar list. If this had been the case, when "ListOfStudents" was changed into a linked list, there wouldn't have been a problem (when the second programmer changed the implementation of the attribute she or he would also have modified any methods that accessed it). The reason why there wouldn't be a problem is that by hiding the information (the seminar list) and encapsulating how students are enrolled in courses, we were able to keep the abstraction the same (we just send a message to "Seminar" asking it to add the student to the seminar list).

INHERITANCE TIPS

1. Look for similarities. Whenever you have similarities between two or more classes, either similar attributes or similar methods, then you probably have an opportunity for inheritance.

2. Look for existing classes. When you identify a new class, you might already have an existing class to which it is similar. Sometimes you can directly inherit from an existing class, and just code the differences of the new class. For example, say our university information system also needed to support university administrators. The "Person" class already has many of the features that an "Administrator" class needs, so have "Administrator" inherit from "Person."

3. Follow the sentence rule. One of the following sentences should make sense: "A subclass IS A superclass" or "A subclass IS LIKE A superclass." For example, it makes sense to say that a student IS A person. If one of the sentences doesn't make sense, then you've found either an aggregation relationship or an Instance relationship (we'll talk about both of these concepts later in this chapter).

4. Inherit everything. The subclass should inherit everything from the superclass. If it doesn't, the code becomes harder to understand and maintain. For example, say class "B" inherits from "A." To understand B, we need to understand what A is all about, plus all the features that B adds on to A. If we start removing functionality, we also need to understand what B ISN'T. This is a lot of work. Besides, if you need to start removing functionality, the sentence probably didn't make sense. You wouldn't have been able to say that "a 'B' IS AN 'A'" instead you would have said "a 'B' IS AN 'A,' except for. . . ." That isn't any good.

5.5 Inheritance

There are often similarities between different classes. Very often, two or more classes will share the same attributes and/or the same methods. Because we don't want to have to write the same code over and over again, we would like to have a mechanism that takes advantages of these similarities. Inheritance is that mechanism. Inheritance allows us to model "is-a" and "is-like" relationships, which lets us reuse existing data and code.

As stated, there are often similarities between classes. For example, students have names, addresses, and phone numbers, and they drive vehicles. At the same time, professors also have names, addresses, and phone numbers, and they drive vehicles. Without a doubt, we could develop the classes for student and professor, and get them both running. In fact, we could even develop the class "Student" first, and once it is running make a copy of it, call it "Professor," and make the necessary modifications. Although this is fairly straightforward to do, it isn't perfect. What if there was an error in the original code for student? Now we'd have to fix it in two places, which is twice the work. What would happen if we needed to change the way we handled names (say we go from a length of 30 to a length of 40)? Now we'd have to make the same change in two places again—that's a lot of dull, boring, tedious work. Wouldn't it be nice if somehow we could only have one copy of the code to develop and maintain?

That's exactly what inheritance is all about. With inheritance we would define a new class that encapsulates the similarities between students and professors. This new class would have the attributes "Name," "Address," and "PhoneNumber," and the method "DriveVehicle." Because we need to name all of our classes, we need to ask ourselves what does this collection of data and functionality describe? In this case I think that the name "Person" is fitting.

Once we have the class "Person" defined, we would then have "Student" and "Professor" inherit from it (see Figure 5.5). We would say that "Person" is the superclass of both "Student" and "Professor," and that "Student" and "Professor" are the *subclasses* of "Person." Everything that a superclass knows or does, the subclass knows or does. For free (actually, for this example you would need to write two lines of code, one saying that "Student" is a subclass of "Person," and

DEFINITIONS

Inheritance— Allows us to take advantage of similarities between classes by representing "is-a" and "is-like" relationships.

Superclass—If class "B" inherits from class "A," then we say that "A" is a superclass of "B."

Subclass—If class "B" inherits from class "A," then we say that "B" is a subclass of "A."

Figure 5.5.
Modeling the fact
that "Professor"
and "Student"
inherit from
"Person."

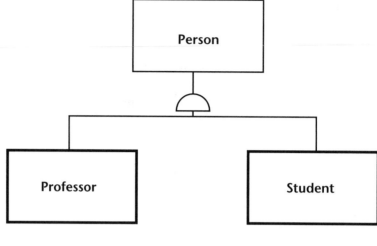

Figure 5.6.
The modeling
notation for
inheritance.

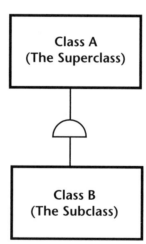

MODELING TIPS

The subclass should
always appear below
the superclass.

The semicircle
should always point
from the subclass to
the superclass.

another saying that "Professor" is a subclass of "Person"). Because "Person" has a name, address, and phone number, both "Student" and "Professor" have those attributes as well. Because "Person" has the ability to drive a vehicle, so does "Student" and "Professor."

5.5.1 Single Versus Multiple Inheritance

When a class inherits from only one other class, we call this single inheritance. When a class inherits from two or more other classes, we call this multiple inheritance. The thing to remem-

Before

After

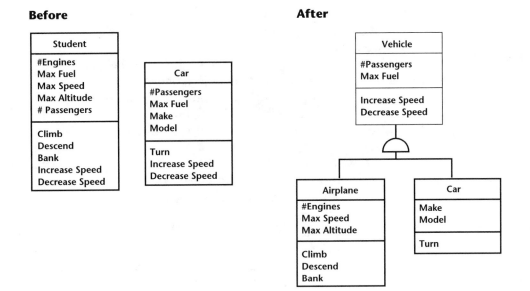

Figure 5.7.
Creating the
vehicle class
hierarchy.

ber is this—the subclass inherits all of the attributes and methods of its superclass(es).

5.5.1.1 Single Inheritance

In Figure 5.7, we see that there are several similarities between airplanes and cars. They both have a number of passengers, a maximum fuel level and they can either increase or decrease their speed. To take advantage of these similarities we create a new class called "Vehicle" and have "Airplane" and "Car" inherit from it. We say that the classes "Vehicle," "Airplane," and "Car" form a *class hierarchy*. We call the topmost class in a class hierarchy (in this case "Person") the *root*. Important: Notice how the attributes and methods of the superclass aren't listed in the subclasses (they've been inherited).

Notice how we have the method "Turn" for "Car" and "Bank" for "Airplane." Turning and banking are the exact same thing! We could have defined a "Turn" method in "Vehicle" and had "Airplane" and "Car" inherit it (this implies that we would have removed "Bank" and "Turn" from the subclasses). This would mean that we would require our users of airplanes (probably pilots) to change the terminology they use to work with airplanes! Realistically this wouldn't work. A better solution would be to define "Turn" in "Vehicle" and have the method "Bank" call it.

5.5.1.2 Abstract and Concrete Classes

"Vehicle" has a lighter outline than does "Airplane" and "Car." This is because we say that "Vehicle" is an *abstract class*, where "Airplane" and "Car" are *concrete classes*. The main difference between abstract classes and concrete classes is that objects are instantiated (created) from concrete classes but not from abstract classes. For example, in the real world we have airplanes and cars, but we don't have anything that is just a vehicle (in other words, if it isn't an airplane or a car we aren't interested in it). This means that we will instantiate airplane and car objects, but we will never create vehicle objects. Abstract classes are created when we need to create a class that implements common features from two or more classes.

5.5.1.3 Multiple Inheritance

In the "before picture" of Figure 5.8 we want to create a new class called "Dragon." We already have the classes "Bird" and "Lizard." A dragon is like a bird, because they both fly. A dragon is also like a lizard, because they both have claws and scales. Because dragons have the features of both birds and lizards, in the "after picture" we have the class "Dragon" inheriting from both "Bird" and "Lizard." This is an example of an "is-like" relationship—a dragon IS LIKE a bird and a dragon IS (also) LIKE a lizard.

Figure 5.8.
An example of multiple inheritance

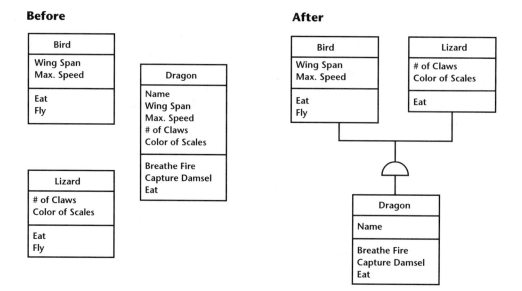

DEFINITIONS

Single inheritance—When a class inherits from only one class, we say that we have single inheritance.

Multiple inheritance—When a class inherits from more than one class, we say that we have multiple inheritance.

Concrete class—A class that has objects instantiated (created) from it.

Abstract class—A class that does not have objects instantiated from it.

Override—Sometimes we need override (redefine) attributes and/or methods in subclasses.

Class Hierarchy—A set of classes that are related through inheritance.

Root—The topmost class in a class hierarchy.

Notice how we listed the method "Eat" for dragon. Although all three types of creatures eat, they all eat in different ways. Birds eat bird seed, lizards eat bugs, and dragons eat knights in shining armor. Because the way that dragons eat is different than the way that either birds or lizards eat, we need to redefine, or *override,* the definition of the "Eat" method. The general idea is that a subclass will need to override the definition of either an attribute (very occasionally) or a method whenever it uses that data, or performs that method in a different manner than its superclass.

5.6 Persistence

Persistence describes the issue of "how do you save objects to a database." To make an object persistent you must save the values of its attributes to storage (onto disk), as well as any information needed to maintain the relationships (both aggregation and instance relationships) with which it is involved. Although relational databases can be used to store objects, object-oriented databases often offer a better storage mechanism.

From a development point of view, there are two types of objects: persistent objects (these stick around) and transient objects (these don't). For example, a customer is a persistent object. You want to save customer objects into some sort permanent storage so that you can work with them again in the future. A customer editing screen, however, is a transient object. Your application creates the customer-editing screen object, displays it, then gets rid of it once the user is done editing the data for the customer with whom they are currently dealing.

5.6.1 Persistence Tips

1. **Business domain (analysis) classes are usually persistent.** You are naturally going to need a permanent (persistent) record of instances of real-world classes like "Student," "Professor," and "Course."

2. **Interface classes are usually transitory.** Interface classes (screens and reports) are almost always transitory. Screens are created and displayed when needed, then once they are no longer in use they are destroyed (removed from memory). Report classes are created, they gather the data they need, manipulate the data, and then output the data. Once this is done the report object is usually destroyed as well. Note: Sometimes you might need to maintain a log of when you printed a report and who/what you sent it to, making the report log persistent.

3. **You need to store both attributes and relationships.** When an object is written to disk, you obviously need to store the value of its attributes. You must also store information about any relationships that the object is involved with, however. For example, if the student Alyssa Ogawa is taking the courses Bio-Medicine 101 and Nursing 301, then we want to make sure that when we store the Alyssa object to disk that we remember the fact that she's taking those two courses.

4. **Consider using an object-oriented database (OODB).** Relational databases are really good at storing straightforward, simple objects, but are often not very good at storing objects that are involved in complex relationships. Object-oriented databases on the other hand are designed to store objects and the complex relationships between them.

5. **Full persistence means you need to store methods as well.** A true OODB will not only include data, but the method code

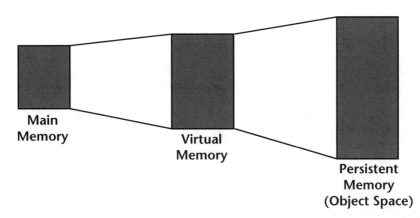

Figure 5.9.
Different ways to
look at memory

Main
Memory

Virtual
Memory

Persistent
Memory
(Object Space)

as well. Remember, an object is made up of both data and functionality (programming). Therefore, to make an object persistent (to save it to permanent storage), you should really be saving both the data and the methods.

5.6.2 Persistent Memory

In the structured world we had the concept of "virtual memory," which was where structured applications run. Virtual memory is the combination of main memory plus any drive space on your computer. Figure 5.9 shows "persistent memory," also called the "object space," which is where object-oriented applications run. Persistent memory is the combination of the main memory on your computer, plus all of the available disk space on your network (assuming you are networked and your OODB is distributed, which they often are). When it gets right down to it, persistent memory is where objects exist/are stored.

5.6.3 Object-Oriented Databases (OODBs)

Object-oriented databases are very good are storing both variable and fixed-length data (pictures and sound bites, as well as strings and numbers), and at maintaining complex relationships between objects. We need to be able to traverse these relationships quickly (so as to get to other objects the current object is related to), and that is exactly what OODBs are tuned for. OODBs are what make persistent memory persistent. Although objects interact with

DEFINITIONS

Persistence—The issue of how objects are permanently stored to disk.

Persistent object—An object that is saved to permanent storage.

Transitory object—An object that is not saved to permanent storage.

Persistent memory—Main memory plus all available storage space on the network.

Figure 5.10.
The instance-
relationship
notation.

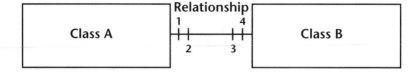

each other in the object space (persistent memory), they are stored in an OODB. Think of it like this—in the structured world you store data in databases, and read it into virtual memory in order to work with it. In the object-oriented world you store objects in OODBs, and bring them into persistent memory so that they may interact/collaborate with each other. In the second volume in this book series we'll take a look at OODBs in greater detail.

5.7 Instance Relationships

In the real world, objects are associated with other objects. We call these associations "instance relationships." The relationships between objects are important because they help us to define how they interact with each other.

As stated, in the real world, objects are associated with (related to) one another. For example, students TAKE courses, professors TEACH courses, criminals ROB banks, politicians KISS babies, and captains COMMAND starships. Take, teach, rob, kiss, and command are all verbs that define relationships between objects. We want to identify and document these relationships, so that we can gain a better understanding as to how objects interact with one another.

Not only must we identify what the relationship(s) are between classes, we must also describe the relationship. For example, it isn't enough to know that students take courses. How many courses do students take? None, one, or several? Furthermore, relationships are two-way streets: Not only do students take courses, but courses are taken by students. This leads to questions like: How many students can be enrolled in any given course and is it possible to have a course with no one in it?

Table 5.1. Converting Optionality and Cardinality to Every-Day English

Optionality	Cardinality	Combination	English Meaning
Must	One	Must have one	One and one only
Must	Many	Must have many	One or more
May	One	May have one	Zero or one
May	Many	May have many	Zero or more

In addition to identifying the relationship, we also need to identify its cardinality and optionality. Cardinality is a fancy word for how many. Optionality is a fancy word for whether or not you have to do it.

When we model instance relationships, we show them as a thin line connecting two classes. Figure 5.10 shows how the line is labeled with one or two words that describe the relationship, and how the cardinality and optionality are shown as symbols on either end of the line.

There are two cardinality symbols: a bar representing ONE, and a bird's foot representing MANY. Similarly, there are two symbols for optionality: a bar for MUST and a circle for MAY. Because there are two symbols for each, we end up with four (two times two) combinations as can be seen in Table 5.1.

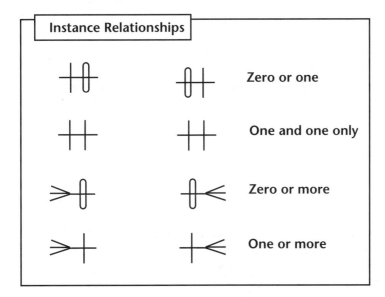

Instance Relationships

Zero or one

One and one only

Zero or more

One or more

Figure 5.11.
The four cardinality/ optionality combinations.

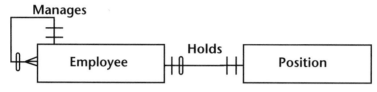

Figure 5.12.
Several classes
and the
relationships
between them.

Figure 5.11 shows how each combination is drawn. Figure 5.12 depicts several different classes and the relationships among those classes.

The relationships in Figure 5.12 would be read like this:

- A student takes one or more seminars.

- A seminar is taken by zero or more students.

- A seminar is a section of a course.

- A course has one or more sections.

- An employee holds one and only one position.

- A position may be held by one employee (some positions go unfilled).

- An employee is managed by one and one only employee.

- An employee manages zero or more employees (some people don't have any staff).

5.7.1 Recursive Instance Relationships

The relationship "manages" between employee and itself is recursive (a class has a relationship with itself). We say that an instance relationship (or as we'll see an aggregation relationship) is recursive when the relationship is between one class and itself. Although recursive relationships are rare, they do occur. For example, a company may be partnered with another company, or an employee may work with another employee.

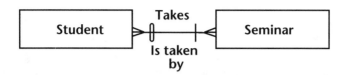

Figure 5.13.
Using two labels
on instance
relationships.

Style Issue
Although relationships are two-way streets, with this notation we
label relationships with ONE label only—the one that is shortest.
Some people suggest that because relationships are bidirectional they
should be documented using two labels, one for each direction. For
example, in Figure 5.13 we see how the relationship between students and seminars would be described using two labels. Personally, I
don't see the value of this—if you know that students take courses,
you can figure out yourself that courses are taken by students. The
bottom line is that all the second label does is clutter up your diagram without adding any significant value.

5.7.2 How Instance Relationships Are Implemented

Instance relationships are maintained through the combination of
attributes and methods. The attributes store the information necessary to maintain the relationship, and methods keep the attributes
up-to-date. This little fact has an important implication—because
attributes and methods are inherited, instance relationships are too!
We'll see why this is important in chapter 6.

*Instance
relationships
are inherited!*

5.8 Aggregation

Sometimes objects are built out of other objects. In this case we say
"an object is an aggregate of other objects." Basically, aggregation
represents "is-part-of" relationships.

Sometimes an object is made up of other objects. For example, an
airplane is made up of a fuselage, wings, engines, landing gear, flaps,
and so on. A delivery shipment is made up of one or more packages.
A team consists of two or more employees. These are all examples of
the concept of aggregation, which represents "is-part-of" relationships. An engine is part of a plane, a package is part of a shipment,
and an employee is part of a team.

> ### MODELING TIP
>
> No matter how good a job you did during CRC modeling, you're almost guaranteed to have missed the full details about instance relationships. So what do you do, make something up and hope for the best? No of course not! You'd go back to your users and ask them what the real situation is, wouldn't you? The problem is remembering to go back and do so. The solution: Mark it as "currently unknown" by putting a question mark beside the part of the relationship of which you are unsure. For example, in Figure 5.14 we think that a position is held by zero or more employees. We know for a fact that it is possible for a position not to be currently filled, but what we aren't sure of is whether or not you can have one or several persons holding the same position. Is job sharing going on in our organization? Do we have generic positions, such as "Bank Teller," that are held by many people? Or is it really one person to one position, as we currently show now? Because we don't know for sure, we mark the relationship with a question mark, indicating to us that we should go back later and verify our "educated guess."

Figure 5.14.
Modeling the fact that you don't always have all the facts!

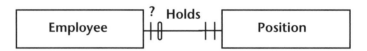

Examples of aggregation appear so frequently, we've decided to give aggregation its own special symbol. Don't worry though, when we model aggregation we show it exactly the same way as we would an instance relationship (i.e., you should show optionality and cardinality), with the addition of a triangle on the relationship pointing from the "part" to the "whole." Hey, it's nice to be consistent!

Just as instance relationships are two-way streets, so are aggregation relationships. Furthermore, the aggregation relationships shown in Figure 5.15 are read exactly the same way that you would read instance relationships.

DEFINITION

Cardinality—A fancy word for "how many?"

Optionality—A fancy word for "do you have to do it?"

- An item is part of one and one only shipment.

- A shipment is made up of one or more items.

- An engine is part of one and one only airplane.

- An airplane has one or more engines.

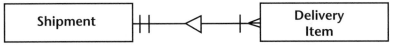

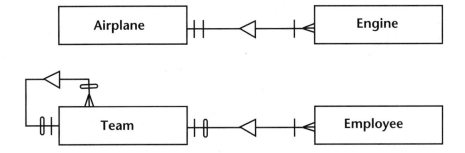

Figure 5.15.
Several aggregation examples.

- An employee may or may not be part of a team.
- A team is made up of one or more employees.
- Any given team may or may not be part of a larger team.
- A team may or may not be made up of smaller subteams.

5.8.1 Aggregation Tips

1. **The "part" is almost always involved with only one "whole."** This at least is true of physical and/or mechanical parts. For example, any given engine is only involved with one airplane (except perhaps during a mid-air collision, but that's another story). However, it is possible that a part can be involved with more than one whole. For example, Figure 5.16 above shows that any given spreadsheet cell is involved with both a row and a column (i.e., the cell "M5" is part of column "M" and row "5"). Furthermore, on the previous page we said that employees may be part of one team only. However, I suspect that we've modeled this relationship wrong (hey, that's an analysis error! I bet we didn't do any use-case scenario testing). I think that it would be reasonable to assume that employees could actually be part of several teams, perhaps

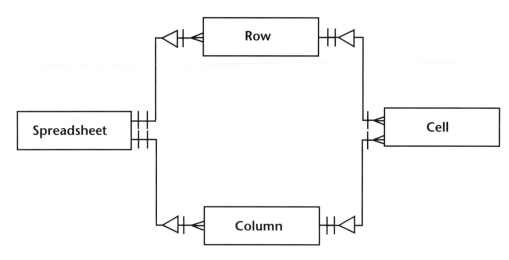

Figure 5.16.
The design of a spreadsheet.

their work team and one or two task forces. In short, although a "part" is usually involved with only one "whole," it isn't always that way.

2. **The sentence should make sense.** It should make sense to say "the part IS PART OF the whole." If it doesn't, you probably don't have aggregation (instead you either have inheritance or an instance relationship).

3. **It should be a part in the real world.** The part should actually be a part in the real world, and should have its own set of attributes and methods.

4. **You should be interested in the part.** An object may actually be a part in the real world, but if you aren't interested in keeping track of it, then don't model it. For example, an airplane maintenance system would be interested in keeping track of engines because they need to keep track of maintenance information about each engine. On the other hand, an air traffic control system isn't interested in keeping track of engines, just airplanes. Therefore an engine would not appear as a class in an air traffic control system.

DEFINITION

Aggregation—
represents "is-part-of" relationships.

5. **Show cardinality and optionality.** Aggregation relationships are a very common type of instance relationship. Just as you show cardinality and optionality for an instance relationship, you need to do the same for an aggregation relationship.

Figure 5.17.
The collaboration/ messaging notation.

6. **Aggregation is inherited.** Like instance relationships, aggregation relationships are maintained by a combination of attributes and methods. Therefore aggregation relationships are inherited.

5.9 Collaboration

When we were CRC modeling we saw that classes often need to work together to fulfill their responsibilities. Actually, it is the real-world objects that are working together (remember, classes represent a collection of similar objects). Collaboration occurs when an object asks another object for information or asks it to do something. Objects collaborate by sending each other messages.

In order to get the job done, objects often need to collaborate (work) with other objects. For example, an airplane collaborates with its engines to fly. In order for the plane to go faster, the engines must go faster. When the plane needs to slow down, the engines must slow down. If the airplane didn't collaborate with its engines effectively, it wouldn't be able to fly.

5.9.1 Messages

Objects collaborate with one another by sending each other messages. A message is either a request to do something, or a request for information. Figure 5.17 shows that a message is modeled as a thick arrow going from the sender of the message to the receiver. A label is drawn above the message line describing what the request is.

5.9.2 Two Types of Collaboration

1. **A request for information.** Objects will often ask other objects for some information. For example, Figure 5.18 shows how students will send a message to a seminar, requesting the number of seats still available in the seminar.

2. **A request to do something.** Objects will often ask other objects to do something for them. For example, Figure 5.18

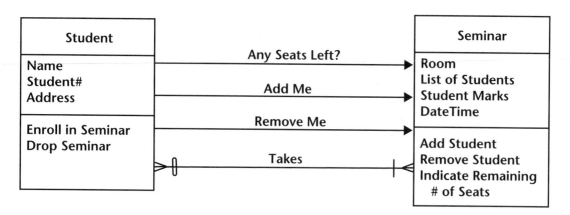

Figure 5.18.
The class
"Student" needs
to collaborate
with "Seminar"
to enroll and
drop.

shows how students will send a message to a seminar asking it to either add them to the seminar list, or to remove them from the seminar list.

5.9.3 Collaboration Tips

1. **There must be some sort of relationship.** The only way that an object can send a message to another object is if it knows about it in the first place. Basically you can't ask anyone for help unless you know how to get in contact with them, can you? Of course not. There has to be either an instance relationship or an aggregation relationship between the two objects for them to be able to collaborate.

Objects collaborate by sending each other messages.

2. **There must be a corresponding method in the receiver.** Collaborations are fulfilled through methods. If an object is asked for information, it must have a method that returns that information. If an object is asked to do something, it must have a method to do it. When it gets right down to it, object-oriented languages effectively implement messages as method (function) calls. Therefore, there must be a corresponding method for every message that an object receives.

An object responds to a message by invoking a method.

3. **There might be a return value.** If the collaboration is a request for information, then there's a return value (the requested information). Messages are shown only as an arrow going from the sender to the receiver, regardless of whether

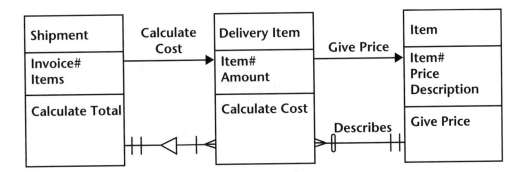

or not there is a return value. In other words, you don't show an arrow going back to the original sender.

4. **There may or may not be parameters.** Some messages have parameters, some don't. Remember, a message is effectively a method (function) call. Just like functions may take parameters, so do methods. For example, consider Figure 5.18. A student can send a message requesting the number of seats left in the seminar. No need for a parameter there. A student can also send a message requesting that he or she be added to the course. You need a parameter in that message (a pointer/handle to the student being added).

5. **Messages show collaboration, not data flows.** Messages are requests. That's it. They aren't data flows. Process diagrams (data-flow diagrams) from the structured world showed data flows, which are movements of data from one part of the system to another.

6. **Sometimes the receiver needs to collaborate.** The receiver of a message may not be able to completely fulfill the request by itself, and may need to collaborate with other objects to get the job done as in Figure 5.19. That's perfectly fine. It is important that each object being collaborated with should always do something, however, and not just pass the buck. Passing the buck often results in "spaghetti code," which can be very difficult to maintain.

Figure 5.19.
Classes collaborating together to calculate the total cost of a shipment.

DEFINITIONS

Collaboration—
Classes work together (collaborate) to get things done.

*Message—*A message is either a request for information or a request to do something.

*Messaging—*In order to collaborate, classes send messages to each other.

5.10 Persistent Versus Transitory Instance Relationships

There are two types of instance relationships: Persistent and transitory. The main difference is that persistent relationships are saved to disk, whereas transitory relationships are only temporary in nature. Persistent relationships are drawn as a complete line, whereas transitory relationships are drawn as a dotted line.

5.10.1 Persistent Instance Relationships

Persistent instance relationships are those that are permanent, or at least semi-permanent in nature. An instance relationship is persistent if information to maintain it is saved to disk. For example, the TAKE relationship between students and courses is persistent. This is important business information that must be stored to disk. The TEACH relationship between professors and courses is persistent for the same reason. All of the instance relationships that we have dealt with so far in this book have been persistent.

5.10.2 Transitory Instance Relationships

Transitory relationships are shown as dotted lines.

Transitory relationships are temporary in nature—they aren't saved to disk. Transitory relationships usually (but not always) involve at least one transitory object, such as a screen or report. The reason for this is simple—if you aren't saving the object to disk, you aren't going to be saving any of the instance relationships that it was involved with to disk either!

Transitory relationships exist between objects for one reason only—so that they may collaborate with one another. For an object to collaborate with another object it needs to know about it. That means that there must be either an instance relationship or a part-of relationship between the two objects. When there isn't a persistent relationship between the two objects, as in Figure 5.20, then a transitory relationship between them is defined so that they may be able to collaborate with each other.

EXPLANATION In Figure 5.20 there is a transitory relationship between the classes "Student" and "Student-Editing Screen." This represents the fact that a student-editing screen edits student information.

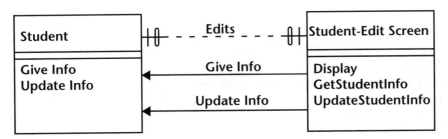

Figure 5.20.
A transitory
relationship
between two
classes.

In our system the information for a student may be edited by only one person at a time, and each editing screen has the capability to edit only one student at a time. The editing screen gets the current information from the student object, displays it in editing mode, and then updates the student object with the new information once it is finished.

The transitory-instance relationship between an instance of an editing screen and an instance of a student exists for as long as the student information is displayed on the screen. Once the screen is closed, or once the user chooses to edit another student, the relationship no longer exists.

We will now consider a second example as shown in Figure 5.21.

EXPLANATION

1. **Reports are transitory objects.** A transcript object exists only for the time that it takes to print itself out. Because transcripts are transitory, any relationship that they are involved with is also transitory.

2. **The transcript was told what student to print itself for.** The transcript was initially passed enough information for it to determine for what student it should be printed. Depending on the environment, this may imply that the transcript object was passed the object ID for the student object, it was passed a pointer to the student object, or it was passed the student object itself. This is how the transitory relationship would be set up. Transcript objects are probably created by some sort of batch job that gets run at the end of every school term. Furthermore, I suspect that the information system given to the school's registrar also has the ability to print transcripts.

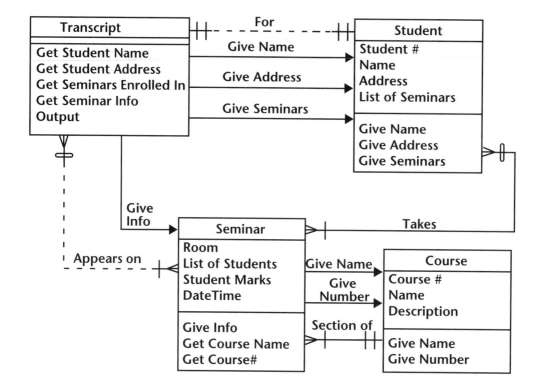

Figure 5.21.
How a report implementation uses transitory-instance relationships.

3. **It first gets the necessary information from the student.** The transcript object sends messages to the student object, obtaining the name and address to print at the top of the transcript. It would also get the list of seminars (in the form of object IDs, pointers) that the student has taken over the course of his or her career. This information is used for the next step.

4. **It then loops through the seminars, outputting the information one seminar at a time.** Once the report header is printed, the transcript object would loop through each seminar one at a time printing out the data for it. This would be the course name and number, the term and year the student took it, and the mark they got in it. Because "Seminar" doesn't know the name and number of the course, it would collaborate with "Course" to get this information.

5.10.2.1 Persistent Versus Transitory Relationships

Persistent relationships are those that are permanent or semi-permanent in nature, whereas transitory relationships are temporary. Persistent relationships are drawn as complete lines, whereas transitory relationships are shown as dotted lines.

5.11 Coupling and Cohesion

Coupling and cohesion may be the two most important principles to come out of the discipline of software engineering. Coupling measures how interconnected two classes are, whereas cohesion measures how much a method or class makes sense. To develop a system that is easy and inexpensive to maintain you want to develop classes that are loosely coupled and highly cohesive.

5.11.1 Coupling

Coupling is a measure of how much two program modules, or in our case classes or methods, are interconnected. When one class relies on another class, we say that they are coupled. When one class interacts with another class, but does not know any of the implementation details of the other class, we say that they are loosely coupled. When one class relies on the implementation (i.e., it directly accesses the data attributes of the other), we say that they are highly coupled.

Loose coupling is very, very good.

High coupling is very, very bad (usually).

Previously we discussed the example of how the class "Student" could implement the "Enroll" function: It could directly access the attribute "ListOfStudents" in "Seminar," or it could send "Seminar" a message asking it to enroll the student in the seminar. Directly accessing and updating "ListOfStudents" might save a few CPU (central processing unit) cycles and run a little quicker, but as soon as the implementation of that attribute changes then we need to modify the code in "Student." As we saw, this wasn't very good. The basic problem is that when two classes are highly coupled, a change in one very often requires a change in the other. This in turn could require a change in another class, and then another, and then another, and so on. High coupling is one of the main reasons why there is such a large maintenance burden. What should be a simple maintenance change can often create months of work, if it can even be done at all.

It's amazing how much code there is out there that people are willing to touch because they're afraid of breaking it.

5.11.1.1 When You Want High Coupling

Every so often programmers are seduced by the dark side of the force and decide to write code that is highly coupled. This only makes sense if you are truly desperate to cut down on the processing overhead in your system. For example, database drivers are often highly coupled to the file system of the operating system on which the database runs. If you can save a few milliseconds accessing data, it quickly adds up when you are accessing hundreds of thousands of objects.

5.11.1.2 Dealing with High Coupling

If you are in a position where you think you need to write highly coupled code, here's my advice.

1. **Avoid it if you can.** High coupling leads to higher maintenance costs, and very often the cost of the processing time that you save isn't as much as the increased cost to maintain the system. Furthermore, faster/bigger hardware might be the solution. Why spend an extra $50,000 maintaining a system when all you need is a faster CPU with more memory that costs $5,000?

2. **Document it thoroughly.** The higher the coupling, the better the documentation has to be. You need to thoroughly document how and why two classes are coupled. Maintenance programmers need to know how the classes are coupled so that they know how the classes will be affected when they make a change. They also need to know why the classes are highly coupled because they might be tempted to "fix" the problem. Code that is highly coupled often looks like it was poorly designed.

5.11.2 Cohesion

Cohesion is a measure of how much a program module, or in our case either a class or method, makes sense. A good measure of the cohesiveness of something is how long it takes to describe in one sentence. The longer it takes, the less cohesive it is. We want to design methods and classes that are highly cohesive. In other words, it should be very clear to us what a method or class is all about.

Small, cohesive methods that do one thing and one thing only are easier to understand and maintain.

5.11.2.1 Highly Cohesive Methods
A method is highly cohesive if it does one thing and one thing only. For example, in the class "Student" we have methods to enroll a student in a seminar and to drop a student from a seminar. Both of these methods do one thing and one thing only. We could have written one method to do both these functions, call it "ChangeSeminarStatus." The problem with this solution is that the code for this method would be more complex than the code for either of the "EnrollInSeminar" or "DropSeminar" methods. That means that the code for "ChangeSeminarStatus" would be harder to understand, and hence harder to maintain. Remember, we want to reduce the maintenance burden, not increase it.

If you can name your method using a strong verb/noun combination, chances are it is highly cohesive.

The name of a method often indicates how cohesive it is. Whenever you see a strong verb/noun combination used for the name of the method, very often it is highly cohesive. For example, consider methods like "GetName," "PrintName," "EnrollInSeminar," and "DropSeminar." Verbs like get, print, enroll, and drop are all very strong. Now consider "ChangeSeminarStatus." Is change as strong or as explicit as the words enroll and drop? I don't think so.

5.11.2.2 Highly Cohesive Classes
A highly cohesive class represents one type of object and only one type of object. For example, for the university information system we model professors, not employees. Although a professor is indeed an employee, they are very different from other kinds of employees. For example, professors do different things than janitors, who do different things than secretaries, who do different things than registrars, and so on. We could easily write a generic "Employee" class that is able to handle all of the functionality performed by every type of employee working for the university. This class would quickly become cumbersome and unmaintainable, however.

Instead, we would be better off defining a class hierarchy made up of the classes "Professor," "Janitor," "Secretary," "Registrar,"

DEFINITIONS

Coupling—A measure of how connected two classes are

Cohesion—A measure of how much a method or class makes sense

and so on. Because there are a lot of similarities between these classes, we would create a new abstract class called "Employee," which would inherit from "Person." The other classes, including "Professor," would now inherit from "Employee." The advantage of this is that each class represents one type of object. If there are ever any changes that need to be made with respect to janitors, you can go right to the class "Janitor" and make them. You don't need to worry about affecting the code for professors. In fact, you don't even need to know anything about professors at all.

5.12 Polymorphism

DEFINITION

Polymorphism—
Polymorphism says that an object can take any of several forms, and that other objects can interact with the object without having to know what specific form it takes.

An individual object may be one of several types. For example, a "Gregory Quinn" object may be a student, a registrar, or even a professor. Should it matter to other objects in the system what type of person Greg is? I would significantly reduce the development effort if other objects in the system could treat people objects the same way, and not have to have separate sections of code for each type. The concept of "polymorphism" says that you can treat instances of various classes the same way within your system.

A Polymorphic Card Game

SCENARIO The poker game had been going on for hours, and it was Slick Scotty's turn to deal (see Figure 5.22). One of the players turns to him and asks "So what'll it be pardner?" Thinking about it, Slick Scotty replies "Draw!" Suddenly, everyone goes wild. The artist who was sitting across the table from Slick Scotty suddenly pulls out a pad of paper and a pencil and starts drawing. The professional card player to Scotty's right starts playing draw poker, and the gunfighter to Scotty's left goes for his guns. "This always happens whenever I say 'Draw!' Stupid $%#&$ polymorphism!" thinks Slick Scotty to himself.

Figure 5.22.
(Opposite page)
"Draw!"

Although polymorphism may have given Slick Scotty a tough time as a card dealer, as you can see, polymorphism has greatly simplified our design.

5.12.1 A Partial OO Design for the Big Card Game

1. **The polymorphism is in the way the dealer tracks the players.** In Figure 5.23 the class "Dealer" has an attribute "Players," which keeps track of the people who are playing the game. The point to be made here is that some of the people playing may be artists, card players, or gun slingers—it doesn't matter. "Dealer" doesn't care what type of person each individual is, it deals with them in all the same way. As far as dealer is concerned, they're only people. Polymorphism is the concept that permits this to happen.

2. **The different subclasses respond to "Draw" in their own way.** In this scenario, Slick Scotty sends out the message "Draw" to each person at the table. The artist object responded to the message by drawing a picture. The professional card player object responded to the message by starting to play draw poker. The gunfighter object responded to the message by drawing his guns. This is a perfect example of polymorphism. The same message, "Draw," went out to different types of objects, and they all did something different (actually, a better way to look at it is that from their point of view, they did the appropriate thing). The interesting thing to note is that Slick Scotty didn't have to send different messages to each object (perhaps "ArtistDraw," "PokerDraw," and "GunFighterDraw"), he just had to send the one message, "Draw."

Figure 5.23.
The person–class hierarchy for the big game.

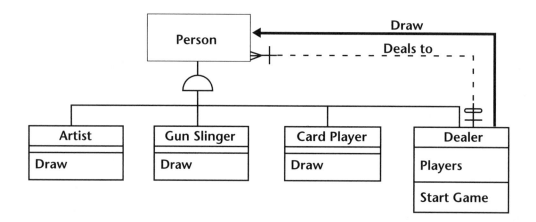

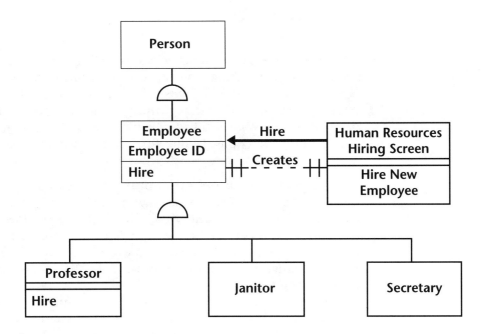

3. **There's still work to be done.** Although each type of object responds to "Draw" in an appropriate manner, it isn't really what we want. We probably need to add a new method called "Play Game" to the class "Person," which would take as a parameter the type of game to be played (i.e., draw poker, stud poker, crazy eights). Note: This isn't a problem with polymorphism, we've just blown it in design by sending a message that these classes already respond to, when we really wanted the classes to do something else. Should've read the documentation first!

Figure 5.24. A partial implementation of a human resources system for the university.

5.12.2 Polymorphism in the University

Let's consider a slightly more realistic example of polymorphism by exploring the design of how the university handles the hiring of new staff (see Figure 5.24).

5.12.2.1 Interesting Points About the Example

1. **Notice how the person class hierarchy has been modified.** We've added a new abstract class called "Employee" that

encapsulates all of the similarities of the different employees at the university.

2. **Notice how there is an instance relationship "Creates."** There is a "Creates" relationship between the class "HumanResourcesHiringScreen" (HRHS) and "Employee." This is a perfect example of a transitory instance relationship. Although some methodologies such as Booch (1993) would have you use a special "instantiates" relationship to show this, I think that an appropriately labeled transitory relationship does the job just as well.

3. **Hiring is where the polymorphism is.** The interesting thing to note is how HRHS collaborates with employee objects. In order to hire a new employee, the "HireNewEmployee" method would instantiate the appropriate object (either a professor, or a janitor) and then send it the message "Hire." If the person is either a janitor or a secretary, the "Hire" method defined in the class "Employee" would be run. If the person is a professor, "Hire" in the class "Professor" would run (we overrode the method "Hire"). This is polymorphic because it doesn't matter what kind of employee the person is, we still interact with them in the same way. As you can see, the concepts of polymorphism and inheritance are very complementary.

5.12.3 Why Polymorphism Is Important

By being able to send the message "Hire" to any kind of employee, there isn't the need for a complicated set of IF or CASE statements in the "HireNewEmployee" method. This method doesn't need to send a "HireProfessor" message to professor objects, "HireJanitor" to janitor objects, and so on. It just sends "Hire" to any type of employee, and the object will do the right thing. As a result, we can add new types of employees (perhaps "Registrar") and we don't need to change the HRHS class at all! In other words, HRHS is loosely coupled to the employee class hierarchy, allowing us to extend our system easily.

5.13 Structured Versus Object-Oriented Applications

Structured applications are built from two parts: Data and programs that work with the data. On the other hand, OO applications are

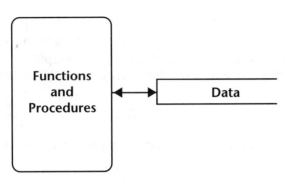

Figure 5.25.
The basic architecture of a structured application.

built from a collection of interacting objects that encapsulate both data and functionality. As you can see, structured and OO applications are based on two completely different development paradigms.

5.13.1 Structured Applications

Using a structured approach, applications are created through separating the data from the functionality. The application's data is stored in a database, whereas the application's functionality is implemented in a program. This is shown in Figure 5.25.

5.13.2 Object-Oriented Applications

Figure 5.26 shows that when an OO application is running, it is really just a collection of interacting objects that have been instantiated (created) from the class definitions. Because the definition of a class includes the definition of both its attributes and its methods, an OO application has both data and functionality (programming).

So What's the Big Deal?
The main difference is that object-oriented applications are modeled from a different viewpoint than structured applications. When we are

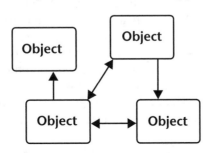

Figure 5.26.
The basic architecture of an object-oriented application.

taking an OO approach, we first look for the objects that are pertinent to the system at hand, and then abstract them into classes. When we are taking a structured approach, we split the application into two sections: the data for the system and the functions and procedures that access it.

An Example
To get a better feel for what is going on, let's walk through a quick example:

What happens in the real world:

> A new student, Reginald Barclay (Reg), enrolls in the university. He goes to the registrar's office, where the registrar enters information about him into the system. When this is completed, the registrar uses the system to enroll Reg in the courses that he wants.

What happens in an OO application:

> The registrar uses the system to display the student editing screen. This is an instance (object) of the class "StudentEditingScreen." Reg's information is entered, and a new student object representing him is instantiated (created). Once the registrar has finished entering the seminars that Reginald wants, the screen object sends messages to both the student object and to the appropriate seminar objects informing them that Reginald has now been enrolled in those seminars. No longer needed, the screen object is de-instantiated (removed from memory).

What happens in a structured application:

> The registrar uses the system to display the student editing screen. The is done by the function "DisplayStudentEditScreen," which is part of the human resources program. Reg's information is entered, and a new student record is created for him in the database. Once the registrar has finished entering the seminars that Reginald wants, new records are added to the database recording the seminars in which he is now enrolled. No longer needed, the screen is no longer displayed.

Let us now consider some comments concerning objects, both transitory and persistent.

DEFINITION

Deinstantiate—To remove an object from the object space (to destroy it, to de-allocate it).

1. **Objects are more powerful than records.** Records only have data, whereas objects can also do things.

2. **Transitory and persistent objects work together in an OO application.** The editing-screen object worked together with student and seminar objects in order to enroll Reg in the university. The editing screen is transitory (it is instantiated, used, and then deinstantiated when no longer needed), whereas the student object and seminars objects are persistent (they would be saved into the database).

Figure 5.27. The Ambler class-modeling notation.

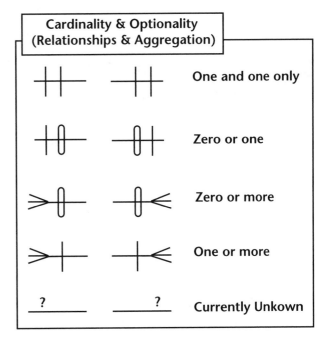

Abstract Class

Class Name
Attributes
Methods

Concrete Class

Class Name
Attributes
Methods

Subsystem (Server)

Contract

Cardinality & Optionality (Relationships & Aggregation)

Aggregation

Inheritance

Persistent Inst. Rel.

Transitory Inst. Rel.

Message

One and one only

Zero or one

Zero or more

One or more

Currently Unkown

5.14 What We've Learned

We've discussed in detail numerous object-oriented terms and concepts in this chapter, and have introduced notation to model these concepts. The concepts and terms are summarized in the box near the beginning of this chapter (p. 118), and the notation is summarized in Figure 5.27. In order to make the OO learning process easier, you might want to photocopy these two pages and put them on your office wall.

References

Booch, G. *Object-Oriented Design with Applications,* 2nd ed., Redwood City, CA: Benjamin/Cummings, 1993.

> *Class models allow us to model*
> *both the results of our analysis and of our design.*

Chapter 6

Developing a Better Understanding of the System: Class Modeling

What class models are.

Why we want to draw class models.

How CRC modeling, use-case scenario testing, and class modeling all fit together.

How to find classes.

How to find attributes.

How to find methods.

How to find object relationships.

How to define inheritance.

How to define collaboration.

How to define aggregation.

How to document class models.

How to take advantage of class-modeling tips and techniques.

This chapter describes the fundamental OO modeling technique—class modeling. You aren't doing OO if you aren't doing class modeling.

Class models are the mainstay of OO analysis and design. In the previous chapter we covered object-oriented concepts and the notation with which to model those concepts. In this chapter we'll review and expand on these concepts to describe how to class model.

Class models are created using all of the modeling concepts and notations discussed in chapter 5. Class models show the classes of the system, their inter-relationships (including inheritance, aggregation, and object relationships), and the collaborations (interactions) between those classes. In short, class models are the mainstay of object-oriented analysis and design. We use them to show both what the system should be able to do (analysis), and how we're going to do it (design).

6.1 Steps of Class Modeling

Because class modeling is used for both object-oriented analysis and design, there are naturally both analysis and design steps in the class-modeling process. In fact, in this chapter we'll see that all of the steps of class modeling have both analysis and design aspects to them. One should note, however, that for the most part the "Find" steps are analysis, and the "Define" steps are design. The steps of class modeling are:

- Find classes

- Find attributes

- Find methods

- Find object relationships

- Define inheritance

- Define collaborations

- Define aggregation

As you can see, there is a fair bit of overlap between CRC modeling and class modeling. For example, both techniques include the steps "Find Classes" and "Define Collaborations." Additionally, the CRC-modeling step "Find Responsibilities" is covered by the steps "Find

Attributes" and "Find Methods" [remember, responsibilities are the things that a class knows (it's attributes), and the things that a class does (it's methods)]. As we discussed in chapter 3, it is this overlap in modeling steps that allows us to take our CRC model and convert it into an object model. Throughout this chapter we'll discuss how to actually go about expanding a CRC model into a full-fledged class model.

So far in this book, we've seen that we perform CRC modeling and use-case scenario testing to gather the user requirements for the system. Although both these techniques are incredibly effective, the main problem with them is that we really can't justify handing-off a stack of index cards to upper management as our analysis document. They just won't go for it. Additionally, although a CRC model provides an excellent overview of a system, it doesn't show the details that we need to build the system. That's why we have scribes to take down the business logic. Basically, we use our CRC model as a base and fill in the details required in a class model from the scribe's notes (see Figure 6.1).

CRC models show the initial classes of a system, their responsibilities, and the basic relationships (in the form of a list of collaborators) between those classes. Although our CRC models of user

CRC modeling and class modeling go hand-in-hand!

Figure 6.1.
Your CRC model and the scribe's notes are used as input for your class model.

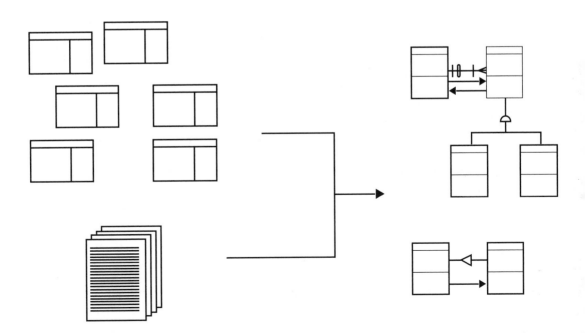

DEFINITION

Class model—
Class models show
the classes of the
system, their
interrelationships,
and the
collaborations
between those
classes.

requirements provide an excellent overview of a system, the
do not provide the details needed to actually build it. Luckily,
those details have been captured in the notes taken down by
the scribe(s) during CRC modeling. We use the CRC model and
the detailed notes as input for our class model. The main goal
in class modeling is to "flesh out" our CRC model, and naturally make improvements to it, in order to document the
results of our analysis and design in a manner that developers
can use to construct a system. This chapter discusses in detail
how to do that.

6.1.1 Finding Classes, Attributes, and Methods

Objects are any person, place, thing, concept, event, screen, or report
that is applicable to your system. Objects both know things (they
have attributes) and they do things (they have methods). A class is a
representation of an object. Classes form the main building blocks of
an object-oriented application. We found most of our classes during
CRC modeling, as well as their attributes and methods.

Two of the steps of CRC modeling included the finding of classes
and the finding of responsibilities. Classes represent a collection of
similar objects. For example, although there are thousands of students who attend university we would only model one class, called
"Student" that would represent the entire collection of students.

To describe a class, we defines it's attributes and methods. Attributes are the information that we store about classes, whereas methods are the things that a class does. For example, students have
student numbers, names, addresses, and phone numbers. Those are
all examples of the attributes of a student. Students also enroll in
courses, drop courses, and request transcripts. Those are all examples
of the things that a student does, which get implemented (coded) in
the form of a method. You should think of methods as the object-oriented equivalent of functions and procedures.

6.1.1.1 Finding Classes
Our CRC model already shows the main classes of our system,
although as we delve deeper into the design of the system we will
find that we need to add new classes to support features, such as
accessing databases and printers. Although these topics are touched

DEFINITIONS

Object—Any person, place, thing, event, screen, report, or concept that is applicable to the design of the system.

Class—A class represents a collection of similar objects. A class is effectively a template from which objects are created.

Attribute—Something that a class or object knows. An attribute is basically a single piece of data or information.

Method—Something that a class or object does. A method is similar to a function or procedure in structured programming.

on briefly in this book, they are addressed in detail in my next book for SIGS.

For each CRC card that we have, we draw it in our class model as a concrete class. Remember, a concrete class is one from which objects are instantiated (created). When we take advantage of inheritance, we'll see how abstract classes are defined. Remember, an abstract class is one from which objects are not instantiated. Classes are shown as rectangles that have three sections: the top section for the name of the class, the middle section is for the attributes of the class, and the bottom section is for the methods of the class.

6.1.1.2 Finding Methods and Attributes

We have already found many attributes and methods during CRC modeling. As we begin to add object relationships and aggregation relationships to our model we will find that we need to add new attributes and methods to our classes to support these relationships. These topics are covered in detail later in this chapter.

6.1.1.3 Converting CRC Cards to Classes

1. **There is one concrete class for each card.** You will draw one concrete class (concrete classes are rectangles with thick borders) for each CRC card. At this stage we are only interested in the class itself, plus its responsibilities. Copy the name of the class into the top section of the class, the attributes into the middle section of the class, and the methods into the bottom section of the class (see Figure 6.2).

Each CRC card is modeled as a concrete class.

Student	
Student number Name Address Phone number Enroll in seminar Drop seminar Drive Car Give name Seminars enrolled in	Seminar

Seminar	
Course# Date/Time Room# List of students Student marks # seats available Waiting list Indicate # seats left Get prerequisites Add/drop student Give student list	Course

Student
Student number Name Address Phone number Seminars enrolled in
Enroll in seminar Drop seminar Drive car Give name

Seminar
Course# Date/Time Room# List of students Student marks # seats available Waiting list
Indicate # seats left Get prerequistes Add/drop student Give student list

Figure 6.2.
Converting CRC
cards into classes

2. **Ignore the collaborators for now.** We'll use the list of collaborators, along with the scribe's notes, to help define collaborations, aggregation, and object relationships.

6.1.2 Finding Instance Relationships

In the real world, objects are associated with other objects. We model these associations on our class models with instance relationships. Instance relationships are important because they define how objects interact with one another, if they interact at all. Our users told us about instance relationships, which were recorded by the scribe during the CRC-modeling process.

Objects are often associated with, or related to, other objects. For example, in our university system we have several associations

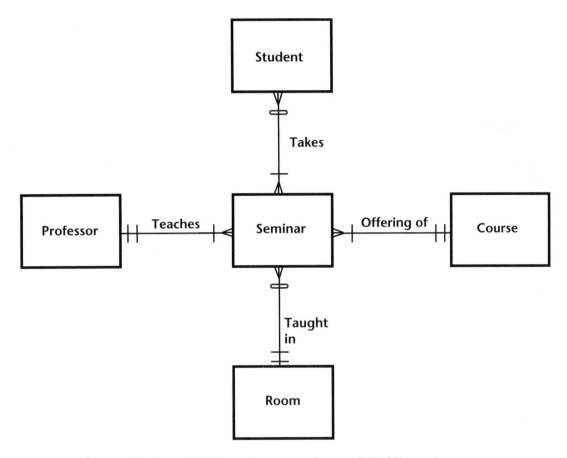

between objects: Students TAKE seminars, professors TEACH seminars, seminars are OFFERINGS OF courses, seminars are TAUGHT IN rooms, and so on. We call these associations "instance relationships," and we model them as lines connecting the two classes whose instances (objects) are involved in the relationship (see Figure 6.3).

Explanation

1. **We must always model cardinality and optionality.** Cardinality shows how many objects are involved in the relationship, and optionality indicated whether or not they have to be involved. For example, in Figure 6.3 a student must take one or more seminars, but a seminar is taken by zero or more students (sometimes a seminar is offered, but nobody enrolls in

Figure 6.3.
Some of the instance relationships between classes in the university system.

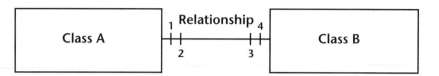

Cardinality (positions 1 & 4):

┼ One   ⪕ Many

Optionality (positions 2 & 3):

┼ Must   ┤├ May

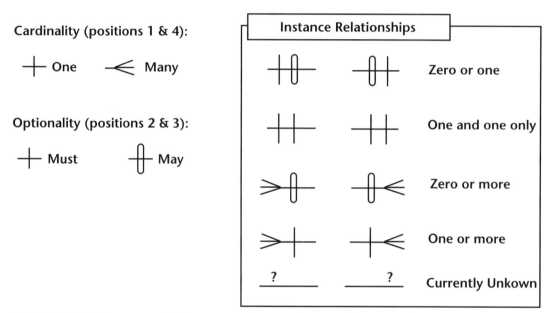

Instance Relationships

Zero or one

One and one only

Zero or more

One or more

Currently Unkown

Figure 6.4.
Instance-
relationship
notation.

it). As a second example, a professor teaches one or more seminars, and a seminar is taught by one and only one professor. Figure 6.4 shows the notation introduced in chapter 5 that is used to describe instance relationships.

2. **Relationships are two-way things.** As we can see in the paragraph above, relationships are two-way processes. Students have relationships with seminars, and seminars have relationships with students. The implication is that when there is a relationship between two classes, we must model the relationship from both points of view. A common problem is that our users will give us the details about the relationship from one point of view (i.e., students take one or more courses) but will forget to tell us about the relationship in the other direction. The main reason for this is that they are very close to the business and will often assume that the relationship is obvious. Unfortunately it often isn't. You should expect that you will need to contact your users to fill

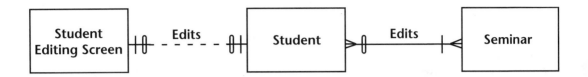

Figure 6.5.
Transitory and
persistent
instance
relationships.

in the details when you are class modeling. Actually, this "problem" points to a reason for having at least one outsider in a CRC-modeling session. What is obvious to an insider usually isn't to an outsider. Chances are the outsider will be asking intelligent questions throughout a CRC-modeling session that would investigate many of these details.

6.1.2.1 Persistent Versus Transitory Relationships

Persistent relationships are those that are permanent or semi-permanent in nature, whereas transitory relationships are temporary. Persistent relationships are drawn as complete lines, whereas transitory relationships are shown as dotted lines. Examples of both are shown in Figure 6.5.

The basic issue here is that of the lifetime of the objects involved. If at least one of the objects isn't persistent, that is, it isn't saved to permanent storage, then the relationship will be transitory.

6.1.2.2 Implementing Instance Relationships

Instance relationships are implemented via the combination of attributes and methods. The attributes describe the relationship, the methods define and update it. Although this is basically a construction issue (construction issues are dealt with in Volume 2 of this series), it is important enough to warrant discussion here.

1. **Relationships are implemented by a combination of methods and attributes.** Attributes such as pointers or object IDs (a unique identifier) are updated by methods to maintain the relationships. For example, Figure 6.6 shows that to maintain its relationship with "Seminar," "Student" has the attribute "Seminars enrolled in" and the methods "Enroll in seminar" and "Drop seminar," which update the attribute. "Seminar" also maintains the relationship that it has with "Student" using the attribute "List of students" and the methods "Add/drop student."

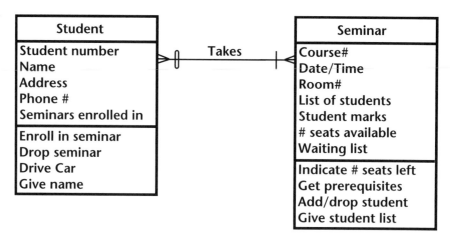

Figure 6.6.
Implementing
the relationship
between students
and seminars.

2. **Relationships can be inherited.** Because attributes and methods are inherited, instance relationships are automatically inherited too! We'll discuss this concept in greater detail in the next section.

3. **You need to understand how objects collaborate with each other.** In our example above "Student" has the attribute "Seminars enrolled in." Because student objects know what seminar objects they are enrolled in, they are able to collaborate with those seminars. Similarly, "Seminar" has the attribute "List of students" which allows seminar objects to collaborate with student objects. If an object needs to collaborate with another type of object, then it needs to maintain information identifying it (either a pointer or object id). Because "Seminar" collaborates with "Student," and "Student" collaborates with "Seminar," they each have to maintain information about the other one so that they know where to send messages (unless of course sufficient information was passed to it in the form of a parameter to a message). We'll discuss collaboration in greater detail in following sections.

DEFINITION

Object ID—An attribute that is a unique identifier for an object. Also called an *OID*.

Style Issue
Although many developers will add the necessary attributes and methods needed to maintain object relationships, others will assume that they exist and not bother to document them on the class model. Both styles are fine, so follow whichever one you like. In this

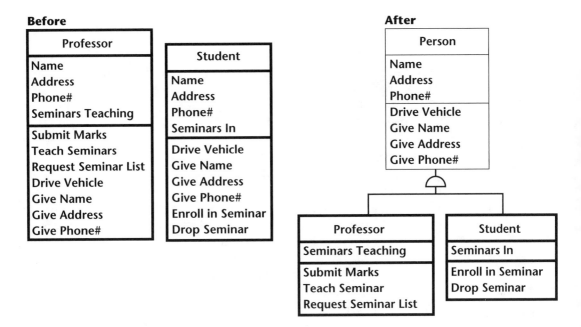

Figure 6.7.
Inheritance.

book we show them whenever it is pertinent to the example at hand, otherwise we leave them out. In my next book, however, we'll delve into this issue in great and gory detail, and we'll show all of the attributes and methods needed to support relationships in those diagrams.

6.1.3 Defining Inheritance

Inheritance allows us to model *is a* and *is like* relationships. We are able to recognize opportunities for inheritance by looking for similar attributes and/or methods between two or more classes.

6.1.3.1 Recognizing Opportunities for Inheritance

Class "A" can inherit from class "B" when it has the same data and performs the same functions as class "B." When "A" inherits from "B" we say that "A" is the subclass of "B" and that "B" is the superclass of "A." Furthermore, we say that we have "pure inheritance" when "A" inherits all of the attributes and methods of "B." Figure 6.7 shows how we create a new class that implements the common features of two existing classes.

Explanation

In the "before picture" of Figure 6.7 there are many similarities between the "Student" and "Professor" classes. Not only do they have similar attributes, but they also have similar methods. To take advantage of these similarities, we create a new class called "Person" and have "Student" and "Professor" inherit from it, as we can see in the "after picture."

Explanation

The difference in Figure 6.8 is that we've pushed up the attributes "Seminars Teaching" and "Seminars In" into the class "Person," calling the new attribute "Seminars." The reason why we did this is because both attributes would have been implemented the same way—as some sort of collection of pointers onto the seminar objects themselves. Although the attribute "Seminar" is used differently by the classes "Professor" and "Student," we can still take advantages of the similarities between the two attributes. This is a perfect example of a design decision.

Something to think about: Would this approach work if professors could also take courses? Why or why not? Would we need to make any changes to our hierarchy, and if so what?

Figure 6.8.
An alternative
inheritance
approach.

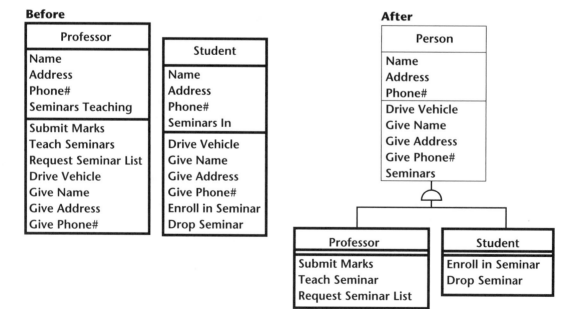

INHERITANCE TIPS & TECHNIQUES

Although we discussed these tips in detail in chapter 5, they're repeated here for your convenience:

- Look for similar methods and/or attributes

- Look for existing classes

- It should make sense to say either:

  - The subclass IS A superclass

  - The subclass IS LIKE A superclass

- Inherit everything

Inheritance Modeling Issues

We've been working on our university information system class model, and somebody notices that we need to add the class "Corporate Donors." Corporate donors are companies that make endowments to the university to pay for new facilities, research, and scholarships. We need to keep track of the name of the company, the address of the headquarters, the name of the contact person at the company, his or her title, phone number, and the contact's office address (many companies have more than one address).

One solution would be to add a new class called "Corporate Donor" and have it inherit from the class "Person," which already has the name, address, and phone number that "Corporate Donor" needs. The problem with this approach is that a corporate donor isn't a person, it's a company. Second, corporate donors don't drive vehicles to the school. Therefore we wouldn't have pure inheritance. A better solution is shown in Figure 6.9.

Explanation

1. **"Address" was pulled out of "Person."** Because it didn't make sense to have "Corporate Donor" inherit from "Person" in Figure 6.9, and because we don't want to implement addresses in two places, we created a class called "Address." Addresses are places, so it makes sense to make them classes. The attribute "Address" in "Person" would now be implemented as either a pointer to an address or as the object ID of the address.

Class Modeling

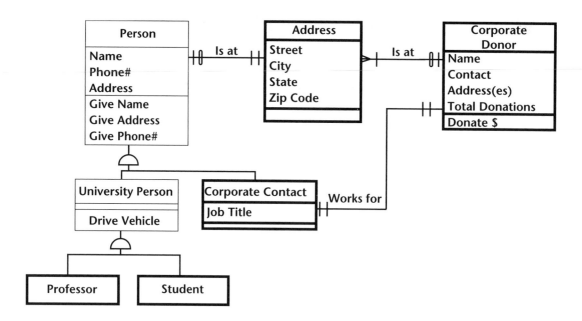

Figure 6.9.
The university
information
system with
corporate
donors added.

2. **"Corporate Donor," "Corporate Contact," and "University Person" were added.** We've added three new classes "Corporate Donor" to keep track of donors, "Corporate Contacts" to keep track of the contacts, and "University Person" to implement "Drive Vehicle" (remember, as far as we're concerned corporate contacts don't drive vehicles on our campus). Note: We didn't show the attributes and methods of "Student" and "Professor" to simplify the diagram.

3. **Instance relationships are inherited.** All of the subclasses of "Person" inherit the instance relationship between it and "Address." Remember, instance relationships are implemented with attributes and methods. Because both attributes and methods are inherited, instance relationships are too.

4. **"Corporate Contact" doesn't need to know for whom it works.** From the point of view of the university, it deals with corporations, and the person acting as a contact is of secondary importance. In our system we need to be able to traverse from "Corporate Donor" to "Corporate Contact," but not vice-versa. This means that "Corporate Donor" must know who the contact person is, but not vice-versa.

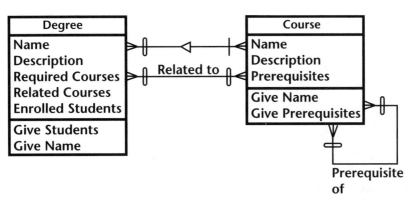

Figure 6.10.
A course is part
of a degree.

6.1.4 Defining Aggregation

Aggregation allows us to model "part-of" relationships. As with instance relationships, our users tell us about part-of relationships during CRC modeling. During class modeling, it is our job to determine whether or not aggregation makes sense in the current context. Basically, aggregation makes sense when the part is a part in the real world and we are interested in keeping track of the individual part.

6.1.4.1 When to Use Aggregation

Aggregation represents a special type of object relationship—it models a "part-of" relationship. We use aggregation when one object is part of another object and we need to keep track of both the whole and the part. Figure 6.10 shows how we might use aggregation in our university system. Some comments on aggregation follow.

1. **The sentence "a course is part of a degree" makes sense.** A degree is made up of a collection required courses, so the sentence "a course is part of a degree" makes sense. A degree is made up of one or more courses, and a course is part of zero or more degrees (some courses are not applicable towards earning a degree).

2. **We can have recursive instance relationships.** The instance relationship "Prerequisite of" is an example of a recursive relationship. It models the fact that a course has zero or more prerequisites, and that any given course is a prerequisite of zero or more courses. It is also possible to have recursive aggregation relationships too. For example, a team may be part of another team (see Figure 6.11).

3. **Is a course really part of a degree?** It is questionable whether a course is really part of a degree. You can't take a degree apart and pull out several courses. It may make more sense to use an instance relationship labeled "Required for" instead of aggregation in this example. When aggregation doesn't work you can often use object relationships instead.

If aggregation doesn't work, try an instance relationship instead.

Aggregation Modeling Issues

Our users just won't leave us alone! Now they want us to keep track of research teams too. Although a research team is led by a professor, both students and other professors may be involved. In an effort to organize their work, a large team may be split up into research sub-teams who are treated as a real team. The changes we need to make to our class model are shown in Figure 6.11. Some additional comments concerning aggregation follow.

1. **"Professor," "Student," and "Person" didn't change.** When we added "Research Team," the only existing class that was affected was "University Person." Because both professors and students can be part of a research team we were able to push this similarity up into "University Person." We couldn't push it all the way up into "Person" because corporate contacts aren't on research teams.

2. **Aggregation is implemented by attributes and methods.** Aggregation is implemented in exactly the same way as instance

---

AGGREGATION TIPS AND TECHNIQUES

Although we discussed these tips in detail in chapter 5, they're repeated here for your convenience.

• The part is almost always involved with only one whole.

• It should make sense to say that one object is part of another object.

• It should be a part in the real world.

• You should be interested in the part.

• Cardinality and optionality must be shown.

• Aggregation is inherited.

relationships—through the use of attributes and methods. That implies that you inherit part-of relationships too. For example, the part-of relationship is between "Person" and "Research Team" (a person is part of a research team). "Professor" and "Student" inherit this relationship (therefore a professor can be part of a team and a student can be part of a team).

3. **We can have recursive aggregation.** We are able to model the fact that some research teams are made up of smaller subteams.

4. **We need to understand how the whole and the parts collaborate with each other.** Just as with instance relationships, we need to understand how the objects collaborate together. For example, because a research team object needs to be able to collaborate with professors and students (perhaps to get their names and phone numbers) "Research Team" needs the attribute "Members," which would probably be a list of object IDs for each university person on the team. "University Person" has the attribute "Teams on" so that each professor and student object can collaborate with the research teams with which they are involved. Note, however, that "Research

Figure 6.11. Adding research teams to the university information system class model.

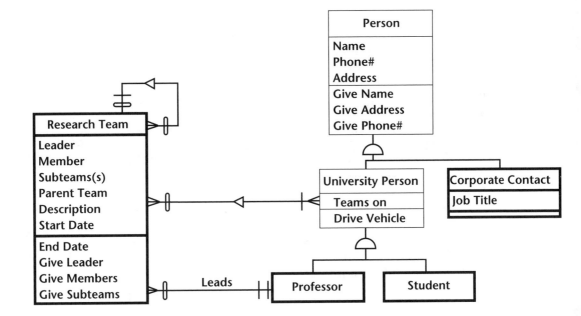

Team" knows who the leader is, but "Professor" doesn't keep track of the teams of which they are the leader (I guess professors don't care about that sort of stuff).

6.1.5 Defining Collaborations

Classes often need to collaborate with other classes to fulfill their responsibilities. Collaboration takes one of two forms: either a request for information or a request to do something. On our CRC cards we recorded the classes that each class needs to collaborate with, and in our notes we defined how those collaborations actually take place. On class models we show collaboration as a message being sent from one class to another.

6.1.5.1 How to Define Collaborations

Collaborations occur whenever one object needs another object to either give it information or to do something for it. Figure 6.12 shows examples of collaboration. Some comments on collaboration follow.

1. **We need either an instance relationship or a part-of relationship between the classes.** In order for an object to send another object a message, it needs to know about it first. Think of it like this: If you don't know how to get hold of someone, you can't communicate with that person, can you?

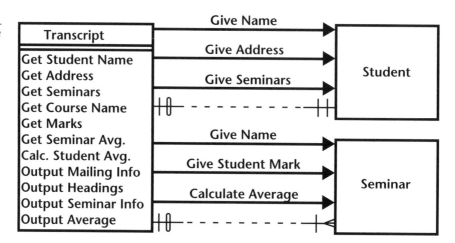

Figure 6.12. The collaboration of "Transcript" with "Student" and "Seminar."

2. **There are "transitory relationships" between "Transcript" and the classes "Student" and "Seminar."** Transitory relationships are ones that are not permanent. They usually occur when an instance of a transitory class (in this case "Transcript") has a relationship with another object (transitory relationships can also occur between instances of persistent classes, although this is not as common). "Transcript" is a transitory class because we don't save it to permanent storage. We instantiate a transcript object, it gets the information it needs, it outputs it, and then we de-instantiate it (i.e., we remove it from memory). While the transcript object exists it has a transitory object relationship with a student object, as well as all the class objects that the student took.

3. **We sent the same message "Give Name" to two different classes.** To get the name of a student we sent it the message "Give Name" and to get the name of a class we sent it the message "Give Name."

6.1.5.2 How Collaboration REALLY Happens

When it gets right down to it, an OO application is basically a collection of objects that are working together to get the job done. Therefore, to fully understand how an OO application works, we need to understand how objects collaborate. Although the example information presented may not be completely relevant to class modeling, it should answer a few questions as to how all this is happening in the system. It's probably of interest to programmers, but might not be to analysts or user representatives. Parental discretion is advised.

The next example (see Figure 6.13) shows how a transcript object collaborates with the appropriate student object to get his or her name so that it can be printed at the top of the report.

Explanation

1. **An object collaborates with another object.** One object sends a message to another object. In this case, the transcript object sends a message to a student object (Paul Manheim) requesting his name.

2. **The method definition is searched for in the class.** Methods are only stored once for the class, and not once for each

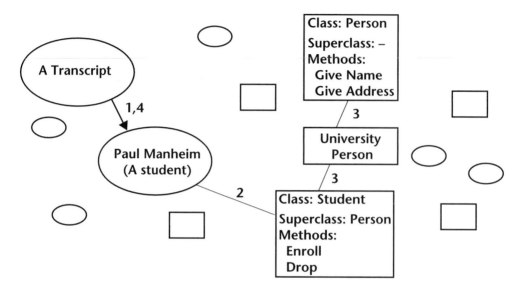

Class: Person
Superclass: –
Methods:
  Give Name
  Give Address

A Transcript

1,4

Paul Manheim
(A student)

3

University
Person

3

2

Class: Student
Superclass: Person
Methods:
  Enroll
  Drop

Figure 6.13.
A transcript
object requests
the name of a
student object.

object (if you had 1,000 students, you wouldn't want to store the code 1,000 times). Therefore, when an object receives a message, the next step would be to go to the appropriate class definition (i.e., a student object goes to the "Student" class definition). Class definitions are stored in the object space once and once only. In our example, we are looking for the "GiveName" method.

3. **The method definition is searched for higher in the inheritance hierarchy.** If the method isn't found in the class definition, the application looks for the method in the superclass of the current class, and so on until it finds the method. The first method with the appropriate template is run (the template of a method includes both its name and the definitions/types of any parameters passed to it). That way, if a method has been overridden (redefined) lower down in a class hierarchy, it will be run, instead of the one defined higher up. In our example, we find "GiveName" in the definition of "Person," which is the superclass of "Student." If we go all the way to the top of the class hierarchy and we can't find the method, then an error occurs.

4. **A return value, if any, is passed back.** The method is run, and a return value, if any, is passed back to the object that

originally sent the message. In our example, the name of the student is returned to the transcript object. Because methods can run other methods for the object, these methods are searched for using the same algorithm as described in step 3.

DEFINITION

Transitory relationship— A nonpermanent relationship between two objects.

6.2 Documenting Class Models

It isn't enough to draw a class model, it also needs to be documented. The bulk of the documentation work is documenting the details about a class, as well as the reasoning behind any trade-offs that you made.

6.2.1 How to Document a Class

To document a class, you must describe it, it's attributes, and it's methods.

1. **Describing Classes.** A class is documented by a sentence or two that describes its purpose. You should also indicate whether or not the class is persistent or transitory, and if there are any aliases (other names that it is called) for the class. This information would then be followed by the documentation for each attribute and method (described in the following example).

   Class: Student

   Description: Students are the main clients of the university. Students come to the university to learn new skills and to gain new insights into themselves and the world in which they live.

   Persistent: Yes

   Aliases: Classmate

   It is important to document the potential alias' for a class because it is very likely that different people in an organization will call the same thing by different names. For example, do banks serve clients or customers? Do truckers drive trucks, vehicles, or lorries? Do children eat sweets, candies, or good-ies? The point to be made here is that we want to ensure that everyone is talking the same language, and that if not we had better document what's going on.

2. **Attributes.** Attributes should be described with one sentence, its type (if appropriate), an example should be given, a range of values defined (if appropriate), and an example given (if appropriate) as shown in the following example.

   Attribute: Name

   Description: The given name of the person, in the format "Last Name, First Name, Initial."

   Format: Student names are alphabetic, at least one charac-ter, but could be of any length.

   Example: Galen, Richard

3. **Methods.** Methods are documented with pseudo-code describing its logic (see the following example).

   Method: Enroll in seminar

   Logic:

   Send a message to the seminar to verify that there is an available seat

   If there is room in the seminar

   Send a message to the seminar to enroll in it.

   Add that seminar to the list of seminars in which the student is enrolled.

   endif

Using CASE (Computer Aided Software Engineering) Tools
There are many affordable object-oriented CASE (computer-aided software engineering) tools on the market, and you should consider using one if you are going to be doing a lot of class modeling. CASE tools provide automated support for documenting your class model. Many CASE tools are as easy to use as a paint program. You draw your class model by clicking on the appropriate icons and dropping class

model symbols onto your diagram. When you double-click on a symbol in your class model, an appropriate editing screen is displayed which you are expected to fill in. It's that simple. You can either keep your system documentation online in an electronic file, or print it out to obtain a hard copy. Object-oriented CASE will be discussed in detail in the second volume in this series.

6.2.2 Documenting Design Trade-Offs

1. **Inheritance.** Inheritance usually doesn't need to be documented, unless you feel that what you did isn't obvious (actually, if it isn't obvious you should first rethink any design decisions that you made to verify that they made sense).

2. **Aggregation.** If you used aggregation and you weren't sure that it was the right idea, you should probably document why you did it. For example, remember how we said that a course is part of a degree, but we weren't sure whether or not to use aggregation or an instance relationship?

   Important: The good news is that in the long run it really doesn't matter whether or not you use aggregation or an

---

DOCUMENTATION TIPS

1. ***Documentation is an important part of systems development.*** It might not be the most exciting part of developing an application, but you must document what your application should be able to do, why it should be able to do it, and how. You should also be documenting what an application shouldn't do, and why. Remember, analysis included the definition of both what is in and what is out of scope.

2. ***Document complicated things.*** If it's complicated, then document it thoroughly (actually, if something is complicated, then spend more time and try to design it so that it's simple). If something is simple, then you don't need to spend a lot of time documenting it.

3. ***Don't overdocument.*** You need to document, but you shouldn't overdocument, either. Remember, users pay you to build systems, not document them. There's a fine line between underdocumenting and overdocumenting, and only through experience are you able to find it.

The more complicated something is, the more it needs to be documented.

Your goal is to produce a system, not a mound of documentation.

instance relationship. They are both implemented in exactly the same way, as a combination of attributes and methods, so from a construction point of view it doesn't matter. From a design point of view, however, it does matter, as it gives the designers something to argue about.

3. **Document any minimums and maximums.** There are often minimums and maximums involved with object and part-of relationships. For example, perhaps professors must teach at least two courses a term, but no more than six. If you are using a CASE tool, most likely you are able to double-click on the relationship line and have an editing screen pop up that would allow you to input the minimums and maximums. If you are documenting the system on paper, you have two options: You can either document these figures in their own special section, or you can include them in the documentation of the appropriate class.

   Important: You should also document the reason for these figures, if you know them (if nobody can supply you with a reason for a minimum or maximum, then you should question why it is needed). Many minimums and maximums exist due to limitations of current technology, and there may not be a valid reason for them.

6.3 Class Modeling Tips and Techniques

This section describes some tips and techniques that you may wish to consider while you are class modeling. Some of these pointers are very straight forward, whereas others you may want to think about awhile.

6.3.1 Class Modeling Pointers

1. **Collaboration goes hand-in-hand with relationships.** You need to have either an instance relationship or a part-of relationship between two classes for their objects to collaborate with one another. A good rule of thumb is that if two classes don't collaborate, then you shouldn't need to maintain a rela-

tionship between them. The basic thinking is this: If the classes never take advantage of the relationship, why have it?

2. **Inheritance and aggregation relationships are often confused.** Developers often get confused about when to use inheritance and when to use aggregation. The thing to remember is that inheritance models "is-a" or "is-like" relationships, whereas aggregation models "is-part-of" relationships. By following the sentence rules (it should make sense to say that a subclass IS A superclass) you should be able to determine when to use each concept appropriately.

3. **A subclass should inherit everything.** A subclass should inherit all of the attributes and methods of its superclass, and therefore all of its relationships as well. When a subclass inherits everything from its superclass we say we have "pure inheritance." The advantage of pure inheritance is that we only have to understand what a subclass inherits, and not what it doesn't inherit. Although this sounds trivial, in a deep class hierarchy it makes it a lot easier if you only need to understand what each class adds, and not what it takes away.

   Strive for pure inheritance.

   Important: We're not saying that we can't override (redefine) attributes and methods. For example, in chapter 5 we saw how the class "Dragon" inherits everything from the classes "Bird" and "Lizard," including the method "Eat." However, in the definition of "Dragon" we needed to override "Eat" because dragons eat differently than either bird or lizards (remember, dragons eat knights in shining armor).

4. **Methods should do something.** This sounds really obvious, but each method of a class should either access or modify the attributes of the class. The basic idea is that a method should do something, and not just pass the buck to other methods.

5. **Minimize coupling.** A class should be dependent on as few classes as possible. Coupling is discussed in detail in Section 6.3.3.

6. **Maximize cohesion.** If you can't describe a class or method with one sentence in less than 15 seconds, then it probably isn't cohesive. Classes should represent only one kind of object, and methods should do one thing and one thing well.

7. **The root of a class hierarchy is usually abstract.** We create abstract classes by capturing the similarities between two or more classes in it. In doing so, we virtually guarantee that the root (the class at the top) of a class hierarchy will be an abstract class (after all, we push similarities up into abstract classes). This doesn't imply that a concrete class can't be the root, it's just that it doesn't happen very often.

8. **Any kind of class can inherit from any other kind.** Both abstract and concrete classes can inherit from either abstract or concrete classes. Remember, you inherit attributes and methods, not whether or not the class is concrete or abstract.

6.3.2 How to Recognize Coupling in a Class Model

A class is coupled to another class when it has knowledge of that other class. Coupling is important because when class "A" is coupled to class "B," a change in "B" could necessitate a change in "A." We want to reduce coupling wherever possible. Figure 6.14 illustrates several sources of object-oriented coupling.

6.3.3 Sources of OO Coupling

Figure 6.14.
Examples of coupling in our university information-system class model.

1. **Coupling via instance relationships.** Whenever two classes are associated via an instance relationship they are coupled. For example, "Student" and "Seminar" are coupled via the instance relationship "Takes." A student object knows what seminars he or she is in, and a seminar object knows what students are taking it. As you can see, "Student" and "Seminar" are coupled via their instance relationship. Similarly,

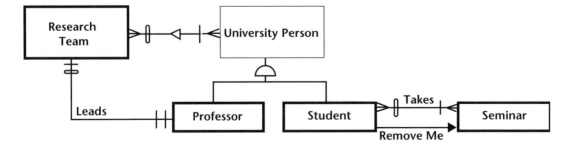

"Research Team" is coupled to "Professor" (a research team object knows who leads it). However, "Professor" is not coupled to "Research Team" via this instance relationship (remember, the class "Professor" does not need to keep track of what research teams that it leads).

Important: A class is coupled to another class only when it has knowledge of that other class. Therefore class "A" can be coupled to class "B" without "B" being coupled to class "A."

2. **Coupling via aggregation.** Just like with instance relationships, part-of relationships also couple classes to one another. For example, "Research Team" and "University Person" are coupled via a part-of relationship. A research team object knows what students and professors work on it, and each student and professor know what research teams they are on, if any. Once again we have two classes coupled via a relationship.

3. **Coupling via collaboration.** In a way, coupling via collaboration is related to coupling via either instance relationships or part-of relationships (remember, without a relationship you can't have collaboration). The main point here is that collaborations increase coupling—not only does an object know of the existence of other objects, it also collaborates with it. For example, "Student" increases its coupling to "Seminar" because it collaborates with it several times.

4. **Direct coupling via inheritance.** Subclasses are highly coupled to their superclasses (a subclass knows and does everything that its superclass does). The only way to reduce this kind of coupling is to not allow subclasses to modify the values of attributes defined in their superclasses. This implies that you need to write methods that change the values of attributes—it's a little extra work, but it makes your system more maintainable in the long run. These methods are called accessors, and will be covered in detail in my next book.

5. **Indirect coupling via inheritance.** Because classes inherit all relationships and collaborations of its superclass, it also inherits any coupling that superclass is involved with.

6.4 Class Modeling Case Study: Part I

Let's take a look at what the class model would look like for the bank. We repeat the description of the case study below for your convenience.

6.4.1 The ABC Case Study

The Archon Bank of Cardassia (ABC) would like to develop an information system for handling accounts. The following is a summary of interviews with employees and customers of the bank.

> **SCENARIO** The bank has many different types of accounts. The basic type of account is called a savings account. Savings account customers do not get a monthly account statement. Instead, they have a passbook that gets updated when they come in. Each passbook page has enough room to hold up to ten transactions, and every time the book is updated the next transaction immediately after the last update printed in the book. The bank already has the passbook printers and printing software in place (we bought it from a third-party vendor).
>
> Customers are able to open and close accounts. They can withdraw or deposit money, or get the current balance. The current balance is displayed on an account update screen that will be part of the teller's information system. This screen displays the account number, the customer's name, and the current balance of the account. An account is associated with a specific branch. Although we now support multi-branch banking, every account is still assumed to have a "home" branch.
>
> A checking account is just like a savings account, except customers can also write checks on it. We sell checks for $30 for a box of 100. Once a customer uses 75 checks, or check #90 comes in (sometimes people make mistakes and rip checks up) we send them a notice in the mail asking them if they want to purchase more checks. Account statements are sent out every month. Checking accounts do not have passbooks, and savings accounts do not have account statements.

We charge $1,200 a year for Private Banking Accounts (PBAs). PBAs are just like checking accounts, but they entitle customers to investment counselling services, as well as other services not available to other clients. A PBA account can be held by only one customer (they're not joint), although a customer may have more than one PBA account. This is exactly as it is for savings accounts. Checking accounts, however, can be joint. This means that a checking account can be accessed by one or more customers (perhaps a husband and wife).

A current account is for our corporate customers. It works like a checking account, with a few extra features. For example, there is a quarterly account statement (which is exactly the same as a monthly account statement, except it is done for an entire quarter) that is sent out in addition to the regular monthly statements. The quarterly statement is sent in the same envelope as the statement for that month. Corporate customers also get to choose the number of checks they are sent (100, 250, 500, or 1000) at a time. Current accounts are not joint, nor can they be accessed through an automatic teller machine (ATM). Furthermore, because of the different service needs of our corporate customers, we deal with them at special branches called "Corporate Branches." Corporate branches serve only corporate customers, and do not serve our retail (normal) customers. Corporate customers can be served at "Retail Branches," although they rarely do because the tellers in a retail branch do not have the necessary background to meet their special needs.

There can be more than one account accessible from a bank card. We currently give cards out to any customer who wants them. Customers access their accounts using two different methods—at an automated teller machine or at a bank branch. ATMs allow customers to deposit, withdraw, and get balances from their accounts. They can also pay bills (this is basically a withdrawal) and transfer money between accounts (this is basically withdrawing from one account and depositing into another).

Everything that can be done at a bank machine can also be done by a real-live teller in a branch. The teller will have an information system that provides the screens to perform all of these functions. Additionally, tellers can also help customers to open and close their accounts, as well as print out account statements for the customer. The account statements are just like the monthly/quarterly statements, except they can be for any time period. For example, a customer could request a statement from the 15th of August to the 23rd of September, and we should be able to print that out on the spot.

Monthly and quarterly account statements are normally printed out on the first Saturday of the following month. This is done by an automated batch job.

Because we have started to put ATMs into variety stores and restaurants (in the past we only had ATMs in branches) we now consider each and every ATM, including those in our "brick-and-mortar" branches, to be a branch as well. That means that ATMs have branch IDs and addresses, just like a normal branch does.

To manage the bank effectively, we split it up into collections of branches called "areas." An area is a group of between 10 and 30 branches. A branch is part of only one area, and all branches are in an area. Each area has a unique name, and is managed by an "area manager." Area managers receive weekly transaction summary reports every Monday morning before 9 A.M. This report summarizes the number and total amounts of all withdrawals, deposits, and bill payment performed at each branch (including ATMs) for the previous week. For brick-and-mortar branches, there is also an indication of how many accounts in total were at that branch at the beginning of the week, how many accounts were opened during the week, and how many accounts were closed during the week, and how many accounts there are now. Finally, all of these figures are summarized and output for the entire area.

To help you read the diagrams a little more easily, the notation is summarized in Figure 6.15.

6.4.2 An Answer to the Case Study

The answer presented below is by no means definitive. Due to the complexity of the case study, the answer has been divided into several parts. This first section overviews the answer, and the next few sections describe pieces of the answer in detail.

6.4.2.1 The ABC Classes

Account—An abstract class that provides all of the basic capabilities of an account.

Account accessor—An abstract class that facilitates the access of accounts by customers.

Figure 6.15.
The Ambler class modeling notation.

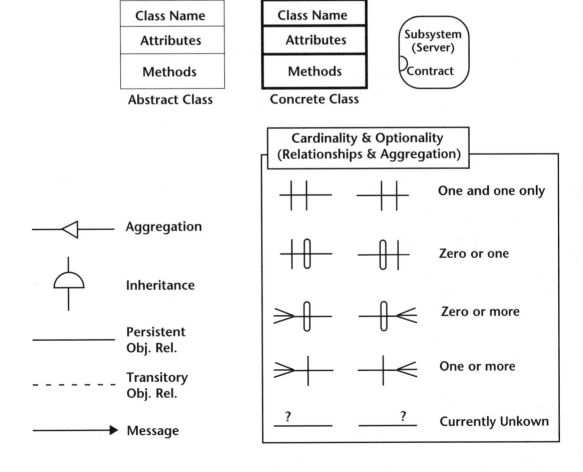

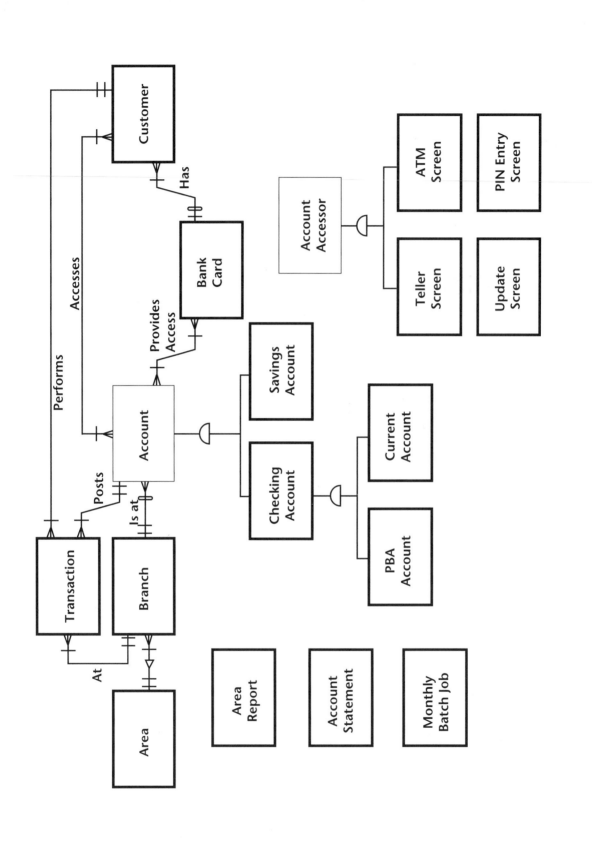

Account statement—A report that shows the transactions processed on an account for a given period of time.

Area—A group of branches within the bank.

Area report—A summary report showing totals for all of the types of transactions for each branch within an area.

ATM screen—The screen (actually a set of screens) display to customers at a bank machine.

Bank card—Bank cards are used to verify the identity of customers.

Branch—A location where the bank does business. Branches can either be traditional "brick-and-mortar" branches or an automated teller machine.

Checking account—A bank account that supports the writing of checks.

Corporate customer—A customer that is a business entity, not a person.

Current account—An account held by a corporate customer.

Customer—A person that the bank does business with.

Monthly batch job—This job is run on the first Saturday of each month. I loops through each account and has the account statement printed out for it.

PBA account—Private banking accounts are for people with significant liquid assets who require investment advice and custom services from the bank.

PIN entry screen—The screen displayed at bank machines that asks customers to input the PIN of their bank card.

Savings account—A very basic kind of account. Savings accounts are the only accounts with a passbook but they have no account statement.

Figure 6.16.
(Opposite page)
The classes for the ABC information system and any permanent relationships between them.

Teller Screen—The main screen of the teller information system. This screen provides the main menu and ties together other screens such as the account update screen.

Transaction—A transaction is posted every time an operation occurs on an account.

Update Screen—This screen displays the current balance for an account, as well as the name and address of the person requesting the update.

6.4.2.2 Missing Classes

1. **We're missing most of the screens for the teller information system.** "Update screen" is only one of several screen classes that would need to be developed for the teller information system. Our case study didn't mention things like a customer editing screen, a deposit input screen, and so on. Normally we would ask our users about them, prototype them, and then develop classes for them. Once you've seen one screen class you've seen them all, however, so "Update screen" is more than sufficient for our purposes.

2. **There isn't a "Loan" class.** Although banks make loans to customers, they weren't mentioned in this case study. The case study is complicated enough as it is, so let's consider loans as out of scope.

3. **There isn't a "Weekly-Batch-Job" or "Print-Check-Bundles" class.** We'll discuss the need for both these classes in the reports section coming up. We'll see that the weekly batch job is exactly the same idea as the monthly batch job, and that a class for printing check bundles is just one more kind of report. The main reason why we left them out was to keep our model as simple as possible.

6.4.2.3 The Account and Customer Class Hierarchies
Customers and their accounts (shown in detail in Figure 6.17) are at the heart of the bank's business. This section shows how simple it can be to implement the core part of your business using object-orientation.

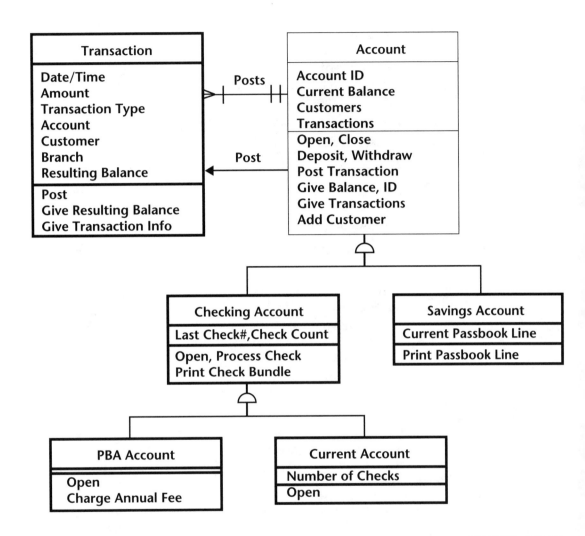

Explanation

Figure 6.17.
The accounts
class hierarchy
and the class
"Transaction."

1. **Accounts post transactions.** Whenever an account is opened, closed, deposited to, or withdrawn from, a transaction will be posted. This allows us to keep track of what happens to the account. Transactions are used in several reports (which are described in following sections).

2. **Open gets constantly overridden.** Each type of account has a different relationship with customers. For example, some

accounts are joint, whereas others aren't. Some accounts are accessed by certain types of people (i.e., current accounts are only for corporate customers). The easiest way to implement the object relationship between "Account" and "Customer" is the following:

- "Account" implements the attribute to keep track of a list of customer(s) that can access it.

- "Account" implements the method to add customers to this list.

- "Account" implements a minimal version of "Open" that allows one retail (normal) customer to access it.

- The subclasses override "Open" to suit their own needs.

The advantage of this approach is that the business logic for restricting access to an account is encapsulated into one method ("Open"). We can define the relationship between an account object and one or more customer objects following the appropriate business rules (i.e., checking accounts can be joint and are only accessed by retail customers) and then we don't need to worry about it anymore. We've managed to implement important, complicated business rules in a simple manner.

3. **Savings accounts keep track of the last passbook line printed.** If a passbook printer cannot detect what line to start printing on, this information will need to be stored online.

4. **Checks require extra processing.** To determine when to send out a new bundle of checks, checking accounts need to keep track of the number of the last check processed, as well as how many checks have been processed in the current bundle. Additionally, because it is possible to have different check-bundle sizes, current accounts need to keep track of how many checks the customer wants sent out in a bundle. Note: This also implies that when a current account is opened, there must be some sort of "Choose check bundle size" feature on that screen.

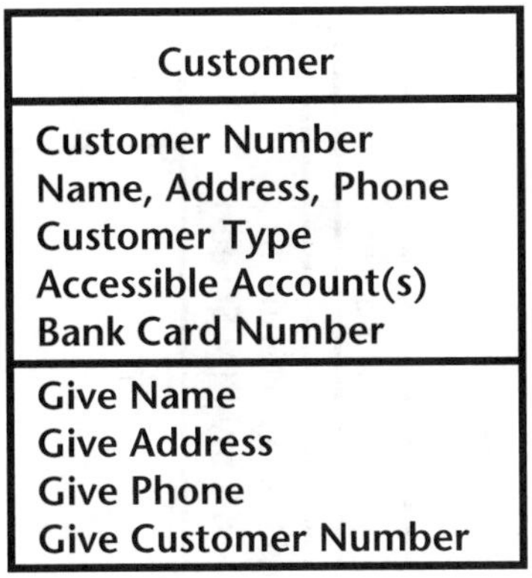

Customer
Customer Number Name, Address, Phone Customer Type Accessible Account(s) Bank Card Number
Give Name Give Address Give Phone Give Customer Number

Figure 6.18.
The class
"Customer."

Explanation

1. **Retail and corporate customers are distinguished by an attribute.** As far as we know from the description of the problem, the only difference between retail (normal) customers and corporate customers is in the types of accounts they can open. We've already taken care of this issue (see Figure 6.18), so for now we don't need the class "Corporate Customer." In the long run, however, we may find that we need to introduce a class for corporate customers that would implement features that retail customers don't have.

2. **We're not showing the real-world behaviors.** A big difference between our CRC model and our class model is the fact that we don't show behaviors. Remember, a behavior is the way in which the real-world acts with the system (for the most part they're use cases). Some of the behaviors of a customer are the fact that they open accounts, close accounts, make withdrawals, and make deposits. Customers do these things in the real world, and it's important to know about them. However, because we won't be implementing any of these behaviors in the class "Customer" we don't show them as methods of that class. Please note that these features get implemented in the screen classes that the customer interacts with to perform them (in this case either at the teller's screen or at a bank machine). This makes sense because from a system point of view, all of these behaviors are initiated by people using the user interface, therefore that's where the code should go.

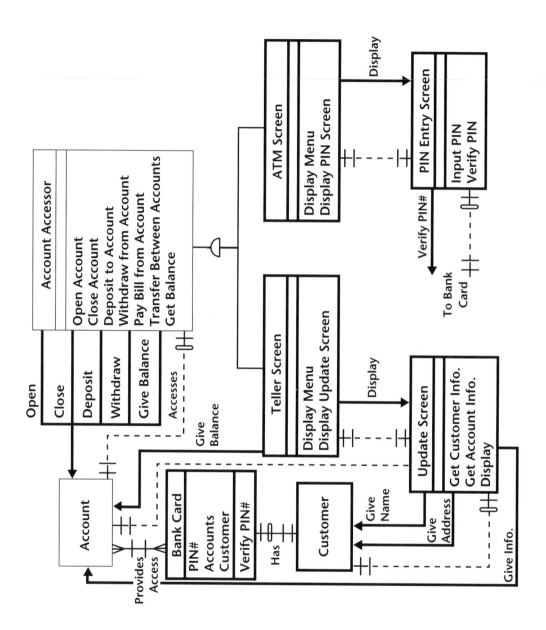

Figure 6.19.
The screen
classes.

6.4.2.4 The Screens
This section discusses some of the screen classes (see Figure 6.19) of the ABC system, and how people interact with them. Remember, screen classes are transitory. They exist only as long as they are displayed. The basic logic of a screen is to get data from other classes, display it, allow it to be edited if appropriate, and then update the classes when the user is finished.

Explanation

1. **"Account Accessor" provides the basic functionality to access accounts.** We've pushed all of the similarities of "Teller Screen" and "ATM Screen" up into the class "Account Accessor." This makes a lot of sense because tellers and ATMs provide the same sort of service: performing transactions on accounts.

2. **Not all the screens are shown here.** We weren't given any details as to how the teller information system and an ATM works. Obviously we need screens to open accounts, close accounts, make deposits and so on.

3. **There are transitory relationships between screens.** Screens are transitory objects (they exist only as long as we need them). This implies that any object relationships or part-of relationships that they are involved in are also transitory.

4. **There are transitory relationships between screens and business classes.** Although a screen is in the process of working with information from another class, there will always be a transitory relationship between them. For example, there is a transitory object relationship between "Update Screen" and "Customer" (the customer name and address is displayed on the screen).

5. **There are several ways to build the interface for this system.** As with any computer system, there is almost always more than one way to build it, and OO applications are no exception. We have two main strategies to choose from:

   a. **Have a menu class that controls the interaction between several screen classes.** This is the strategy that we've already taken in our model. The advantage is that it is easy to identify each screen (it's a class). The disadvantage is that we would probably find that we would need to break "Account Accessor" up into several classes—one that handles opening accounts, one that handles closing accounts and so on. This would happen because we have a "Make Deposit" screen for both an ATM and for the teller information system. They both do the same sort of thing, but do it in a different way.

There are always design trade-offs!

Design trade-off: Splitting up "Account Accessor" is very cumbersome. Although it does have the virtue of supporting "pure inheritance," which says you must inherit everything, a better solution would be to leave "Account Accessor" alone and have all screens inherit from it. For example, the class "Open Account Screen" would inherit from "Account Accessor" to inherit all of the account-opening functionality. At the same time it would inherit the ability to withdraw from accounts, which it doesn't need. Although this strategy would go against pure inheritance, it has the significant advantage of encapsulating all of the account access functionality in one class, making it easier to find and maintain.

b. **Have an information system class that does everything.** We could create one class that handles the teller screens, and one class that handles ATM screens (both would still inherit from "Account Accessor"). Although all of the interface functionality would be in one place, these classes would be very large and cumbersome, and likely very difficult to maintain.

6. **We could have used aggregation between the screens.** Instead of using transitory instance relationships, we could have used transitory part-of relationships. For example, if we rename the class "Teller Screen" to "Teller Information System," it makes sense to say that an account update screen is part of a teller information system.

7. **Transfer is performed by "Account Accessor" and not "Account."** A transfer is basically a withdrawal from one account and a deposit into another. "Account Accessor" already knows how to withdraw from an account and deposit

to an account, so it makes sense to put "Transfer" there. On the other hand, it would be difficult to have "Account" handle a transfer because an account only knows how to withdraw from or deposit to itself, and not another account.

8. **Bank cards help to provide security.** The main purpose of a bank card is to be able to verify the PIN of the corresponding card in the real world (i.e., there is one instance of a bank card object for every physical bank card that exists). A customer sticks his or her card into an ATM, the ATM reads the magnetic strip on the card, asks the user to input his or her PIN, and then sends a message to the bank card object asking it if the right PIN has been entered. If so, the person is given access to his or her accounts.

6.4.2.5 The Reports

This section discusses some of the reports (see Figure 6.20) prepared by this system. Reports are transitory classes—They exist as long as it takes to generate and print the report. The basic logic of a report is to get the data, crunch the data, and then output the data. Some comments on the reports follow.

1. **The monthly batch job needs to be scheduled.** The purpose of the monthly batch job is to loop through all of the checking, PBA, and current accounts and have the appropriate account statement printed for them. We've made the assumption that the batch job can be scheduled somehow—either it is automatically run by the system once a month or a person is assigned to running the job.

2. **We need a weekly batch job to print area reports.** Just like we print account statements monthly, we print area reports weekly, hence the need for a weekly batch job. We didn't include it in our model so as not to complicate it. The weekly batch job would be implemented in the same way as the monthly batch job.

3. **"Account Statement" is robust.** When we run an account statement, we pass it a "from date" and a "to date" that indicates the time period for which it is to be printed. That way we can have the "standard" monthly statement printed for

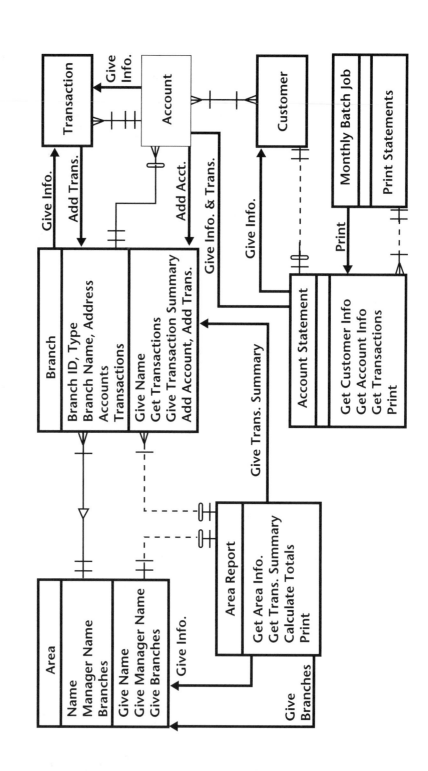

Figure 6.20.
The area report
and the account
statements.

checking accounts, as well as quarterly statements done for current accounts.

4. **Accounts are able to give transaction information for a specific time period.** Accounts keep track of all of the transactions that they post. As a result, they are able to provide a list of transactions for a specific time period, information that is needed for account statements.

5. **We've implemented "Account Statement" as a standard report.** The basic logic of a report is to get the data, crunch the data, and then output the data. This is exactly how we've implement "Account Statement." It gets customer, account, and transaction info, and then outputs it (as we'll see in a minute, there isn't any data that needs to be crunched here).

6. **We've implemented "Area Report" using a different strategy.** Whereas the account statement has its reporting logic encapsulated in one class, "Account Statement," the logic for the area report is spread out among several classes. The first thing an area report does is get a list of the branches within the area. It then sends a message out to each branch requesting that it calculate it's weekly summary. The branch then gathers the transactions for the week [when a transaction is posted, the branch that it is performed at is informed (that's the "Add Transaction" message)]. The branch then summarizes the transactions and passes the information back to "Area Report." As you can see, the bulk of the work is being done by "Branch," not by "Area Report."

The advantage of this strategy is that if your operating system supports multitasking you can have several branches calculating their totals at once, significantly reducing the time it takes to generate this report. The disadvantage is that the logic for area reports is spread out amongst multiple classes, making the classes involved less cohesive (for example, "Branch" implements both branch things and area report things). Both ways to implement reports work well, you just need to decide which way you want to go. As always, there are design trade-offs.

7. **We need a "Print Check Bundles" class.** Just as account statements and area reports are printed, so are bundles of

checks. Printing checks is no different than printing account statements—both are reports. Once an account realizes that it is running out of checks, it would send a message to a class called "Check Bundle," which would then go about the task of printing checks out and getting them mailed to the customer. Because this is so similar to the other reports we've shown in our model, we decided not to include this in our model to simplify it.

8. **Transactions need to keep track of the resulting bank balance.** The opening balance for the period is one of the first things printed on an account statement. Although we could always calculate the opening balance by taking the current account balance and backing out all transactions back to the beginning of the account statement, this is very processor intensive (for a quarterly report, there could potentially be hundreds or even thousands of transactions on a report). A better way is to have transaction objects keep track of the resulting balance from the transaction. We use this figure to calculate the opening balance for the month by backing out the amount of the first transaction for the period. For example, let's say we're printing an account statement for the period July 1st through July 31st. The first transaction of the period was a deposit of $40 made on the 4th, resulting in a balance of $100. Therefore, the opening balance on the first of July must have been $60 ($100–$40). The advantage of this approach is that it is simple and quick. The disadvantage is that it increases the storage space required for transactions.

6.5 Class Modeling Case Study: Part II

Users will often request that new features be added to a system. The mark of a good system design is that it should be easy to extend and/or modify the functionality of an existing application. So let's see what happens.

6.5.1 The ABC Case Study: Part II

You banking system has been in place for 6 months and it's running fine. During this time, the bank has been preparing to expand into other countries. Not only will the bank do business in the United States, it will also start doing business in Canada, Mexico, Great Britain, and France.

> **SCENARIO** We want to be able to do business in each of those countries in their own currencies. For example, Mexican accounts will be handled in pesos, Canadian accounts in Canadian dollars, French accounts in Francs, and so on. Because many of our customers do business internationally, it is certain that some customers will have accounts in several countries.
>
> ABC's corporate strategy is to be second to none in the banking industry. That means we must provide the best service to our customers. As a result, our accounts must be very robust, which means if somebody wants to transfer money between an American account and a Mexican account, he or she can do it. If someone wants to deposit $20 American into a British account, he or she can do it. At both a teller and an ATM.

6.5.2 An Answer to the Case Study

Figure 6.21 shows only the additions that need to be made to our class model. Some comments concerning the case study follow.

1. **Accounts need to know their currency type.** We could have created account class hierarchies for each type of currency, but that wouldn't work well. The easiest way to handle accounts with non-American currencies is to have the

Figure 6.21. The modifications to our class model that are needed to support different currencies.

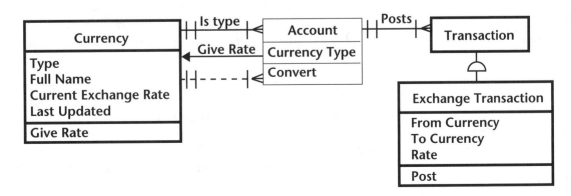

account know what currency it is in. Any transactions processed on an account will be in its currency. For example, a deposit of 500 into an account whose currency type is Mexican pesos would be a deposit of 500 pesos. When we deposit 500 into an account whose currency type is Canadian dollars, it's a deposit of 500 Canadian dollars.

2. **The "Deposit" and "Withdraw" methods will change.** We've been told that we need to be able to process transactions for various currencies on all accounts. For example, we should be able to withdraw 20 American dollars from an account whose currency is French francs. This means that the "Deposit" and "Withdraw" methods defined in "Account" must be told what currency the transaction is being done in, and if it is different than the currency of the account then it must first make the conversion. This implies slight changes to the "Deposit" and "Withdraw" methods, as well as the methods in "Account Accessor" that call them.

3. **The method "Convert" was added to "Account."** Accounts need to be able to convert currencies back and forth. All instances of "Currency" know the exchange rate to convert into American dollars. For example, say we want to deposit 5 British pounds into a Canadian savings account. We need to convert the pounds into Canadian dollars before we can deposit it. To do this, the account sends a message to the British pound instance of "Currency" to get the exchange rate (say the going rate is 1 pound equals 2 American dollars). It then sends a message to the Canadian dollar instance of "Currency" to get that exchange rate ($1 Canadian equals $0.66 American). Therefore, the exchange rate for British to Canadian must be 3 (2/.66), giving us a deposit of 15 Canadian dollars.

4. **During conversions, there is a transitory relationship between "Currency" and "Account."** There is always a persistent relationship between "Currency" and "Account" called "Is type." During conversions, there can sometimes be a transitory relationship between "Currency" and "Account" as well. This relationship is set up when we need to convert

non-American funds to/from a non-American account. For example, there had to be a transitory relationship between the Canadian savings account object and the British pound currency object for them to be able to collaborate (account was able to set it up because "Account Accessor" told it what currency the deposit was being made in.

5. **Exchange transactions are now posted.** We've added a second new class called "Exchange Transaction," which inherits from "Transaction." Every time we perform a transaction in which we need to exchange currencies we must post an exchange transaction instead of a normal transaction. We need to do this because the exchange rates are always changing, and customers want to see on their account statements what rate they were given when they did the transaction. For example, when we deposited the British pounds into the Canadian account an exchange transaction was posted for a $15 deposit. This implies that the "Post Transaction" method in "Account" will need to know which type of transaction to post.

6. **The "Open" methods will change.** When accounts are opened they'll need to be told what currency they will be in. Furthermore, the "Open Account Screen" class in the teller information system will now have to provide the ability to open the account in any kind of currency that ABC supports.

7. **We'll need to determine how to update the exchange rate.** We weren't told how exchange rates are updated. Either the rates are input periodically via an editing screen (which we'll need to write), or electronically via some sort of currency trading system (with which we'll need to interface). Either way, we still have some more coding to do on top of what we've already got.

8. **The modifications were actually quite trivial.** Expanding into other countries is a major step for any company. We were able to support this move with very minor modifications to our existing system design. How many banks out there today do you think could accomplish this as easily?

DEFINITION

Class model—
Class models show
the classes of the
system, their
interrelationships,
and the
collaborations
between those
classes.

6.6 What We've Learned

Class models are the mainstay of object-oriented analysis and design. In this chapter we learned how to model object-oriented concepts in a simple yet effective manner. We discussed each OO modeling step in detail, and saw how we can model systems using object-oriented techniques.

6.6.1 Class Modeling

Although a CRC model provides an excellent overview of a system, it doesn't show the details that we need to build a system. That's why we have scribes to take down the business logic. To model the details that developers need, we use the combination of our CRC model and the scribe's notes as a base from which we can create a class model. In other words, the main goal in class modeling is to "flesh out" our CRC model and document the results of our analysis and design in a manner that developers can use to construct a system. The steps of class modeling are reviewed below.

6.6.1.1 Finding Classes, Finding Attributes, and Finding Methods
Two of the steps of CRC modeling were to find classes and to find responsibilities (which are methods and attributes). As a result, we've already found most of our classes , attributes, and methods already.

Classes are shown as rectangles consisting of three sections (see Figure 6.22): In the top section we show the name of the class, in the middle section we list the attributes of the class, and in the bottom section we list the methods of the class.

Figure 6.22.
The class
"Student."

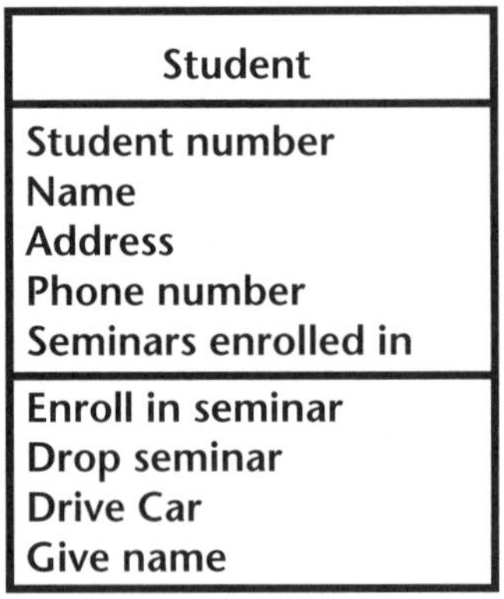

Student
Student number Name Address Phone number Seminars enrolled in
Enroll in seminar Drop seminar Drive Car Give name

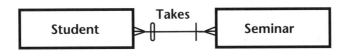

Figure 6.23.
The instance relationship between students and courses.

6.6.1.2 Finding Instance Relationships

We use instance relationships to model the associations between classes. When we are modeling instance relationships, we need to consider cardinality (one vs. many) and the optionality (may vs. must) of the relationship from both directions. For example, in Figure 6.23 we see that a student takes one or more courses and that a course is taken by zero or more students.

Instance relationships are implemented through the use of attributes and methods. Attributes are used to describe the relationship, whereas methods modify the values of the attributes so as to set up/maintain the relationship.

6.6.1.3 Defining Inheritance

Inheritance models is-a and is-like relationships. We use the concept of inheritance to take advantage of the fact that there are often similarities between two or more classes. We inherit both attributes and methods. This implies that we are able to inherit object relationships.

The concept of "pure inheritance" tells us that a subclass should inherit everything from its superclass. This makes the subclass easier to understand, which in turn makes it easier to maintain.

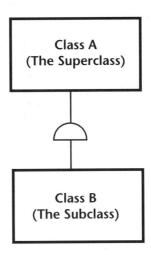

Figure 6.24.
The modeling notation to show inheritance.

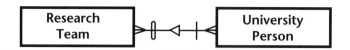

Research
Team

University
Person

Figure 6.25.
The part-of
relationship
between
"University
Person" and
"Research Team."

You know you've correctly identified an opportunity for inheritance when one of the two following sentences makes sense: "The subclass IS A superclass" or "The subclass IS LIKE A superclass."

6.6.1.4 Defining Aggregation

The concept of aggregation allows us to model "part-of" relationships. You should think of part-of relationships as a special form of instance relationship. Figure 6.25 shows how a university person is part of zero or more research teams and that a research team is made up of one or more university people. You know you've correctly identified a part-of relationship when the following sentence makes sense: "The part IS PART OF the whole."

6.6.1.5 Defining Collaborations

Whenever a class needs information from another class, or needs it to do something, they collaborate. Classes collaborate by sending messages to each other. In order for classes to collaborate, there must be either an instance relationship or a part-of relationship between them. Figure 6.26 shows how "Student" first requests information from "Seminar" as to how many seats are left, and then requests that the student be added into the seminar.

Figure 6.26.
"Student"
collaborates with
"Seminar."

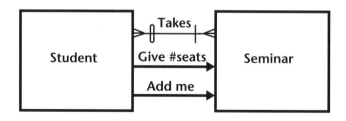

*Object-orientation will completely change
the way that you develop systems.*

Chapter 7

Putting It All Together: OO in Practice

What We'll Learn in This Chapter

When to use OO techniques.

When not to use OO techniques.

How to take a "waterfall approach" to OO development.

How to take an iterative approach to OO development.

It isn't enough to know how to draw class models. You also need to know when you should use OO techniques, and how to go about actually developing object-oriented systems.

The techniques used in OO development are ideal for several types of systems, yet are not so ideal for others. Just like you don't want to try to fit a square peg into a round hole, you don't want to use OO for projects when it doesn't make sense. The text that follows outlines when OO techniques are appropriate.

1. **To develop complex systems.** The easiest way to deal with complexity is to break it down into smaller components, and then deal with each component in turn. The OO paradigm is based on the concept of defining systems based on a collection of interacting objects. This strategy allows us to break down a complex system into smaller components, in this case collections of similar objects called classes. It is easier to deal with one class at a time than it is to deal with the entire system as a whole.

2. **To develop systems that are prone to change.** If the system that you are developing is prone to change, you should consider taking an OO approach to developing it. Remember, OO leads to systems that are extensible (easy to change). With the ever-increasing pace of change in the business world that our systems are designed to support, extensibility will become more and more important as time goes on. If our business rules change, our systems must change too.

3. **To develop systems with graphical user interfaces (GUIs).** GUIs are complicated. Consider how much programming must go into something as simple as a window. A window can be moved, resized, opened, closed, minimized, maximized, and so on. Would you want to have to program that yourself? I sure wouldn't. Call me lazy, but I'd rather let somebody else write it, and then reuse their work (most likely through the use of inheritance). OS/2, Motif, X/Windows, the Apple Macintosh, and MicroSoft Windows are all examples of environments that use graphical user interfaces.

4. **To develop systems that are based on the client/server model.** In the client/server (C/S) model, a client machine (usually a PC or workstation) is connected to one or more servers (usually a high-powered PC, mini, or mainframe) via a network. Client machines provide the front-end (the inter-

face), whereas the server(s) provide access to data and functionality. In a way, doesn't a server sound a lot like a class? Although there is a little more to it than that, in the next book, we'll see that the only way to effectively design client/server systems is to take an OO approach.

5. **To develop systems where structured techniques don't seem to work.** Many organizations are turning to OO techniques because they failed when using structured techniques for a new application. We need to remember that structured techniques were created in the mid-1970s, when we were developing large, mainframe-based batch-transaction processing systems. Now in the 1990's we are developing smaller (sometimes), PC/LAN-based online systems with GUI front-ends (see Figure 7.1). It should come as no surprise that structured techniques just don't cut it for the systems of today.

6. **To develop systems within an organization that is willing to try new approaches.** For OO to be successful, your organization must be willing to try new approaches to systems development. Virtually all organizations want to develop

Figure 7.1.
Systems
development
in the 1990s.

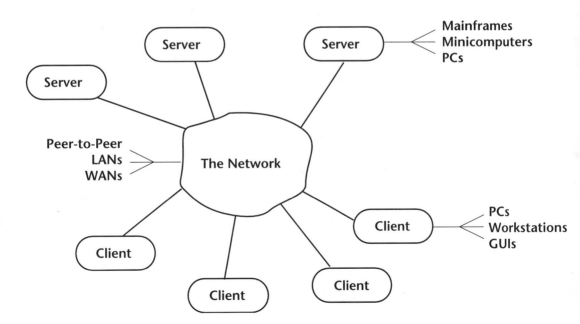

complex, GUI, and/or client/server-based applications, yet few are willing to modify the way that they approach systems development. The systems that we are creating today are completely different than those of only 5 or 10 years ago. The systems have changed, and so must our approach. Managers and developers alike must be willing to cast aside their preconceived notions and embrace the OO mind-set. Only then will your project succeed.

OO should not be used . . .

1. **To develop systems for which structured techniques are ideal.** Remember, structured techniques were specifically created for a certain style of system. As we discussed earlier, these systems are typically large, mainframe-based, batch-transaction applications.

2. **To develop systems when you can't use OO throughout the entire development life cycle.** This is mainly a language issue. Although OO languages are common in the PC and Unix worlds, for the most part you still can't get OO languages for many mainframe and mini platforms. Because the benefits of OO are achieved throughout the entire development life cycle, it isn't advisable to use OO if you can't do OO programming. Similarly, use an OO language only when you have an OO design.

7.1 A New Development Strategy

In this book we have claimed that OO development techniques are superior to structured development techniques. OO development techniques are better because they offer greater opportunities for reuse, extensibility, and improved quality. Remember, Improved quality results from increased involvement of users in the development process. With structured development, users are involved with the analysis and user acceptance testing of a system. With OO development, users are involved in the analysis, design, testing, and user acceptance testing of a system.

Structured Development Steps	Object-Oriented Development Steps
• Initiation Ⓤ	• Inititiation
• Analysis Ⓤ	• CRC Modeling/Prototyping ⓊⓊⓊ
• Design	• Use-Case Scenario Testing ⓊⓊⓊ
• Construction	• OO Modeling
• System Testing	• OO Construction
• User Acceptance Testing Ⓤ	• OO System Testing
• Implementation	• User Acceptane Testing ⓊⓊ
	• Implementation

Ⓤ = User Involvement

7.1.1 The Steps of Object-Oriented Development

1. **Project initiation.** Project initiation doesn't change under OO. You still need to gather initial user requirements, perform a feasibility study, and put together a development. If there are any changes, it's in the way that you choose team members. We'll cover this topic in a future volume when we discuss management issues.

2. **CRC modeling/prototyping.** Here's the first major difference between the way we've presented OO as compared to traditional/structured techniques: For the most part, users do the bulk of the analysis. As we saw in chapter 3, CRC modeling is a simple, iterative analysis technique that goes hand-in-hand with prototyping. CRC models provide a very good overview of a system and provide the basis for class models, which are the mainstay of OO modeling.

3. **Use-case scenario testing.** Use-case scenario testing, a component of CRC modeling, is a technique in which users find and fix errors where they are most commonly made—during analysis. Remember, developers are good at building systems right, what we aren't good at is building the right systems. Chapter 4 explained a straightforward technique to dramatically reduce the cost of finding and fixing errors, while at the same time increasing the quality of the system and preparing the bulk of the user acceptance test plan.

Figure 7.2.
An object-oriented "waterfall" system development life cycle.

4. **OO modeling.** For our purposes, there are two main types of model about which we need to be concerned: class models and state models. A class model shows the classes in the system, and the way in which they are related and interact with one another. A state model documents the various states that an object may be in, describing the different business rules that are applicable, depending on the current state the class is in. Chapters 5 and 6 covered basic class modeling, whereas the second volume in this series will discuss advanced class and state modeling.

5. **OO construction.** Programming is programming, or so some might say. In the second volume in this series we'll describe OO programming tools in detail, discussing what to look for in an OO programming language and reviewing several of the leading OO languages. We'll also cover database topics, describing object-oriented database systems (OODBMSs) and discuss in detail the issues involved in using relational database technology to store objects.

6. **OO system testing.** Although many structured testing techniques can be used for OO testing, the very nature of OO requires that we adopt new testing principles. The second volume in this book series provides insight into how your testing process must change to meet the needs of OO development.

7. **User acceptance testing.** User acceptance planning is the same in the OO world as in the structured world. The only difference is that the bulk of the user acceptance test plan is created as part of use-case scenario testing.

8. **Implementation.** Implementation is no different in the object world than in the structured world.

7.1.2 What's So Different About OO Development?

1. **OO requires that we work with our users more.** Users do the bulk of the analysis. This is radically different as compared to structured development, in which developers interview users, perhaps do some prototyping, and then produce some sort of analysis document (sometimes). With the way that we have presented OO development, the people who understand the business do the analysis.

2. **OO puts a greater emphasis on analysis and design.** We do CRC modeling, prototyping, use-case scenario testing, class modeling, and state modeling. These are all analysis and design tasks. If you don't get the analysis and design right, it doesn't matter how good of a programmer you are.

3. **OO benefits are achieved throughout the entire development life cycle.** This means that you need to understand how OO changes analysis, design, and testing, in addition to OO programming. That's why this book describes the entire development life cycle, and not just part of it as other books do.

4. **OO development requires a new mind-set on the part of developers.** You have to work with your users more. You have to concentrate more on analysis and design. Communication and modeling skills become imperative. This won't be an easy transition for many developers, but it is a transition that they MUST make.

5. **OO development requires a culture change within IS departments.** As individuals, developers must look at their jobs in a new manner. As a group, developers must change the way in which they work together to serve the needs of their clients. In other words, the OO development process requires a change in your development culture.

6. **OO development is iterative in nature, not serial.** Although we talk about doing analysis, and then design, and then testing, and then implementation, we'll see that with OO we'll often be performing several of these tasks simultaneously. Although the OO Waterfall System Development Life Cycle (SDLC) presented above is very comfortable to us, we'll see in the next section that an iterative approach, such as the Pinball SDLC [Ambler, 1994] is more appropriate for OO development.

The OO paradigm will change the way that you interact with your users and with your fellow developers.

7.1.3 The Pinball SDLC (v2.0)

In the previous section we discussed the basic steps of object-oriented development, putting them into the context of the waterfall system development life cycle. Because many organizations currently use the waterfall SDLC for structured development, they will find an OO version of it very comforting. However, experience has shown us that the serial nature of the waterfall SDLC does not serve us very well (remember our extremely high rate of project failure). Experience has also shown us that an iterative approach to systems development appears to improve our chances for successfully developing an application. The Pinball SDLC [Ambler, 1994] of Figure 7.3 is an iterative, OO SDLC, the basic idea being that the game of pinball is an excellent metaphor for systems development.

7.1.3.1 The Necessary Features of an OO SDLC

1. **It should reflect the steps of OO development.** This is an easy one, we'll take the steps of the OO version of the waterfall SDLC and expand on them as necessary.

2. **It should be fairly simple.** Nobody wants to be burdened by a complicated SDLC.

3. **Developers should want to follow it.** Otherwise, why bother creating it in the first place? Taking into account that developers are generally a weird group of people, an SDLC that they would be willing to follow should probably be a little weird too! That's why the metaphor that developing a system is just like playing a game of pinball might actually work.

7.1.3.2 The Pinball Metaphor

1. **The ball.** The ball represents the current version of the application or system under development.

2. **The bumpers.** The bumpers represent the steps of OO systems development. Unlike structured development, which for the most part is serial in nature, OO development is an iterative process. Instead of doing analysis, then design, then programming, then testing, with OO development you may do a little bit of analysis, then some design and programming, then go back to analysis. Although you perform the same OO development tasks over and over again, the order in which you do them is never quite the same. It's exactly the same when you are playing pinball. The ball is constantly bouncing off the same set of bumpers, yet doing so in a different order each game.

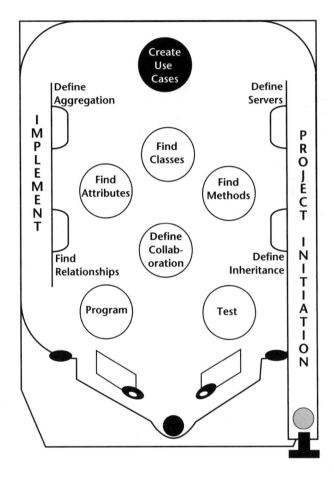

Figure 7.3.
The Pinball SDLC.

3. **The points.** The points scored during the game represent the benefits achieved by the project. When the ball bounces off a bumper, the player scores some points. When the project goes through a development step, some benefits are derived for the company (one hopes).

4. **The player.** The player represents the project manager. Just like the player guides the ball through the game, the project manager guides the project through development The better the player, the more points she or he can score. The better the project manager, the more benefits she or he will achieve for the company.

5. **The machine.** The pinball machine represents the way in which an organization develops systems. Just like every pinball machine is similar yet different, so is the way that every organization develops systems.

6. **The paddles.** The paddles represent project resources. A pinball player uses the paddles to keep the ball bouncing between bumpers, whereas a project manager commits resources such as money, time, and people to keep a project going.

7. **The hole.** The hole represents a major transition point in the life of a project. During play the ball sometimes goes down the hole. When this happens, either the ball is put back into play, or the game ends. Every so often throughout the life of a project, development work stops. At this point one of two things will happen—Either development begins on a new version (the ball is put back into play) or the project is finished (the game is over).

8. **The quarter.** Putting in the quarter represents the project feasibility study. Sometimes you put a quarter into a pinball machine and the game is activated, and sometimes the machine just eats your quarter. It's exactly the same with project feasibility studies: Sometimes the project is a good idea and you get approval for it, sometimes you don't. In both cases you've invested something—either a quarter or your time and effort. Additionally, in both cases you may or may not get to play the game.

9. **The plunger.** The plunger represents management approval to begin the project. The player pulls on the plunger to get the ball rolling, and management gives its approval to get the project going.

7.1.4 *The Steps of the Pinball SDLC*

The bumpers of the pinball machine represent the iterative steps of object-oriented development. Although we have discussed many of the analysis and design steps of OO development, we haven't discussed the complete development life cycle yet. Until now.

7.1.4.1 *Project Initiation*
Project initiation doesn't change under the OO paradigm. We still need to do a feasibility study. Feasibility studies address the issue of

Table 7.1. Steps of OO Development

OO Waterfall SDLC Steps	OO Pinball SDLC Steps
Initiation	Initiation
CRC Modeling	Find classes, attributes, and methods. Define collaborations.
Use-Case Scenario Testing	Testing
OO Class Modeling	All of the find and define steps
OO Construction	Program
OO System User Acceptance Testing	Testing
Implementation	Implement

whether or not your organization should go ahead with a project. A feasibility report will include a cost/benefit analysis indicating whether a project is economically viable, an indication of whether the project is operationally viable, and an indication of whether it is currently possible to build the project.

The one main difference is that for your first OO project you will likely need to sell the concept of the OO paradigm to upper management during the project initiation phase. This means you will have to consider training/re-tooling issues, language issues, methodology issues, and so on. A future volume will discuss this issue in detail.

7.1.4.2 Programming

With the OO approach, programming should be only 10% to 15% of the entire development effort. As we've seen throughout this book, the majority of the OO development process concentrates on analysis and design. One of the advantages of object-orientation is that very little effort is needed to go from designing to programming. The reason for this is simple—Both OO programming and OO design are based on the same principle, which is the building of systems out of reusable components called objects. When you are coding in an OO environment, you are basically filling in the details for a class.

In the next book, we'll see that OO programming is usually done with an object-oriented language, such as C++ or Smalltalk. Furthermore, object-oriented fourth-generation languages (especially for client/server environments) are also becoming popular. We'll talk about the strengths and weaknesses of some of the more popular OO languages in the next book.

7.1.4.3 Testing

We still need to verify that our systems work! On the one hand object-oriented testing is similar to structured testing in that both white/clear box- and black-box testing is applicable. On the other hand it is different from structured testing because instead of unit and integration testing, we now have method, class, and integration testing. The next book will discuss OO testing techniques in detail, explaining them and showing why OO testing is different than structured testing.

7.1.4.4 Implementation

Implementation of an OO project should be little different than what your organization has done in the past. When you implement might change, however, because you are developing the system in an iterative manner, you may be in a position to implement small parts of the system at a time. This enables you to get functionality out into the hands of your users quickly, and at the same time make it appear that you are doing some work. Implementing in small steps is often radically different than what many developers are currently used to. With the ever-changing business environment, gone are the days of the multiyear project. We need to be able to give our users systems quickly. That means quick releases, and one way to do that is implementing in small steps.

7.1.4.5 Defining Servers

Object-oriented analysis and design are made up of eight steps: find classes, find attributes, find methods, find instance relationships, define inheritance, define aggregation, define collaborations, and finally define servers. We've covered the first seven steps in great detail in this book, but we really haven't discussed how to define servers at all. That's because it's complicated.

A *server* is a collection of two or more classes that work together to fulfill contracts. A *contract* is a service provided by a server. For example, say we had an "Accounts" server that was made up of the

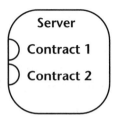

Figure 7.4.
The class modeling notation for a server.

"Account" class hierarchy and the class "Transaction." Contracts provided by this server would be "Open," "Close," "Withdraw," "Deposit," "Give Balance," "Give Account ID," and "Give Transactions." These contracts represent the collection of all of the messages received by the classes of the "Accounts" server from other classes outside of the server (see Figure 7.4).

    The reason why we want to organize a system into a collection of interacting servers is straightforward: When you are developing systems following either a client/server or a peer-to-peer architecture you need to distribute both the data and the functionality of the system across several computers. You want to do this in such a way as to effectively utilize your hardware. The short version of how you define servers is that you analyze the messages sent back and forth between classes, and from that information you decide what class belongs on what computer. This topic will be covered in detail in the next book.

> **DEFINITIONS**
>
> **Server**—A server is a collection of two or more classes that work together to fulfill contracts.
>
> **Contract**—A contract is a service provided by a server.

7.2 Where to Go from Here

On the one hand, the object-oriented learning process can be long and difficult. Furthermore, there is no guarantee for success. On the other hand, you've gotten a really good start at it by reading this book. Now it's time to move on down the never-ending road of continuous learning.

7.2.1 Advice for Overcoming the OO Learning Curve

1. **Read upcoming books.** If you think this book was great, wait till you see the next book. We're going to cover advanced OO design issues, OO construction, and OO testing. You're going to love it.

2. **Pick up some other books.** Following this chapter is a selected reading list of some really good books. Although each takes a different approach to OO development, you'll find that there are many similarities among them. You should seriously consider reading at least one or two of them.

3. **Subscribe to some magazines and/or journals.** There are several object-oriented analysis and design magazines and journals, as well as numerous OO programming magazines. They provide cutting-edge advice regarding OO development techniques. It's really worth your while to start reading some of them.

4. **Read, read, read.** I can't stress this strongly enough, you have to do a lot of reading. Object-orientation is relatively new, and significant work is being done on it all the time. You need to keep up with the latest and greatest techniques, and the only way you can do this is by reading.

5. **Take some OO courses.** There are a lot of great object-oriented development courses out there, so sign up for a few of them. There is a lot of value in classroom training, and I highly recommend it. Take at least one OO analysis and design course, an "Intro to XXX Programming," course, and an "Advanced XXX Programming" course, in which XXX is your language of choice. OO can be hard to pick up on your own, and talking to an expert can really help.

6. **Bring in a mentor.** OO mentors are people who help with the skills–transfer process. They are usually consultants or architects internal to your organization. The key is that they are OO experts who have the communication skills necessary to convey their expertise to others. OO mentors can help to significantly reduce the OO learning curve, while at the same time increasing the chance of success for your project. OO mentoring will be covered in detail in a future volume.

7. **Sign onto the Internet.** There are several interesting newsgroups (a newsgroup is an electronic public forum where people can submit their ideas regarding a certain topic) that discuss object-oriented development issues on the Internet. Even if you don't participate in the discussions, there is

always some valuable advice being given daily. A list of some of the newsgroups that you may wish to consider joining follows:

> comp.object
>
> comp.databases.object
>
> comp.lang.c++
>
> comp.lang.smalltalk
>
> comp.software-eng

8. **Go to object-oriented conferences.** The newest OO tools and techniques can always found at conferences such as OOPSLA (Object-Oriented Programming, Systems, Languages and Applications) and Object Expo. These conferences are advertised months in advance on the Internet and in related magazines/journals.

9. **Don't forget that OO requires a mind-set change.** It takes a long time to get up to speed in object-orientation. You have to completely change the way that you think about systems, and that doesn't come easily, so don't get frustrated. You can do it if you want to.

10. **Don't forget that OO is more than just programming.** It isn't enough to use a programming language like C++ or Smalltalk. You need OO analysis and design skills if you want to become a successful OO developer. It isn't what you want to hear, but many developers are destined to fail miserably because they refuse to accept this fact.

7.2.2 OO Career Choices

The greatest opportunities occur during periods of change, and object-orientation represents a major change in the way that we develop systems. If you dream of getting ahead in your career, object-orientation is one path that you should seriously consider. Throughout the 1990s and into the next millennium there will obviously be countless opportunities for object-oriented programmers, analysts, and designers. There are also some not so obvious opportunities as well, such as:

OO Mentors. Object-oriented experts who are actively involved in skills transfer, including both formal and informal training, design and code walkthroughs, and OO project management consulting. OO mentors are often consultants, although many firms are currently in the process of creating their own "home-grown" mentors to work internally on projects.

OO Quality Assurance Experts. Object-oriented systems have to be tested, and we're going to need people who can do it.

OO is here today.

OO will be here long into the future.

OO Architects. The role of "OO Architect" is becoming more and more common within the strategic planning groups of IS (Information System) departments. Object-orientation is a large field, and organizations are finding that they need an OO expert who can aid in the strategic planning process for their IS department.

The bottom line is that there is a lot of opportunity for developers in the object-oriented world. Object-orientation is here today, and will

Table 7.2. When and When Not to Use OO

When to use OO	When not to use OO
To develop complex systems	To develop large, mainframe-based batch-transaction systems
To develop systems that are prone to change	To develop systems when you can't use OO for the entire development process
To develop systems with graphical user interfaces	
To develop client/server systems	
To develop systems where structured techniques don't seem to work	
To develop systems in an organization that is willing to try new approaches	

be here long into the future. You need to make the right career choices now if you want to be successful tomorrow.

7.3 What We've Learned

In this chapter we've discussed when to use OO techniques and when not to (see Table 7.2 for a reiteration). We've also covered two styles of OO system development life cycles: The serial OO Waterfall approach and the iterative Pinball approach. Finally, we discussed what you should consider doing to continue your education in the object-oriented paradigm.

7.4 Parting Words

This book was written for you, the developer. We hope that this book has helped you to gain a better understanding of the object-oriented

---

The Steps of OO Development
(Regardless of whether or not you take
a serial or iterative approach!)

Project Initiation

OO Analysis
- Find classes
- Find methods
- Find attributes
- Find object relationships

OO Design
- Define inheritance
- Define aggregation
- Define collaboration
- Define servers

OO Programming

OO Testing

Implementation

Overcoming the OO Learning Curve

Read the other books in this series.

Pick up some other books.

Subscribe to some magazines and/or journals.

Read, read, read.

Take some OO courses.

Bring in a mentor.

Sign onto the Internet.

Go to object-oriented conferences.

Don't forget that OO requires a mind-set change.

Don't forget that OO is more than just programming.

---

paradigm and how to use it effectively. More importantly, we hope that you've acquired new insights into this career that we call system development. We wish for all of you success and prosperity in both your careers and your personal lives. May you live long and prosper.

AMBLER'S OBSERVATION

OO Developers

Do it with class.

Further Reading

You should consider reading at least two or three of the object-oriented development books listed below. Object-orientation is a young field, and there is a lot of value in learning several related yet different techniques. Furthermore, it is also wise to read some non-OO books.

Object-Oriented Development Books

Booch, G. (1993). *Object-Oriented Design with Applications,* 2nd Ed. Benjamin/Cummings.

Coad, P. & Yourdon, E. (1991). *Object-Oriented Analysis,* 2nd Ed. Yourdon Press.

Coad, P. & Yourdon, E. (1991). *Object-Oriented Design.* Yourdon Press.

Coad, P. & Nicola, J. (1993). *Object-Oriented Programming.* Yourdon Press.

Gamma, E., et al. (1995). *Design Patterns—Elements of Reusable Object-Oriented Software.* Reading, MA: Addison Wesley.

Love, T. (1993). *Object Lessons.* New York: SIGS Books.

McGregor, J.D. & Sykes, D.A. (1992). *Object-Oriented Software Development: Engineering Software for Re-Use.* New York: Van Nostrand Reinhold.

Meyer, B. (1988). *Object-Oriented Software Construction*. Englewood Cliffs, NJ: Prentice-Hall.

Rumbaugh, J., Blaha, M., Premerlani, W., Eddy, F., & Lorenson, W. (1991). *Object-Oriented Modeling and Design*. Englewood Cliffs, NJ: Prentice-Hall.

Yourdon, E. (1994). *Object-Oriented Systems Design—An Integrated Approach*. Yourdon Press.

Interface Design Books

Laurel, B. (1990). *The Art of Human-Computer Interface Design*. Reading, MA: Addison Wesley.

Mayhew, D. (1992). *Principles and Guidelines in Software User Interface Design*. Englewood Cliffs, NJ: Prentice-Hall.

Non-OO System Development Books

Borenstein, N.S. (1991). *Programming as if People Mattered*. Princeton, NJ: Princeton University Press.

Demarco, T. & Lister, T. (1987). *Peopleware—Productive Projects and Teams*. Dorset House.

Page-Jones (1988). *The Practical Guide to Structured Systems Design*. Yourdon Press.

Yourdon, E. (1992). *Decline and Fall of the American Programmer*. Yourdon Press.

Other Good Books

Beck, N. (1995). *Shifting Gears—Thriving in the New Economy*. New York: Harper Collins.

Potter, B. (1988). *The Way of the Ronin—Riding the Waves of Change at Work*. Ronin.

Senge, P. (1990). *The Fifth Discipline—The Art and Practice of the Learning Organization.* New York: Doubleday.

Magazines and Journals

Journal of Object-Oriented Programming (JOOP)

Object Magazine

Report on Object-Oriented Analysis and Design (ROAD)

Software Development

Appendix A
A Visual Glossary

The following glossary describes the object-oriented terms used throughout this book.

Abstract class—A class that does not have objects instantiated from it. Abstract classes are shown as rectangles with thin lines.

Class Name
Attributes
Methods

Abstract class notation.

Abstraction—The definition of the interface of a class (what it knows and does).

Actor—A real-world person or organization that interacts with the system.

Aggregation—Represents is-part-of relationships.

Analysis error—An analysis error occurs when a user requirement is either missing or misunderstood.

Aggregation notation.

Attribute—Something that an object or class knows. An attribute is basically a single piece of data or information.

BDE (Business Domain Expert)—A person, usually a user, who knows the business.

Behavior—An action that an actor takes in the real world that is not implemented in the system.

Appendix A

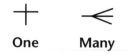

Cardinality notation.

Cardinality—A fancy word for "how many?"

Class—A class represents a collection of similar objects. A class is effectively a template from which objects are created.

Class hierarchy—A set of classes on a class model that are related through inheritance.

Class model—Class models show the classes of the system, their interrelationships, and the collaborations between those classes.

Class modeling—The act of creating a class model. Class modeling is both an analysis and a design effort.

Client—Any class that sends a message to another class.

Cohesion—A measure of how much a method or class makes sense.

Collaboration—Classes work together (collaborate) to get things done. Collaborations come in one of two forms—either a request for information or a request to do something. In order to collaborate, classes send messages to one another.

Collaborator—The receiver of a message (request) during collaboration.

Class Name
Attributes
Methods

Concrete class notation.

Concrete class—A class that has objects instantiated (created) from it.

Contract—A contract is a service provided by a server.

Coupling—A measure of how connected two classes are. Coupling occurs through instance relationships, aggregation, inheritance, and collaboration.

CRC card—A standard index card broken into three sections: the name of the class across the top, the responsibilities of the class along the left, and the collaborators of the class along the right.

CRC modeling—The act of describing a system through the use of CRC cards. CRC modeling is done by a group of BDEs who are led by a facilitator. The business logic details are recorded by a scribe.

Deinstantiate—To remove an object from the object space (to deallocate it).

The Name of the Class	
Responsibilities	**Collaborators**

The layout of a CRC card.

Encapsulation—The definition of how to implement what a class knows or does, without telling anyone how we did it.

Extensibility—The ease with which something can be modified.

Facilitator—A person who leads a CRC modeling session. The facilitator should either be a trained meeting professional or the project leader.

Information hiding—The restriction of access to attributes.

Inheritance—Allows us to take advantage of similarities between classes by representing is-a and is-like relationships. A subclass inherits all of the attributes and methods of its superclass.

Instance—Just as we say that a data record is an occurrence of a data entity, we say that an object is an instance of a class.

Instance relationship—An association between two classes.

Instantiate—When we create a student object, we say that we instantiate it from the class "Student."

Mentor—An object-oriented expert who aids in the skills-transfer process. Some of the tasks performed by mentors include doing both formal and informal training, as well as design and program walkthroughs.

Message—A message is either a request for information or a request to do something.

Inheritance notation.

Label →

Messaging
notation.

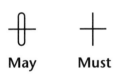

May　　**Must**

Optionality
notation.

Messaging—In order to collaborate, classes send messages to each other.

Method—Something that an object or class does. A method is similar to a function or procedure in structured programming.

Multiple inheritance—When a class inherits from more than one class, we say that we have multiple inheritance.

Object—Any person, place, thing, event, screen, report, or concept that is applicable to the design of the system. An object is an instance of a class.

Object relationship—A term used interchangeably with instance relationship.

Object ID—An attribute that is a unique identifier for an object. Also called an OID.

Object space—Persistent memory.

OO—This is an acronym that is used interchangeably for two terms: Object-oriented and object-orientation. For example, when we say OO programming, we really mean object-oriented programming. When we say that this is a book that describes OO, we really mean that it is a book that describes object-orientation.

Optionality—A fancy word for "do you have to do it?"

Override—Sometimes we need to override (redefine) attributes and/or methods in subclasses.

Paradigm—A "paradigm" (pronounced para-dime) can best be described as an overall strategy or approach to doing things. Many people consider a paradigm to be a specific mind-set.

Persistence—The issue of how objects are permanently stored to disk.

Persistent memory—Main memory plus all available storage space on the network. Objects exist and work together in persistent memory, which is also referred to as the object space. Although we call it persistent memory, both persistent and transitory objects will exist in it, the difference being that transitory objects aren't saved to permanent storage.

Persistent object—An object that is saved to permanent storage.

Pinball SDLC—An iterative, OO system development life cycle.

Polymorphism—This means that an object can take any of several forms, and that other objects can interact with the object without having to know what specific form it takes.

Project success—A project is considered a success when it meets all of the following criteria: it is on time, it is on budget, and it meets needs of its users.

Prototype—A model of something. For example, a rough sketch of a screen would be considered a prototype for it, as would an electronic screen created with the use of a prototyping tool.

Prototyping—The act of creating a prototype.

Responsibility—A responsibility is anything that a class knows or does. In class modeling, the responsibility of a class is the collection of its attributes and methods.

Root—The topmost class in a class hierarchy.

Scribe—A person who records information. Scribes are used in CRC modeling sessions to record the detailed business logic that does not fit on CRC cards.

SDLC (System Development Life Cycle)—The process by which systems are built.

Server—A server is a collection of two or more classes that work together to fulfill contracts.

Single inheritance—When a class inherits from only one class, we say that we have single inheritance.

Subclass—If class "B" inherits from class "A," then we say that "B" is a subclass of "A."

Superclass—If class "B" inherits from class "A," then we say that "A" is a superclass of "B."

Transitory object—An object that is not saved to permanent storage.

Transitory relationship—A nonpermanent relationship between two objects.

Use case—A use case describes a real-world scenario that a system may or may not be able to handle.

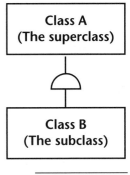

Superclasses and subclasses.

Use-case scenario testing—The process of having a group of BDEs act out use-case scenarios in order to ensure that their CRC model handles them correctly.

Waterfall SDLC—A serial system development life cycle popularized in the 1970s.

Appendix B

Notation Summary and the Pinball SDLC

Photocopy the following three pages and hang them on your wall. Having a summary of the notation, as well as a summary of the steps of OO development, right there in front of you will make both the learning and development process go that much smoother.

The Ambler Class Modeling Notation is shown below:

Class Name
Attributes
Methods

Abstract Class

Class Name
Attributes
Methods

Concrete Class

Subsystem
(Server)

Contract

Aggregation

Inheritance

Persistent
Inst. Rel.

Transitory
Inst. Rel.

Message

Cardinality & Optionality
(Relationships & Aggregation)

One and one only

Zero or one

Zero or more

One or more

?   ?   Currently Unkown

The Pinball System Development Life Cycle

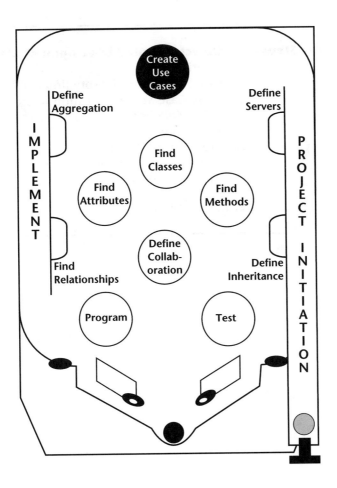

The Steps of OO System Development

Structured Development Steps
- Initiation Ⓤ
- Analysis Ⓤ
- Design
- Construction
- System Testing
- User Acceptance Testing Ⓤ
- Implementation

Object-Oriented Development Steps
- Inititiation
- CRC Modeling/Prototyping ⓊⓊⓊ
- Use-Case Scenario Testing ⓊⓊⓊ
- OO Modeling
- OO Construction
- OO System Testing
- User Acceptane Testing ⓊⓊ
- Implementation

Ⓤ = User Involvement

Index

A

Abstract classes	132, 186
Abstraction	125
Acting out scenarios	97
Actor classes	40, 43
Actors	55
Aggregation	133, 139, 175
and collaboration	144
and inheritance	143, 185
documenting	183
example	141
recursive	177
Aggregation Tips	141, 176
Ambler class	
modeling notation	159, 191

Analysis errors	88, 111
Application backlog	14
Architects	226
Arranging the	
CRC cards	55
Associations	166
Assumptions	107
Attributes	120, 122, 134
documenting	182

B

Beck and Cunningham	28, 51
Behaviors	
example	197

BFC
 (better, faster, cheaper) 7, 8
Booch, Grady 156
Brainstorming 33–34,
  36, 97
 issues to be discussed 37
 rules 35
Business analysts 91
Business classes 41
Business Domain
 Experts 28, 30
Business relationships 57
Business rules 97, 107–108

C

Cardinality 136–137, 167
 symbols 137
Career choices 225
CASE 21
CASE(*See* Computer Aided
 Software Engineering) 182
Class 4, 27
Class hierarchy 133, 186
 example 195
Class model 58
 extending 205
Class modeling 162
 documenting 181
 steps 162
Class Modeling Tips 184
Classes 117, 120
 abstract 132, 186
 concrete 132
 documenting 181
 naming conventions 121
 notation 124
 transitory 134
Client/server 16–17, 212

Cohesion 150, 185
Collaborate 45
Collaboration 48–49, 56,
  99, 178
 and aggregation 144
 and instance
  relationships 144, 170
 and messages 145
 example 50, 179
 tips 144
 types 143
Collaborator 27
Computer Aided
 Software Engineering 182
Concrete classes 132
 and CRC cards 165
Contract 222
Cost of fixing errors 89
Coupling 149,
  185–186
 sources 186
CRC card 66, 77, 83
CRC model 26, 93
CRC modeling 91, 116,
  163, 215
 disadvantages 68
CRC modeling room 34
CRC team 28
CRCcards
 and concrete classes 165
CRCmodel
 converting to class
  model 163
CRCmodeling
 advantages 64
 steps 83
 tips 62
Creating "testing"
 use-case scenarios 95
Creeping featuritis 96
Culture change 20

D

Data flows	145
Defining aggregation	175
Defining collaborations	178
Defining collaborators	47
Defining inheritance	171
Defining servers	222
Defining use cases	52
Deinstantiate	159
Documentation	
aggregation	183
attributes	182
class models	181
classes	181
inheritance	183
methods	182
Documentation tips	183

E

Education	20
Encapsulation	125
End-user computing	17
Extensibility	6

F

Facilitator	29, 30, 32, 36, 57
Finding attributes	165
Finding classes	36, 164
Finding instance relationships	166
Finding methods	165
Finding responsibilities	44

G

Graphical User Inberface (GUI)	16, 212
Greenbaum & Kyng	33

H

HCI (*See* Human-computer interaction)	93
Human-computer interaction boundary	93

I

Implementation	222
Improved quality	7
Information hiding	126
Inheritance	129, 171
and aggregation	143, 185
and instance relationships	139
documenting	183
multiple	130
pure	185
single	130
Inheritance notation	130
Inheritance tips	128, 173
Instance relationships	133, 137
and collaboration	144, 170
example	138
implementation	169
and inheritance	139
notation	136
persistent	146

Instance relationships
(*continued*)

   recursive   138, 175
   transitory   146
Instantiation   122
Interface classes   41
Internet   224
Internet newsgroups   224
IS budgets   12

J

Jacobson   26, 33, 53
JAD (Joint Application
   Design)   32
James Champy   36
Jargon   63

L

Learning curve   223
"legacy" systems   12

M

Maintenance burden   12
Management support   64
Mentors   224, 226
Message parameters   145
Messages   143
   and collaboration   145
Messaging   145
Methods   120, 122–123,
                 185
   documenting   182

Michael Hammer   36
Mind-set   225
   change   20
Multiple inheritance 130, 132
   notation   132

N

Newsgroups   224
Notation   191
Notation summary   159

O

Object   4, 36
Object Expo   225
Object ID   170
Object space   3–4, 136
Object-orientation
   benefits   6, 20
   drawbacks   21
   career choices   225
   learning curve   223
   what's different   216
   why?   212
Object-oriented
   concepts   118
   summary   118
Object-oriented
   databases   135
Object-oriented
   paradigm   2, 22, 120
Objects   117, 120
Observers   30
OID (*See* Object ID)   170
OO   4, 2, 216
   definition   22

OO benefits   20
OO career choices   225
OO learning curve   223
OO SDLC   218
OODB (*See* Object-oriented
    database)   134
OOPSLA   225
OOSDLC
    pinball   217
    waterfall   215
Optionality   136–137, 167
    symbols   137
Override   133, 185
Overriding
    example   195

P

Paradigm   2
    structured vs.
        object-oriented   3
Part-of relationship   139
Peer-to-peer   16–17
Persistence   133, 146
Persistent instance
    relationships   146
Persistent memory   135
Persistent relationships   169
Personal computers   16
Pinball SDLC   217
    steps   220
Polymorphism   152, 156
Programming   221
Project initiation   220
Project success   8–9
Prototyping   58, 66, 215
    advice   61
    steps   60

Pseudo-code   99
Pure inheritance   185

Q

Quality Assurance   226

R

Real-time   16
Recursive aggregation   177
Recursive instance
    relationships   138, 175
Relationships   134
Report classes   43, 147
    example   201
Reports   38, 147, 201
    implementation   148
Responsibilities   44, 55
    example   46–47
Responsibility   27
Reusability   6
Root   133

S

Screen   38
Screen classes
    example   199
Scribe   104
Scribes   29, 31, 51
Server   222
Silver bullet   21
Single inheritance   130

Structured
  development   48, 156
Structured techniques   213
Subclass   129, 133
Superclass   129
System development
  life cycle   64

T

Testing   89, 216,
    222
The object-oriented
  paradigm   4
Top-down design   116
Training   20
Transitory classes   134
Transitory instance
  relationships   146
  example   147, 179,
    199
Transitory objects   135
  example   199
Transitory relationships   169

U

Use case   52
Use-case scenario   52
  description   53
  example   104
  testing   111, 116
Use-case scenario card   52
  example   54
Use-case scenario
  testing   33, 91, 215
  advantages
  disadvantages   95
  steps   111
Use-case scenarios   96
User acceptance test plan   93
User acceptance testing   216
User requirements
  definition   96

W

Wirfs-Brock et al.   26, 52

SIGS BOOKShelf

SIGS BOOKS

Applying OMT
Kurt W. Derr

Applying OMT is a how-to guide on implementation processes and practical approaches for the popular Object Modeling Technique (OMT) created by James Rumbaugh et al. The book begins by providing a thorough overview of such fundamental concepts as modeling and prototyping and then moves into specific implementation strategies using C++ and Smalltalk. By using a typical business application as a case study, the author illustrates the complete modeling process from start to finish.

1995/557 pages/softcover/ISBN 1–884842–10–0/Order# 205/$44.00

Dictionary of Object Technology
The Definitive Desk Reference
Donald G. Firesmith & Edward M. Eykholt

Dictionary of Object Technology is the only reference of its kind dedicated to the terminology used in the object technology field. With over 3,000 main entries and over 600 pages, this long-awaited and much needed dictionary is cross-referenced by major components and includes complete appendices specific to industry standards, programming languages, and more languages.

1995/628 pages/hardcover/ISBN 1-884842-09-7/Order# 206/$55.00

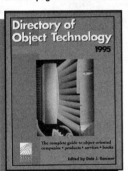

The Directory of Object Technology 1995
Edited by Dale J. Gaumer

This book puts the entire OO industry at your fingertips. It is the most comprehensive object technology resource guide available. It will help you define and then identify the products and services you need. Divided into five separate sections, the Directory provides a complete listing of vendors, products, services, and consultants.

1995/softcover/385 pages/ISBN 1-884842-08-9/Order #C501A-600/$69.00

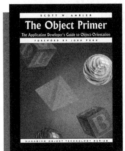

The Object Primer
The Application Developer's Guide to Object-Orientation
Scott W. Ambler

The Object Primer is the ultimate introductory text on object-oriented (OO) technology. By reading this book, you'll gain a solid understanding of object-oriented concepts and object-oriented analysis techniques.

This book provides all a developer needs to know to get started using object-oriented technology immediately.

November 1995/250 pages/softcover/ISBN 1-884842-17-8/Order# 550/$35.00

What Every Software Manager Must Know to Succeed with Object Technology
John Williams

This book shows managers what object technology is and how to manage it effectively. It provides readers with a no-nonsense approach to object technology management, including effective guidelines on how to track the development of projects. This is the only book available that truly addresses the issues that managers must deal with when implementing object technology.

1995/294 pages/softcover/ISBN 1-884842-14-3 /Order# 250/$35.00

Managing Your Move to Object Technology
Barry McGibbon

Written for software managers, **Managing Your Move to Object Technology** clearly defines and illustrates the management implications associated with the transition to object technology. Although other books may cover the technological benefits of OT, this is one of the few to address the business management issues associated with new technology and the corporate environment. It covers what OT will do to the corporate culture, not simply what it will do for it.

1995/288 pages/softcover/ISBN 1-884842-15-1/Order# 350/$35.00

Getting Results with the Object-Oriented Enterprise Model

Thornton Gale and James Eldred
Foreword by James J. Odell

Enterprise modeling is the primary tool used in business reengineering.

Historically, the number one problem with enterprise modeling has been the lack of formalism. **Getting Results with the Object-Oriented Enterprise Model** tackles this dilemma head-on and prescribes a formal methodology based on object technology.

December 1995/Approx. 500 pages/softcover/ISBN 1-884842-16-X
Order# 750/$45.00

The Blueprint for Business Objects

Peter Fingar

The Blueprint for Business Objects provides a clear and concise guide to making informed decisions about emerging object technology and to mastering the skills you need to make effective use of the technology in business.

Based on the workplace experiences of several major corporations, this book presents a framework designed for business and information systems professionals. It provides the reader with a roadmap, starting at the level of initial concepts and moving up to the mastery level.

1995/Approximately 300 pages/ Order #850/ISBN 1-884842-20-8/ $39.00

Reliable Object-Oriented Software Applying Analysis and Design

Ed Seidewitz and Mike Stark

Reliable Object-Oriented Software presents the underlying principles associated with object-orientation and its practical application. More than just another text on methodology, Reliable Object-Oriented Software focuses on the fundamental concepts related to the process of software development and architectural design in order to lay the basis necessary for the development of robust, maintainable, and evolvable software.

November 1995 /425 pages/ softcover /ISBN 1-884842-18-6
Order# 450/$45.00

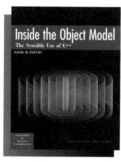

Inside the Object Model

David M. Papurt
Foreword by James J. Odell

Inside the Object Model serves two key functions: it teaches object-oriented analysis and design from first principles and clearly explains C++ mechanisms that implement object-oriented concepts.

Drawing on nearly ten years of programming and teaching experience, David M. Papurt thoroughly describes the relationship between the basic principles and concerns of object modeling and the C++ rogramming language. Each chapter uses independent examples to illustrate key concepts described in the text, and features helpful icons that clearly identify important ideas and dangerous pitfalls.

1995/540 pages/softcover/ISBN 0-884842-05-4/Order# 400/$39.00

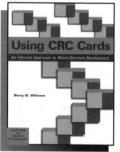

Using CRC Cards

An Informal Approach to Object-Oriented Development
Nancy M. Wilkinson
Foreword by Rebecca J. Wirfs-Brock

In this book, the author draws on her years of project experience to describe how CRC cards can contribute at all stages of the software lifecycle. It includes practical examples of how to utilize CRC cards in projects using either formal or informal development techniques. **Using CRC Cards** also provides a detailed look at how designs created with CRC cards can be mapped to an effective and efficient implementation in C++.

1995/243 pages/softcover/ISBN: 1–884842–07–0/Order# 800/$29.00

Object Lessons

Tom Love

In this usable guide to developing and managing OO software projects, well-respected consultant and OOP pioneer Tom Love reveals the absolute do's and don'ts in adopting and managing object-oriented technology. **Object Lessons** is filled with applicable advice and practical suggestions for large-scale commercial software projects.

Written in a personable yet concise style, this dependable guidebook reaveals "trade secrets" and demonstrates how to put theory into practice, all with an emphasis on minimizing risk and maximizing return.

1994/275 pages/softcover/ISBN 1-9627477-3-4/Order# 101/$29.00

Using Motif with C++
Daniel J. Bernstein

As more software industry professionals gain experience in both object-oriented (OO) development and the graphical user interface (GUI), it is clear that GUI libraries offer several advantages over other kinds of libraries, and that they are fun to use.

This book provides step-by-step instructions on how to create a library for programming GUIs in the C++ language. Written for both beginning and experienced Motif programmers, this book is both a tutorial for writing a portable Motif-based interface library in C++ and a reference for enhancing and maintaining such software.

1995/392 pages/softcover/ISBN 0-884842-06-2/Order #500/$39.00

Objectifying Motif
Charles Bowman

Objectifying Motif describes methods and techniques on ways to combine the power of object-oriented programming in C++ with GUI development under Motif. The book is a complete guide for both beginning and advanced OO programmers on how to combine these two distinct paradigms to achieve the greatest benefit.

Specifically, the reader will learn, step by step, to design and develop a portable GUI library based on X/Motif. This book also provides the source code to this library, called MWL. MWL is a fully functional library derived from the author's years of experience and can be used as is.

1995/513 pages/softcover/ISBN 1-884842-13-5/Order# 204/$39.00

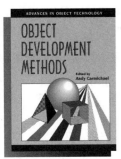

Object Development Methods
Edited by Andy Carmichael

Object Development Methods addresses how object technology can be applied to systems analysis and design. An international roster of contributors compares the leading methodologies of Booch, Rumbaugh, Jacobson, Shlaer/Mellor, Colbert, Graham, Coad/Yourdon, and Texel among others. This book provides significant insight into the contrasting viewpoints and advantages, common concepts and underlying structures of different object-oriented methods.

1995/363 pages/softcover/ISBN 0-9627477-9-3/Order# 300/$39.00

Objectifying Real–Time Systems
John R. Ellis

This book exemplifies the evolution of popular Real-Time Structured Analysis (RTSA) techniques into the object development era – Real-Time Object-Oriented Structured Analysis (RTOOSA). Objectifying Real-Time Systems also includes a diskette of source programs used as examples throughout the book, letting the reader to experiment and verify executions without having to key-in code.

1995/542 pages/softcover/ISBN 1-9627477-8-5/Order# 200/$44.00

An Object Methodology Overview
Written and Narrated by Doug Rosenberg

An Object Methodology Overview is a CD-ROM designed to help users select the proper methodology for their specific project. This state-of-the-art training tool offers an in-depth comparative overview of various popular OOA and OOD methods and highlights the best application of each methodology. It includes information on seven methodologies: OMT (Rumbaugh), Objectory (Jacobson), The Booch Method, Coad/Yourdon, CRC Responsibility Driven Development (Wirfs-Brock), Martin/Odell, and Shlaer/Mellor, and more.

1995/1 CD/Order# 6AD01A-700/~~$995~~ **$795**

CALL FOR AUTHORS

Become a part of SIGS Books. We are currently seeking authors for our three exciting book series:

- **Advances in Object Technology**
Focuses on the latest developments and trends in object-oriented programming and programming languages, object-oriented requirements, object-oriented domain analysis and object-oriented design.

- **Managing Object Technology**
Provides readers with timely and accurate information on a wide range of issues related to business objects.

- **SIGS Reference Library**
Presents state-of-the-art reference material on object technology. As object technology evolves, the Reference Library will provide the resources necessary to insure its success.

FOR MORE INFORMATION...on how to become part of SIGS books, contact Donald Jackson at:
Donald Jackson, Editorial Director, SIGS Books
71 West 23rd Street, 3rd Floor, New York, NY 10010
Phone: (212) 242-7447/ Fax: (212) 242-7574
E-Mail: donald_jackson@sigs.com

Developing Visual Programming Applications Using Smalltalk
Michael Linderman

Developing Visual Programming Applications Using Smalltalk uses object-oriented visual programming environments to illustrate the concepts of object-oriented software construction. It introduces blueprints as a method to record visual programming applications and includes sample applications using Visual Smalltalk, VisualAge, and VisualWorks.

March 1996/Approx. 300 pages/ISBN 0-884842-28-3
Order # 283/Prepub price

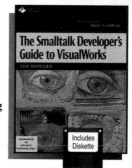

The Smalltalk Developer's Guide to VisualWorks
Tim Howard
Foreword by Adele Goldberg

The Smalltalk Developer's Guide to VisualWorks provides an in-depth analysis of the popular application development tool produced by ParcPlac/Digitalk. Designed to enhance development acumen, this book serves as a guide to using VisualWorks to its full potential.

1995/645 pages/softcover/ISBN 1-884842-11-9/Order# 203/$45.00

Deploying Distributed Business Software
Ted Lewis

Written in a clear and concise style, this is a must-have guide for technical managers and leaders who want the latest information on distributed and client/server computing. Comprehensive yet readable, the book analyzes software technology and standards in database, visual programming, groupware, middleware, remote access, and programming technology.

December 1995/Approx. 250 pages/softcover/ISBN 1-884842-19-4
Order# 650/$35.00

Rapid Software Development with Smalltalk
Mark Lorenz

This book will help professional software developers write Smalltalk code faster without sacrificing software quality. The book covers the spectrum of OO analysis, design and implementation techniques and provides a proven process for architecting large software systems. It includes techniques derived from real OO projects that are directly applicable to on-going projects of any size.

1995/237 pages/softcover/ISBN 1–884842–12–7/Order# 900/$29.00

ORDER FORM

❑ **YES!** Please send me the following books:

Title   *Author*

_____

_____

_____

_____

Subtotal: _____
Shipping: **$5**
Total*:   _____

❑ Enclosed is my check (payable to SIGS Books.)
Please charge my
    ❑ Amex ❑ Visa ❑ Mastercard

Card # _____

Exp. _____

Signature_____

Please add $5 shipping and handling in U.S. ($10 shipping in Canada, $15 everywhere else).
*NY State residents add appropriate sales tax.
Prices subject to change without notice.

Name _____

Address _____

_____

City/State/Zip_____

Phone *(in case we have trouble with your order)*

_____

SIGS Guarantee: If you are not 100% satisfied with your SIGS book, return it within 30 days for a full refund (less S+H).

Return this form to:
SIGS Books
71 West 23rd Street,
New York, NY 10010
For faster service, call

1-800-871-SIGS

Fax: 1-212-242-7574 • http://www.sigs.com